Dare To Be Excellent

Case Studies of Software Engineering Practices That Worked

Edited by
Alka Jarvis and Linda Hayes

with original contributions by
Steve Blair—Phoenix Technology
Vern Crandall—Digital Technology International
Martha Coacher—PKS Information Services
Linda Hayes—WorkSoft Inc.
Dick Holland—Primark Investment Management Services Ltd.
Kambiz Hooshmand—Cisco Systems
Alka Jarvis—Cisco Systems
Cynthia L. Snow—Intel
Dave Moore—Royal Bank of Canada
Bob Underwood—International Business Systems

ISBN 0-13-081156-4

Prentice Hall PTR
Upper Saddle River, NJ 07458
http://www.phptr.com

Editorial/production supervision: *Kathleen M. Caren*
Copyeditor: *Camie M. Goffi*
Cover design: *Alamini Design*
Cover design director: *Jerry Votta*
Manufacturing manager: *Alan Fischer*
Marketing manager: *Kaylie Smith*
Acquisitions editor: *Bernard Goodwin*
Editorial assistant: *Diane Spina*

©1999 Prentice Hall PTR
Prentice-Hall, Inc.
A Simon & Schuster Company
Upper Saddle River, New Jersey 07458

Prentice Hall books are widely used by corporations and government agencies for training, marketing, and resale.

The publisher offers discounts on this book when ordered in bulk quantities. For more information, contact: Corporate Sales Department, Phone: 800-382-3419; Fax: 201-236-7141; E-mail (Internet): corpsales@prenhall.com

Or write: Prentice Hall PTR, Corporate Sales Dept., One Lake Street, Upper Saddle River, NJ 07458.

Printed in the United States of America
10   9   8   7   6   5   4   3   2   1

ISBN 0-13-081156-4

Prentice-Hall International (UK) Limited, *London*
Prentice-Hall of Australia Pty. Limited, *Sydney*
Prentice-Hall Canada Inc., *Toronto*
Prentice-Hall Hispanoamericana, S.A., *Mexico*
Prentice-Hall of India Private Limited, *New Delhi*
Prentice-Hall of Japan, Inc., *Tokyo*
Simon & Schuster Asia Pte. Ltd., *Singapore*
Editora Prentice-Hall do Brasil, Ltda., *Rio de Janeiro*

Dedication

For my siblings, Bharat, Kumi, Jyoti and Raksha,
from whom I have learned so much and
who are always there for me.

For Steve, an individual who is a constant inspiration in life,
the one and only who came up with the book title
and was the guiding light behind this book.

Alka Jarvis

Contents

Foreword ix

Preface xi

Acknowledgments xv

CHAPTER 1 1

REQUIREMENTS (Texas Instruments)

    Company Profile 1
    Basic Concepts of Requirements 2
    Reasons To Implement 4
    Elicitation And Analysis Of DI Business
        Requirements 8
    Lessons Learned 21
    Conclusions 22

CHAPTER 2 25

PROJECT PLANNING (Intel Corporation)

    Company Profile 25
    Intel Corporation's LANDesk Products 27
    Anti-Virus Products 33
    Anti-Viral (AV)Technologies 38
    Virus Protection Software 40
    The Revival Plan 44
    Cultural Issues 47
    The Result—a New Generation of Award-Winning,
        Sustainable LDVP Products 62
    Lessons Learned 64
    Conclusions 65

CHAPTER 3 . . . . **67**

TECHNOLOGY PROJECT MANAGEMENT PROCESS
(PKS Information Services)
Company Profile 67
Reasons to Implement 69
Company Philosophy 73
Technology Project Management Process 74
Culture Change 86
Implementation 88
Final Results 88
Lessons Learned 89
Conclusions 90
TPMP Sample 90

CHAPTER 4 . . . . **127**

PROJECT SUPPORT OFFICE (Royal Bank Financial Group)
Company Profile 127
Reasons To Implement 128
Culture Change 133
Project Office 136
Challenges 141
Customer Satisfaction 142
Conclusions 144

CHAPTER 5 . . . . **147**

INSPECTIONS AS AN AGENT OF CHANGE
(Primark Investment Management Services Limited)
Company Profile 147
Reasons to Implement 148
Measures of Software Quality 150
What Do We Mean By Process? 156
How Did We Get Started? 167
Lessons Learned 176
Culture Change 187
Strategic Plans 189
Challenges 194
Conclusions 195

CHAPTER 6 . . . . **197**

SOFTWARE RELIABILITY ENGINEERING
(Digital Technology International)
Company Profile 197
Basic Concepts and Goals of Software
Reliability Engineering 198
Reasons To Implement. 200
Solutions To the Problem 205
Culture Change 207
Project Plan/Time-Line 212
Implemention 214
Results 216
Lessons Learned 218
Conclusions 219

CHAPTER 7 . . . . **221**

RELEASE PLANNING (Cisco Systems)
Company Profile 221
Reasons To Implement. 222
Release Process 225
Culture Change 251
Lessons Learned 251
Conclusions 252

CHAPTER 8 . . . . **253**

RELEASE METRICS (TANDEM Telecom Network Solutions)
Company Profile 253
Introduction 254
Reasons for Implementation. 255
Obtaining Buy-In. 257
Assessing Measurements 258
Description of the Rating. 260
Calculating the Confidence Rating 263
Implementation 267
Release Management in Action 269
Results 271
Lessons Learned 272
Conclusions 273

CHAPTER 9 . . . . **275**

CREATION OF A SOFTWARE DEVELOPMENT PROCESS HANDBOOK
(Phoenix Technologies Limited)
Company Profile 275
Why Phoenix Created a Process Handbook 276
Cultural Issues 276
Drafting the Software Development Handbook. 278
Lessons Learned 296
Continuous Improvement. 296
Conclusions 297

CHAPTER 10 . . . . **299**

MANAGING CLIENT/VENDOR RELATIONSHIPS
(International Business Systems)
Company Profile 299
Reason To Implement 300
Description of Process. 302
The Handoff 304
Approach. 307
Cultural Change 330
Project Plan/Time-Line 330
Results 331
Lessons Learned 332
Conclusions 332

Acronyms/Abbreviations **335**

References. **339**

Index **343**

Foreword

Welcome to the real world!

Far too much is written about software engineering by the academic crowd, and far too many lectures are held by them at conferences. Real practitioners are generally too busy doing their normal, hectic work to write a book or publish a paper. It is admirable that the editors have organized this work of case studies so we can see the reality from the shop floor.

You will find much conventional wisdom challenged here. You will find a collection of experiential facts and figures from some of the authors. Two things struck me.

I found myself actually acquiring new and interesting insights which I did not previously have. The other was the breadth of approach to the problems which characterized most of the cases. Time and again we are reminded that software engineering means dealing with Marketing, Sales, executives, the help team and politically/organizationally-handicapped customers. We are reminded that the solutions to defects are not necessarily testing, or inspection or reliability models, but a broad and realistic view of the real customer and how they use the system.

We are reminded that real organizations need training and re-training. Executives need to be more than just supportive, they need to be well-informed and actively committed.

We are constantly reminded that just doing things to get ISO 9000 certification or CMM levels is not enough. You have to take the underlying intent seriously. You have to make getting a result uppermost, not getting a certificate.

I was also happy to see the many small organizations represented here, because even people from large corporations all seem to work in "small" organizations.

It is refreshing to see that writers have gotten back to the basics of W. Edward Deming's philosophies, good design, and total systems management, which so many narrow theorists ignore.

I hope this book encourages more such books, and that readers will feel stimulated to write down and share their experiences. Especially important is the challenging and modifying/tailoring of conventional wisdom, as well as giving numeric facts to illuminate the experiences.

I encourage the potential reader to spend a day with this book. You will not fail to come away with at least one great insight, which will save you a year of wasted improvement effort!

Tom Gilb

Preface

Software development has matured to the point where known engineering practices don't need to be defined, they need to be applied. We know what needs to happen, but the inevitable details of how to make it work are often a stumbling block. Too many times, discipline is sacrificed to competing needs and schedule constraints: Taking the time to do things may be viewed as an impractical ideal.

Nothing could be further from the truth, of course. Doing things right reaps continuous rewards that are no less valuable for being difficult to measure: reduced rework and support costs, improved time to market, and increased customer satisfaction. Because it is hard to measure the costs you avoid, but easy to track the costs you incur, the investment in process improvement may be more obvious than the rewards.

The trick is to follow the spirit of a process, not necessarily the form: depending on the size of the project and organizational environment, it may be wise to condense or circumscribe certain aspects. Fit the practice to the situation instead of the other way around.

There are quite a lot of software engineering practices in the world that are viewed to bring "success" to your software development, and there are several books on theories of development practices. Often, you are at a loss to identify companies who may have implemented these theories. So, the question comes up: *How do I know the theories described in a book really work?* The best way to understand a process and how to implement it is through actual examples, which is what this book is all about.

The authors have extensive experience in several software engineering quality improvement techniques to know that what one large company does may not be appropriate for another small company, or that what works for a software development organization in one industrial segment may not work the same way in another. Over the years we have encountered software developers, quality assurance managers, ISO implementors, students, executives, managers, supervisors, consultants, and testers who asked us to give them examples of companies that introduced a process change and the logistics as well as the results of this change. This question inspired us to embark upon a journey to capture real scenarios.

We know most of you are faced with immediate problems of managing software development and do not have time to benchmark or improve current processes based on what has worked for others. Unfortunately, software development does not excel by implementing one or two simple techniques. It is an accumulation of many complex processes which requires integration of project controls and technical knowledge. Quality is built into software products through careful project management and processes that have been known to reduce defects and increase productivity.

Until now (this is the first!), there has been no book that describes case studies of software engineering principles under one cover. We have chosen a variety of companies, big and small, from different aspects of the overall industry such as financial, telecommunications, service, consulting, etc. Each of these companies chose a software improvement path and made a commitment to follow the path to see the ultimate results. Each company stumbled upon different roadblocks that they had to overcome.

This book presents what each company did, what their reason was for implementing the new process, what were the cultural issues, and what were the final results. So many times, we see an organization trying to implement a process change and then abnormally ending the project in search of a "quick fix." The cases

of the companies represented in this book show a lot of persever-
ance, dedication, and good "follow-through." The companies may
not resemble your own, it is the way they applied a practice to make
it succeed for them that is the most instructive: Not just what did or
didn't work, but how and why. You can learn universal principles
from the mistakes and successes of others.

This book seeks to convey an understanding of what worked in
the software development process and how managing that process
to obtain quality software while improving the overall productivity
helped each company achieve a particular goal. Each chapter provides a comprehensive description of the process adhered by a specific company.

- Chapter 1: Focuses on requirements.
- Chapters 2, 3 and 4: Describe different aspects of project
  planning, project management, and project support office.
- Chapter 5: Provides details of using inspections as an agent of
  change.
- Chapter 6: Highlights software reliability.
- Chapter 7: Talks about release planning.
- Chapter 8: Gives you guidance on release metrics.
- Chapter 9: Talks about creation of a Software Development
  Process Handbook.
- Chapter 10: Discusses managing client/vendor relationships.

While we know the importance of software measurements, we
have decided to direct our readers to Grady (1987).

This book captures case studies of companies who mastered an
area of software development and who, by example, can guide your
own efforts.

Acknowledgments

We would like to thank all the companies and individuals who participated in the development of this book. We owe a great deal to these companies and their visionary management teams, and wish to acknowledge each contributor for their support, suggestions, and ideas.

The credit is due to many people, but a few individuals stand out: Lauren Gilbertson, Christer Johansson, Barry Christian, Dan Kohnke, Van Hanson, and Anthony Romano from International Business Systems; Alan Braithwaite, Alan Butt, Chris Russell, Colin Cook, Corey Ercanbrack, Dana Doggett, David Brighton, Eric Blair, Evan Simper, Francis Robbins, Gary Sarff, Gordon Roylance, James Rose, Jeff Compas, Ken Knapton, Lynn Snow, Matt McMullin, Mark Christensen, Randy Templeton, Suzette Rose, Tom Bogart, and Yuki Bernardi from Intel; Phil Howard and Robin Gray from TI; Pam Anderson and Les Bell from Royal Bank; Charles Corbalis, Michael Kalt, and Afsaneh Laidlaw from Cisco Systems; and Edna Clemens from Tandem Telecommunications Network Solutions.

We particularly wish to thank Tom Gilb for his unparalleled enthusiasm and Steve Devinney of Quality Assurance Institute for his continuous support.

We would like to especially acknowledge Dawn Piazza for her technical and administrative support, as well as Kathleen M. Caren, Production Editor, and the copyeditor, Camie M. Goffi. Our special thanks to our publisher, Bernard Goodwin, whose assistance was a major contributor in the completion of this book.

CHAPTER
1

Requirements

Texas Instruments

1.1   COMPANY PROFILE

Texas Instruments (TI) is the world leader in digital signal processing (DSP). With revenues of $9.9 billion and 43,500 employees spread across North America, Europe, and Asia, TI holds 6,000 patents and annually invests over $1 billion in research and development. Two out of three digital cellular phones carry TI technology, as well as nine out of ten high-performance hard-disk drives and one out of every three modems (1996 data). TI is the world's fastest growing modem chipset vendor.

Over the past fifty years, TI was the first in many areas of technological revolution, such as the first silicon transistor, integrated circuit, handheld electronic calculator, single-chip microprocessor and single-chip digital signal processor—all essential building blocks of the information age. Their latest breakthrough, digital light processing™ (DLP), is a revolutionary improvement of image quality in projection systems.

The DLP technology was developed at TI's corporate research lab and think tank. In the mid to late 1980's Dr. Larry Hornbeck, an international award-winning researcher in advanced semiconductor technology, engineered a way to put individually addressable, movable mirrors on a semiconductor micro-chip. Imagine hundreds of thousands of mirrors on a chip the size of your thumbnail, each separately controlled! This chip, a digital mirror device (DMD), could be used to produce color images of a resolution far surpassing existing technologies.

DLP has three key advantages over existing projection technologies. The inherent digital nature of DLP enables noise-free, precise image quality with digital gray scale and color reproduction. DLP is more efficient than competing transmissive liquid crystal display (LCD) technology because it is based on the reflective DMD and does not require polarized light, thus increasing light efficiency. Finally, close spacing of the square mirror means that the image has a 90% "fill factor" of density as compared to 70% or less for LCDs.

1.2   BASIC CONCEPTS OF REQUIREMENTS

What are requirements, anyway? The following story, though not explicitly about requirements, illustrates their elusive nature:

The new superintendent of an office building was concerned about the continuous complaints from tenants about how slow the elevators were. The bids he obtained to upgrade or replace the elevators were astronomical and would no doubt be refused by the building's owners. He finally consulted a man who claimed to be an expert in problem-solving.

The consultant asked the superintendent, "What's the problem?" The superintendent replied, "The tenants are complaining about the elevators being too slow."

"And why is that a problem?" the consultant countered. "Well, if they are unhappy they may move out of the building," the superintendent responded.

"I see, and why is that a problem?" he asked again. "If they move out, the building will lose revenue," the superintendent explained.

The consultant asked yet again, "And why is that a problem?" "If the building loses revenue under my management, I'll lose my job," the superintendent pointed out.

"Okay," said the consultant, "I think I now have an appreciation for the situation, but I'd like to verify some things. Do you mind if I talk to a few of your tenants?"

"You're more than welcome to", answered the superintendent.

A few days later, the consultant returned, and announced to the superintendent, "After a thorough review of all the facts and careful analysis of the problem, I have a solution. I feel confident we can solve your problem for around $500".

"How can you possibly fix the elevators for only $500?" he asked.

"I'm not going to fix the elevators," said the consultant, "because there's no problem with them. But, what I'm going to do is install mirrors on the walls beside them. Your tenants will pass the time by admiring and grooming themselves while waiting. Time will fly by, and you'll never hear another complaint about slow elevators".

Requirements are traditionally the cornerstone of most projects. They define the scope and effort, and ultimately determine the schedule. However, as a project takes shape, usually additional requirements are discovered. This "scope creep" typically impacts resource loading and slides the schedule.

But, what if this approach was turned completely upside down, so that the schedule was paramount, resources were fixed, and the only variable was the requirements? Often a radical view can yield dramatic results.

1.3   REASONS TO IMPLEMENT

An emerging technology division of TI was founded to capitalize on the DLP technology, the Digital Imaging venture project (DI). After some study, DI arrived at the decision to capitalize on this technology not by selling the chips themselves, but by leveraging original equipment manufacturers (OEMs) to reach the end-user market. DI would build an "engine" (later called a "platform") around the chip that could be incorporated into finished products such as projectors, televisions, copiers, printers, and other devices that produced images. By January, 1995—after two-and-one-half years of intensive development—the division entered into delivery commitments with its partners and began the transition into production manufacturing.

1.3.1   SETTING THE STAGE

Now the division was charged with accomplishing yet another unprecedented task, this one in the area of information systems. The challenge was to have a system in place to support the business environment by October 2, 1995. To do it, they had to take extraordinary measures. By their willingness to take a radical approach to achieve the impossible, they proved that if necessity is the mother of invention, pressure is the crucible of clarity. Breaking boundaries creates intense forces that crystallize focus, purpose, and efficiency; under pressure, coal is converted into diamonds.

This is the story about how DI successfully implemented the core capability of the three fundamental modules of SAP[1] in 12 weeks, a task often requiring years. What is interesting and instructive about it is not why we did it—our circumstances were anything but commonplace—but what we discovered about eliciting, prioritizing, and managing requirements in a situation where we had no choice but to innovate, and how we played the hand we were dealt. The principles we proved can and should be applied to every project, every time.

Not only did DI successfully implement SAP in twelve weeks, an unprecedented achievement, we continued to deliver new capability

---

1. SAP is the trademark of SAPAG.

on a quarterly cycle and eventually every month. In so doing, we discovered the keys to getting the right things done at the right time. A "time-box" approach was thrust upon us, setting the cycle time by identifying time as the fixed variable.

We responded with a *"rolling release"* strategy that forced prioritization, accelerated decisions, and increased release frequency. In this context, a "release" is defined as the availability of incremental functionality through the configuration of SAP. This combination created a discrete but constant flow of functionality that not only delivered on a record schedule, but also continues to make DI's information technology more responsive to the business than traditional scope-based release cycles.

1.3.2 THE LAUNCH PAD

The system production date having been established, DI sought to build the information systems infrastructure necessary to support its new phase of operations. A 27-year TI veteran was recruited to establish basic business systems. This experienced IT manager had experience in all phases of information systems with a special interest in requirements, including previously assisting in the formalization and documentation of a requirements elicitation and definition process for TI.

We started with a virtually blank slate. DI's operations had previously been limited to development, and its basic business processes and operations were still in the formative stage. The first months of 1995 were spent interviewing operations managers, compiling basic requirements, writing a white paper on what was needed, and evaluating available PC solutions for the short term. There was no time to develop a customized system or implement a large-scale commercial one—or so we thought.

Meanwhile, another division of TI—the semi-conductor group—was in the process of making the decision to acquire and implement SAP. SAP is an enterprise-level application suite that tightly integrates all phases of operations from Manufacturing to Sales and Distribution and Finance. It offers an enormous range and depth of capability and is used by some of the largest corporations in the world. Although SAP delivers a reference model that covers a comprehensive set of business processes, these must be mapped to the business at hand before they can be implemented.

The semi-conductor undertaking was enormous and would span years. Senior TI management wanted a pilot project that would act as a scout with this application package. In late April, we decided to investigate the possibility of implementing SAP as a pilot. Theoretically, since the DI organization was still in its infancy, it would not have the complexity of dealing with legacy system conversions and could thus move quickly. On the other hand, a hard deadline of October was looming, and DI was still defining its business with its processes, leaving most of the detailed requirements as yet unknown.

A six-week feasibility study was conducted by an outside consulting firm to determine if such a rapid SAP implementation was even conceivable. The study concluded that, while never done before, it might be possible, but only if stringent guidelines were followed. So the decision was made to utilize SAP.

1.3.3   COUNTDOWN

On June 1, Andersen Consulting (Andersen), who was assisting the semi-conductor group in their SAP effort, was asked to be DI's implementation partner. The first order of business was to refine the guidelines from the feasibility study and develop estimates for delivery capability based on time and resource availability. The following principles were adopted to assure success:

◆ "Bare bones" approach—only 20% of the core capability, as projected to support the first year of business, could be included in the October installation.

◆ DI would have to initially adopt processes supported in SAP, rather than adapting them via modifications, extensions, or customization of reports.

◆ Andersen would lead the project at the DI headquarters and provide configuration services from their Solution Center, located in Cincinnati, Ohio, as there was no time to recruit and train DI personnel.

- ◆ Andersen would provide a set of process templates to "jump-start" the overall effort.

- ◆ The SAP modules included would initially be limited to Finance and Control (FI/CO), Material Management and Production Planning (MM/PP), and Sales and Distribution (SD).

- ◆ DI had to form a strong, active, and decisive steering team to sponsor and direct the effort.

These principles were agreed to, while the management team added another key item to the list. To expedite decisive actions, we instituted the concept of "no blame" for mistakes. DI management set the tone of "embracing mistakes" as an essential part of the learning process, reducing the blame which often becomes a detriment to progress. This idea was paramount to fostering rapid, creative decision-making. Another basic principle was to "think from scratch", thus breaking traditional or long-standing patterns of thought and behavior in favor of innovation and invention.

The necessity of using outside consultants during the first phase of the project was dictated by the demanding schedule. There was no time for an internal learning curve. However, DI did not want to remain dependent on the consultants after system start-up. Thus, a "roll-off" plan was devised whereby the expertise of the consultants was transferred to DI personnel in a formal and orderly way.

Due to the overriding constraint of time, a "time-box" approach to project management was also applied. Unlike traditional projects, where the requirements drive the resources and schedule, the time component was the primary driving factor in the prioritization of tasks. Thus, the only controllable variable was requirements, as schedule and resources were fixed.

The time-box method also dictated a "rolling release" strategy. That is, instead of focusing on a single and complete release of functionality, releases would be evolutionary over time, each building upon the previous one. Concurrently, the business itself was evolving with many areas still recruiting personnel, defining their strategies and objectives, and identifying the information system requirements. These moving targets would have to be synchronized to maximize the effectiveness of the strategy.

Now in the beginning of July, with only 12 weeks remaining until the production start date, the elicitation and analysis of DI system requirements began.

1.4 ELICITATION AND ANALYSIS OF DI BUSINESS REQUIREMENTS

Since only 20% of the core functions would be installed as the first release, it was critical that decisions made today supported, and not hindered, future releases. The concept is similar to building a foundation sufficient to support a 20-story building, even if only two stories are being built today. This placed special emphasis on not just the elicitation of requirements, but also the analysis and capacity to provide incremental growth.

It was understood that the infrastructure had to be designed holistically yet constructed incrementally, in proper relationship to the processes it would support. This structure must prove the framework for the business directives as determined from the strategies and policies aligned to the company's vision.

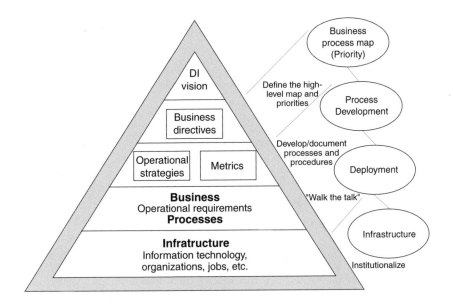

Figure 1-1: Business Driven Processes

Figure 1-1 is an illustration of the interrelationships that would guide the analysis and decision-making process. Within this structure, the first order of business was to agree on the overall vision and business model. This model would determine the selection of appropriate business processes, which in turn would drive the definition of detailed system requirements.

DI's vision was to revolutionize imaging by changing the fundamental building blocks of a picture, whether projected or printed. To accomplish this vision, the company needed to establish name recognition for its technology while leveraging OEM contracts to reach end-users with finished products. This dictated a product life cycle strategy that supported the needs of the OEMs, including potential requirements for customization to target a particular market niche. This strategy required flexibility and responsiveness in both the processes and information systems that supported the business.

For management to monitor and fine-tune the operational strategies, some form of metrics were needed. These metrics had to be decided upon to assure that the infrastructure could provide them. In other words, the highest level of analytical information is available only if all of the supporting detail data is already present. This relationship is depicted in Figure 1-2.

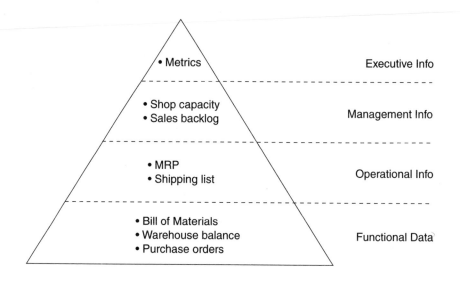

Figure 1-2: Information Hierarchy

This overall structure provided a context to requirements that would assure they were traceable to the business, one of the qualities of good requirements.

1.4.1   THE BUSINESS PROCESS MODEL—REQUIREMENTS REPRESENTATION

The entire founding team at DI were veterans of TI, and they had no difficulty at all expressing their desired business model, but were spoiled by the world-class systems they were accustomed to. The real challenge was to calibrate the business team back to basics. The project team tackled this by first capturing their view of the business, which is charted in Figure 1-3.

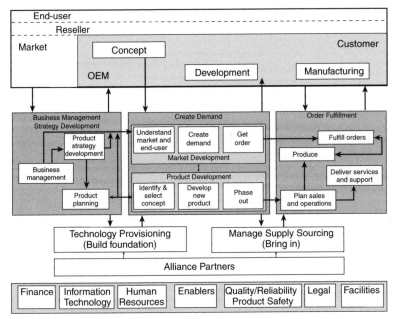

Figure 1-3: Business Process Model

Although this representation adequately depicted a "business view" of the process, it was significantly different than the one Andersen Consulting had developed, which tied more closely with the way SAP is implemented.

The challenge was to map DI's model to the Andersen model, since there was no time to modify the SAP software if the deadline was to be met. This mapping illustrated how management's view of the business process model would be expressed as high-level requirements of the SAP system. It is depicted in Figure 1-4.

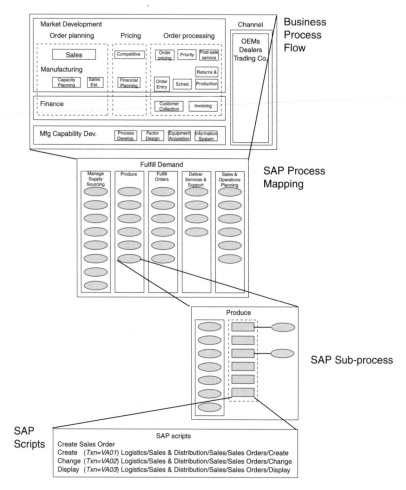

Figure 1-4: Order Fulfillment Process

Once the two models were mapped, requirements representation began in earnest.

1.4.2   REQUIREMENTS REPRESENTATION

Because SAP is sold and delivered in modules of functionality, the requirements teams, called "tracks", were similarly aligned: Material Management/Production Planning (MM/PP), Finance and Control

(FI/CO), and Sales and Distribution (SD). Each track was comprised of key managers who were experts in their area. The initial session was a four-hour meeting to determine the scope of requirements for the first release. Because the participants were highly experienced and accustomed to customized, world-class information systems, their expectations were high; the scope after the initial session was already spiraling out of the realm of possibility.

The first pass yielded a set of "scenarios", each of which described a particular required process. These scenarios provided specific details to the requirements and were utilized later for requirements review and validation. Additionally, these scenarios proved a useful tool for user training. The utility of the scenario approach was very appropriate for the tight schedule goal.

To narrow the scope and provide a consistent framework for evaluating requirement scenarios, Andersen provided a set of templates based on a hypothetical electronics company called "Acutronics". As mentioned previously, SAP delivers support for business processes, but they are not usable without configuration. Andersen had pre-configured about 850 processes into templates, called "scripts", for the hypothetical company. For example, one script included the creation, deletion, and maintenance of a chart of accounts. When the scripts were compared to the scenarios already gathered, it became clear that some scripts were over-defined, some were under-defined, and some didn't exist.

Given that manufacturing would have to occur before Sales and Marketing could fulfill orders, the next round of prioritization was determined by functionality, with MM/PP as the first critical need. Then, because the accounting year would commence in January, FI/CO was next, then SD. This did not mean that just MM/PP would be considered in the first round, only that it would receive a greater amount of functionality. Later releases would focus on the other tracks. The initially selected requirements subset was then prioritized and grouped by track. Almost half were in MM/PP; the other half were roughly equal between FI/CO and SD.

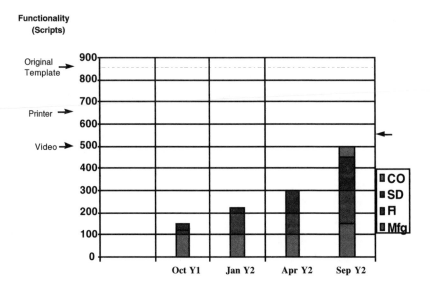

Figure 1-5: Phased "Focus"

Within the allocation guidelines, track managers were next asked to sift the 850 scripts down to those they "positively, absolutely, had to have" to commence operations in October. The first round of scope sessions resulted in an almost 50% reduction, to about 450 scripts. Unfortunately, based on the schedule and resources, this was still far too many for an October deadline; a realistic target was around 150.

Now it was becoming painful. Having already been asked only for absolutely essential requirements, another 60% cut by the tracks seemed impossible. Thus, the ensuing sessions were, in a word, grueling. The next pass resulted in pruning to approximately 200; still too many. Now at "bare bones" in each track, it became necessary to defer some FI/CO and SD functionality to the MM/PP track for October. The final count reached was 147!

Aside from the difficulty of pruning functionality already felt to be essential, it soon became clear that there were conflicts in integrating processes between the groups. To resolve these, several sub-teams were formed. From the start, one of the guiding principles was to have a strong steering team willing to meet daily, if required. This team, comprised of the fewest number of people with decision authority, spent whatever time was necessary to resolve issues.

A rule was established to streamline conflict resolution and decision-making. No issue would go undecided for more than one week. This acted as a catalyst to force business process engineering to happen quickly. But inevitably, hurried decisions were not always correct. For example, when deciding whether processes for incoming materials inspections were needed, the expectation was that supplier parts would be of sufficient quality that no incoming inspection would be necessary. An admirable goal, but of course, it later proved to be impractical for a start-up business just entering production, having new products and all new supply chains.

Remember that DI was started as a development group and was just transitioning into production. The founding management team had only a few people, all pulled from different existing TI businesses—semi-conductor, defense, and consumer products; the rest were brilliant in technical fields, but novices at the realities and practicalities of running a profitable new startup business. The trick was to achieve a balance between academic idealism and practical experience.

During these sessions of deciding how DI would run their business, processes as they were defined were submitted to Andersen Consulting's Cincinnati Solution Center for configuration. This procedure yielded its own set of questions and issues. The team in Cincinnati was getting 80% closure on most processes, with the remaining 20% awaiting detail resolution. The teams were inundated with requests for responses, such as how many warehouses would be needed, what were the part numbering schemes, and so forth. With a score of people configuring these processes in Cincinnati, the details needed for the configuration process shifted the focus from a higher to lower level of detail, requiring 2-3 more weeks of hard-core decisions.

Also, at this time it became evident that the acquisition and delivery of the necessary hardware to run SAP would not make the October deadline. A decision was made, and permission from SAP granted, to allow DI to begin system production utilizing the hardware at Andersen's facility in Cincinnati. A three-month Service Level Agreement had to be negotiated.

1.4.3   VALIDATION

The ultimate proof of requirements definition is validation. It is one thing to identify, define, and configure a requirement and quite another to validate that it does, in fact, meet the true business need (as highlighted in the anecdote about the superintendent's elevators). This has special significance in an integrated environment such as SAP, where a single event can trigger a "domino" effect. One transaction can immediately impact multiple areas, in contrast to a functionally split system where batch feeds between systems have inherent checks and balances. For example, if you ship an order, the customer's receivables balance and credit exposure is recalculated at once, possibly blocking their next shipment.

At this point there was no test strategy, plan, environment, or data in place for validating the system, nor was there a planned freeze date for development. Given the criticality of the processes being implemented and the high degree of integration, it was crucial that validation occur within a compressed schedule and in parallel with the final stages of configuration.

Testing began in September, utilizing Andersen personnel and borrowed resources from the DI customer base. The testing went well and provided two distinct results. First were the normal results of testing: errors, corrections, and additional modifications. Second, and much more important, was the list of business risk areas (those areas where the system results were not what the business assumed). This list was comprised of results where the software did not "fail" in the traditional sense, but completed a process behind the scenes, such as triggering revenue account summarization segregated by sales item categories. Due to the need for the validation of these types of results, emphasis was placed on integration and system test with cross-functional teams assigned to each test scenario. This proved key to the success and effectiveness of the compressed test phase. This capability greatly assisted in the statusing, prioritization, and follow-up of changes identified during validation testing.

As the production date drew nearer, new issues became apparent. SAP provides highly sophisticated security and access levels according to assigned roles. A shipping clerk, for example, cannot change the credit limits for a customer whose shipment is blocked for credit reasons. DI realized that defining all the roles was simply not possible by the deadline date. This meant that all users had to initially be given extensive access to SAP functionality. There was inherent risk in this approach, but with the extremely qualified team and the narrowly defined scope of operations, it was believed acceptable.

Many process issues uncovered during validation could not be resolved before the deadline either because they required too much time to modify, or begged questions that still had to be answered. This meant that the validation team had to document where the "land mines" were buried so that the users would know which areas were problematic and either avoid them or compensate in other ways. These were published as the list of "shall nots". All in all, the validation results produced a "GO" decision.

1.4.4 LIFT-OFF

On October 2, DI went live with SAP. DI was operating on SAP after a record-breaking 12-week implementation phase. This date was set even before SAP was selected as DI's enterprise system, thus creating the ultimate time-box. The business processes only recently imagined, let alone defined, were in full swing.

However, because of the "rolling release" strategy, the commencement of production was really the beginning of the next release, only 12 weeks away. Not only were the teams still chipping away at their prioritized list of changes, but a veritable mountain of issues began to arise from production. Unexpected events, new decisions, and the inescapable intrusion of reality began to settle in.

What is interesting about this phase is that it occurs in any project, no matter how long the initial schedule. Whether 12 weeks or 12 months, the proof of any system is in production, and all the time in the world cannot predict the exigencies the real world produces. In this case, the short interval before the next release acted as a pressure-valve: if a problem arose, relief was in sight within weeks, not months or years.

Since Manufacturing was the primary business function in operation at the beginning, it generated the most additional requests. The carefully planned segue from Manufacturing into Finance and Sales and Distribution began to slide. In fact, over the next year, the planned versus actual distribution is represented in Figure 1-6.

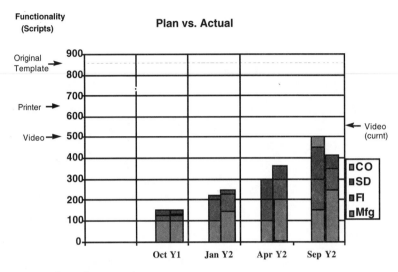

Figure 1-6: Phased "Focus"

The incremental functionality did not only continue in the business process area, but as operations escalated, additional needs for information to manage the company came to light. In addition to adding new scripts, the team now had to add the analyses and reports that management required to make decisions and monitor results. Following the pyramid approach to building up information capabilities, the approximate functionality after the first year is depicted in Figure 1-7.

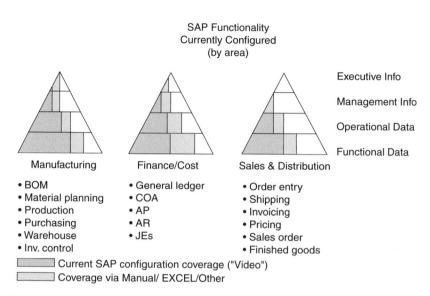

Figure 1-7: SAP Functionality Currently Configured By Area

1.4.5 ONGOING REQUIREMENTS MANAGEMENT

Ironically, once the initially planned set of functionality was released, follow-on capabilities actually came in shorter increments. The versatility of SAP's configurable nature, combined with the continual refinement of DI's business model, generated an unending stream of requirements. The responsiveness that was forged by the early efforts now became institutionalized with releases continuing on a quarterly schedule, and individual modifications or corrections achieving monthly, if not weekly turnaround. IT became an enabler of business evolution, not a drag on the changing business.

This state of affairs was made possible by the continuation of the management models adopted by previous necessity. The steering team, set up for the initial launch, remained in place, supported by Change Control Boards (CCBs) in each area.

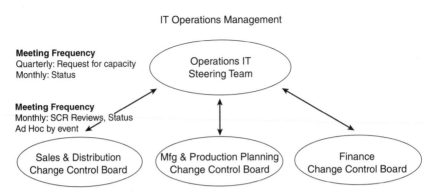

Figure 1-8: IT Operations Management

The Operations IT Steering Team (OITST) continued its responsibility for prioritizing new requirements. They approved all projects and schedules, and empowered a champion for each. This team also represented IT within the business community, listening for and recognizing the implications of IT on the business, alerting staff on issues needing review, and communicating IT plans to the rest of DI. The members kept each other informed of any changed or new business directives, and provided overall feedback on the IT organization's performance.

CCBs were also created for each functional area, and each has a representative on the OITST. These boards reviewed the status of the backlog for their track, provided direction for future projects, set their respective priorities, and resolved issues. When appropriate, recommendations were submitted to the OITST for consideration.

These management structures remain in place today, as do the basic principles and approaches set in place during initial delivery. These principles include the time-box approach to constraining and prioritizing requirements within a fixed schedule, as well as the rolling release approach to delivering a continuous stream of discrete functionality.

1.5   LESSONS LEARNED

Even successful projects, in retrospect, can be improved. After a year in production to evaluate the effectiveness of the project approach, we took time to reflect on the lessons that were learned.

1.5.1   COMPOUNDED CUMULATIVE RISKS

Although start-up business problems were expected, the compounding effect of cumulative risks was underestimated. The idealistic expectations of engineers and optimistic plans of Manufacturing were compromised by a flood of variables: OEM requirements for customization of the engine exceeded expectations, chip yields (the rate at which quality chips can be produced) were below plan, and suppliers did not meet the lofty goal of defect-free shipments. Production requirements had not been thoroughly defined. As a consequence, the system was often not prepared to handle these issues.

1.5.2   DICTATED VS. ADOPTED CHANGE

Next, although the decision to accept SAP's reports was dictated by time limits, these reports often did not prove to be sufficient. Therefore, it became necessary to provide a significant number of management reports produced both by outside means (manually, through spreadsheets or other utilities), as well as the customization of SAP reports. An interesting phenomenon was observed in this area: Although senior management was encouraging change, they were laggers in adapting SAP's "on-line" reporting for their own needs.

The key to supporting change, DI discovered, was to build one level at a time. Incremental change is easier to make and modify than large-scale, monolithic modifications.

1.5.3   INTEGRATED REQUIREMENTS

Third, the integrated nature of SAP was more demanding of process design than traditional point solutions. Decisions were far-reaching and many areas lacked sufficient definition for proper configuration within SAP. This led to a constant evolution of the system as both the strategies and needs of the business continued to evolve.

Balancing the need for consistent, non-contradictory requirements (both essential characteristics) against flexibility is highly complex in a tightly integrated environment.

1.5.4   REWARDS AND RISKS OF RESPONSIVENESS

Last, the configurable nature of SAP allowed flexibility and tailorability, thus reducing cycle time and increasing responsiveness. This was one of the key attractions of SAP for DI, and for TI's semiconductor group as well. The rate of change in DI's business as it evolved was supported by a capability for rapid turnaround of change requests. This shorter interval between changes reduced the risk of large mistakes, while continually providing the end-user community with a constant stream of new capability.

However, responsiveness does have its down-side. Processes, requirements, and testing are of necessity more informal, resulting in less documentation, which means, ultimately, that knowledge is not as transferable. Although DI was built with a star team, turnover is a fact of corporate life and the loss of formality will, if left unchecked, someday take its toll.

1.6   CONCLUSIONS

Although most projects aren't quite as dramatic as a 12-week SAP implementation, and most companies aren't starting from scratch, the basic principles that DI adopted toward requirements are applicable to almost any project.

1.6.1 TIME-BOXING

The concept of "time-boxing" a project has the innate appeal of pre-dictability. Whereas almost all traditional, requirements-based projects suffer from delays due to scope creep, a time-boxed project adheres to a rigid deadline. Aside from improving conformance to schedules, this highly-focused approach demands prioritization—first things first, second things second, and so forth.

What is interesting about this approach is that even requirements-based projects eventually become time-boxed as the deadline ap-proaches. In this case, the order becomes switched and the schedule all-consuming. As the deadline nears, requirements become the only variable. Were the right ones done first? Prioritization of key require-ments is critical.

1.6.2 ROLLING RELEASE

Time-boxing must be coupled with—or maybe even mitigated by—a rolling release strategy. With a greater frequency of smaller releases, users whose requirements don't make the first cut have less time to wait, thus reducing the pressure to make the immediate release. This has the added benefit of providing enough functionality to make us-ers productive in the short term, probably more quickly than if they waited for all their requirements in one larger but later release.

A more subtle effect is that when requirements prove to be incom-plete or inaccurate, the effect of change is narrowed. A design deci-sion may be more easily reversed or changed when it has a smaller impact. Also, the shorter interval until the next release means errors are less costly and easier to remedy. This reduced cycle time makes the system more responsive to the needs of the business.

1.6.3 MANAGEMENT CULTURE

These concepts must be supported by a strong management culture with a bias toward making decisions quickly, without the threat of blame or recrimination. Awaiting the arrival of all relevant informa-tion to make a perfect decision might sound ideal, but in reality, circumstances change and the business evolves so fast that all of the information may never be known, except in retrospect, and a delay can do more damage than a bad decision.

1.6.4 QUALITIES OF GOOD REQUIREMENTS

As a result of this project and those we have participated in previously, we recommend that during the requirement phase of your project, you strive to follow the steps below and insure that each of your requirements possess as many of the characteristics listed as possible.

Steps in the Requirements Process

- ◆ **Elicit:** Seek input from all affected or interested parties.

- ◆ **Analyze:** Review and understand the requirements.

- ◆ **Represent:** Chart, graph, or otherwise depict their overall structure.

- ◆ **Review:** Obtain input from all contributors.

- ◆ **Track:** Trace and maintain them as the project/business evolves.

Characteristics of Good Requirements

- ◆ **Unambiguous:** Not subject to more than one interpretation.

- ◆ **Complete:** Not lacking any essential information.

- ◆ **Consistent and Non-contradictory:** Not in conflict with others.

- ◆ **Unique:** No duplication or overlap.

- ◆ **Testable:** Objectively verifiable.

- ◆ **Feasible:** Practical within project limitations.

- ◆ **Traceable:** Linked to the larger context.

- ◆ **Modifiable:** Adaptable to change.

- ◆ **Usable:** In a form easily adopted and managed.

C H A P T E R
2

Project Planning

Intel Corporation

2.1 COMPANY PROFILE

Intel Corporation began modestly in 1968 with a handful of people, a new type of design, and a fragile technology, all housed in a little rented building. Intel engineers built the first functional 64-bit memory chip. It didn't sell. Then the 256-bit memory chip was produced. It was a marvel of 1969 technology, but didn't sell. The tradition of following one chip with another that contained more transistors, however, was born. Finally, the 1024-bit chip became a big hit. The new challenge became how to satisfy demand for it. Intel had practically 100 percent share of the memory chip market segment. In the early 1970's, other small American companies entered the memory chip business. By the end of the 1970's, there were a dozen players in the business. With each succeeding generation of memory chips, some company, not necessarily the same company, got it right—and it wasn't always Intel. Japanese memory producers began to exert a presence as well.

Managers from Hewlett-Packard reported that quality levels of Japanese memory chips were more consistent and better than those produced by American companies. An internal investigation at Intel substantiated the frightening news. Japanese producers began taking over the world semiconductor market. Intel fought hard to improve quality and reduce costs, but the Japanese producers fought back. Recognizing that, as an American company, Intel couldn't match the Japanese producers' high-quality, low-priced, mass-produced parts, Intel spent heavily on R&D (Research and Development). Engineers explored niche markets for memory chips and other technologies.

A dedicated group of engineers had worked for years on technology for microprocessors, the brains of the computer. Microprocessors, as well as memory chips, are built with silicon chip technology, but microprocessors perform calculations. Memory chips simply dynamically store information. In 1981, Intel's leading microprocessor was designed into the original IBM PC. By 1985, when financial losses on memory chips were hemorrhaging the company, the "386" microprocessor was ready to go into production. Its development was based on a technology developed in a corner of an old production plant.

In 1985, co-founder and CEO Gordon Moore guided Intel out of the memory chip business. Andy Grove, having thought of Intel as "memories are us," agonized over abandoning Intel's identity. It took months to finalize the decision. While closing the door on memory chips, Intel opened the door on microprocessors.

Intel searched for a new identity for the corporation. "We decided to characterize ourselves as a microcomputer company" [Grove96]. Public statements, literature, and advertising had their part in telling the story, but the phenomenal success of the 386 created the conviction. The microprocessor stepchild was formally adopted. By 1992, mostly owing to the microprocessor's success, Intel became the largest semiconductor company in the world, larger even than the Japanese companies that had beaten Intel in chip memories.

Gordon Moore's prediction became the law of the digital age: Microchips will double in power and halve in price every 18 months. The Intel386^{TM} of 1985 had 275,000 transistors; the Intel486^{TM}

processor of 1989 had 1.2 million transistors; Intel's Pentium® processor of 1993 had 3.1 million transistors; and the Intel Pentium II processor of 1997 has 7.5 million transistors.

2.2 INTEL CORPORATION'S LANDESK PRODUCTS

Today, Intel's identification with microprocessors is so strong that it's difficult to get noticed for non-microprocessor products. Management, however, well remembers the "strategic inflection point" that moved the company from memory chips to microprocessors. Since that time, there continue to be numerous stepchildren coming out of R&D. The LANDesk software products represent one such stepchild. Gordon Moore, in the early 1990's said that "half our staff would need to become software types in five year's time" [Grove96]. The LANDesk charter is to deploy, manage, and protect the PCs sold with Intel architecture microprocessors.

2.2.1 INTEL CORPORATION, UTAH SITE HISTORY

Intel's LANDesk software products are produced as part of the Systems Management Division (SMD) of the Small Business and Networking Group of Intel Corporation. The software groups of SMD found their roots in Utah seven years ago. Dana Doggett, the seventh engineer hired by the fledgling Novell Corporation, became an expert at NetWare. He branched out to write software that made NetWare more usable. His LANSchool and Print Server products caught the attention of LANSystems, Inc., a New York-based systems integrator. They offered to buy Dana's source code. Dana's burgeoning business, once encouraged by Novell, was now causing a conflict of interest. Remembering back to 1987, Dana recalls:

> Leaving Novell was a traumatic experience. I had worked into a senior position with the company. Netware-386 was still being architected and my wife and I (with 3 children) had recently purchased our first home. However, we sold our home and moved back to a rental to reduce our expenditures. LANSystems, from New York, offered me a job to continue work on the Print Server. They

had named the product LANSpool and its sales were going well. LANSystems allowed me to work for them from my home in Utah and modem in all new software. I accepted this position. I was given the title of VP of Development. LANSpool exploded! It seemed as if every NetWare customer in the world wanted several copies. LAN Magazine called it the Product of the Year and LAN Times called it the "Breakthrough Product of the Year." LANSystems was so pleased that they asked me to expand my "Utah Development Center." Now the basement bedroom of my rental house was no longer large enough. I found the cheapest office space in the valley: two vacant rooms behind an established hair salon. I furnished the rooms with folding tables and chairs.

Ed Ekstrom was hired to manage the growing group, now selling four products. Ed was an unstoppable force when it came to building a company. Within six months, he had established Utah as the true headquarters for the software division of LANSystems. Growth continued until LANSystems had two distinct divisions: the Utah-based software company, and the New York-based integration company. Intel's Network Products Division (NPD) bought the Utah software group in May of 1991. NPD was responsible for a hardware-based Print Server, NetPort, and needed better NetWare expertise.

By year's end, Intel pulled LANSpool from the product mix, assigning it to the Print Server group in Oregon. At that point, 90% of our revenues were coming from LANSpool. We needed to re-invent ourselves and do it quickly. Ed Ekstrom was fully up to the challenge and in several months had re-focused us on desktop management software. This was a new software category invented by Ed and gave us long-term direction for our other products. Our new anti-virus product, LANProtect, shipped right after our re-direction. Either by fate or by luck, the first global computer virus scare, Michelangelo, hit right when we announced LANProtect. Once again, sales exploded and we again had sufficient revenues to develop Ed's vision of desktop management.

A full suite of desktop management software products now falls under the umbrella of the LANDesk development operation in Utah. The suite includes LANDesk Virus Protect (an outgrowth of LAN-Protect), LANDesk Management Suite, LANDesk Server Manager, LANDesk Client Manager, and LANDesk Configuration Manager.

2.2.2 LANDESK PRODUCT MULTI-DISCIPLINARY TEAMS

Successful software products today need focused attention from multi-disciplinary teams to include Marketing, Human Factors, Engineering, Documentation, Quality Assurance, Sales, and Support. Intel's Systems Management Division (SMD) is organized to allow close interaction of multi-disciplinary team personnel, yet maintain autonomy for the disciplines. The multi-disciplinary teams are organized vertically for accountability purposes. This allows, for example, the support team to rally around customer needs even when the engineers they work with daily want to prioritize a customer request differently. Multi-disciplinary team members sit and work together in a horizontal team for development purposes. Almost all team members report to the Business Unit Managers (affectionately referred to as "BUMS"). BUMS usually work as two-in-a-box. The LANDesk Retail Product BUMS in Utah have finance and marketing expertise, respectively. Figure 2-1 clarifies the vertical accountability concept, as well as the horizontal development organization.

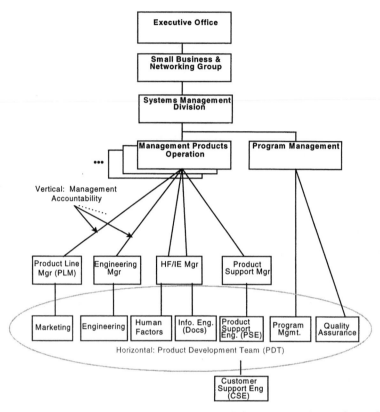

Figure 2-1: Vertical Management Accountability vs. Horizontal Product Development Team

Figure 2-1 shows a subset of the extensive Marketing, Software Development, Manufacturing, Sales, and Support infrastructure of Intel, but includes the groups our software engineering team works with regularly. The Product Development Team (PDT) members sit in close proximity and interact daily. The roles of the multi-disciplinary PDT members are described below:

Marketing: The marketing team understands the history, present, and (hopefully) future of our product line. They set long- and short-term product goals, identify and prioritize product functionality needs, and chart revenues.

Engineering: The software engineering team contains both software development and test engineers. The test team sports the same academic credentials as the development team, and codes regularly. Depending on the current mix and needs of the team, test engineers may perform a sustaining role, or development engineers may substitute as test engineers. We attempt to have an equal number of development and test engineers.

Human Factors (HF): This team represents customer usability issues. A recent point of interest: human factors engineers have historically concerned themselves with the intuitive and the customers' desire. Today, human factors must also equally consider what look-and-feel customers will become used to in future major products (such as operating systems and browsers). Our human factors engineers are responsible for the product prototype and engineering documentation.

Information Engineering (IE): This documentation group is primarily responsible for the on-line help, hardcopy manuals, and virus encyclopedia. The documentation team and human factors engineers participate in all design meetings. They create product prototypes and record design meeting decisions. This team, in conjunction with the software engineering team, actually creates Engineering's required process documents.

Product Support Engineering (PSE): Customer support is layered to include field and telephone support, who escalate unsolved problems to product support engineers (PSEs). Multiple PSEs work on a daily basis with the product development team (PDT). One is focused on the development of new products. This individual sits in our design meetings to represent both customer enhancement and support needs, prepares the training materials for the customer support engineers (CSEs), rangers, and field sales team, and does such training as well.

The sustaining PSEs act as interfaces between Customer Support and Engineering. Issues that can't be resolved by Customer Support are escalated to these PSEs. They verify and filter these escalations. Issues which need Engineering's attention are reproduced then discussed at a sustaining GOST ("Get Our Stuff Together") meeting where Marketing and PSEs assign priorities. The issues are passed to the engineering team for resolution. This might sound like a lengthy process—but isn't since we sit in close proximity. This paper will not discuss the sustaining process in detail, but be assured that all relevant information is tracked in a controlled and backed-up defect tracking system.

The PSEs overlap their work enough that one can easily cover for the other when needed. The LDVP products have dedicated PSEs at remote sites also. They telecon into our regular GOST meetings.

Program Management: The program management team was instituted in SMD a year ago. With site and product offering growth, we were losing the close physical and communication contact inherent in small organizations. The Project Management independent reporting office (note the direct report to the division level) owns schedules and reporting. They insure that a defined process is followed and provide upper management monthly updates on all products and teams. These updates are consistent in format and matter.

Quality Assurance (QA): The QA team conducts inspections and reviews of required documentation, and schedules and conducts the Change Control Board (CCB) meetings. CCB meetings are held whenever a change to an "approved" document is needed. For example, Marketing may desire an enhancement after the marketing and engineering documents have been reviewed, signed, and approved. The change request must be presented at a CCB meeting where the impact can be assessed by all multi-disciplinary team members on the PDT. The request will be accepted or rejected. Marketing owns the product, so they have veto authority to insist that a change be made, but they will clearly understand the impact before exercising that veto. Engineering is also subject to CCB review. When an upgrade product is started, the PDT reviews all open enhancements and defects in the tracking system. They decide which will be addressed/fixed in the upgrade. If Engineering later wants to add/remove a defect from the list, it must be done via the CCB meeting.

2.3 ANTI-VIRUS PRODUCTS

> More than any other person, Andy Grove has made real the defining
> law of the digital age: the prediction by his friend and Intel co-
> founder Gordon Moore that microchips would double in power and
> halve in price every 18 months or so. And to that law Grove has
> added his own: we will continually find new things for microchips to
> do that were scarcely imaginable a year or two earlier [Isaacson97)].

Anti-virus products have unique development and sustaining needs.
Consider the dichotomy that one or more anti-virus products has
been in PC Magazine's top ten selling retail products for years, yet
there remain only a handful of anti-virus vendors worldwide! The
reason lies in their complexity (multiple types of computer viruses,
multiple types of detection) and the rapid birth rate of new viruses.

2.3.1 WHAT IS A COMPUTER VIRUS?

Viruses are pieces of renegade and damaging code that attach to files
or embed in macros within application files. Once in memory, a virus can infect other executable files, disk boot areas, or macro templates. Simply opening a file can spread a macro virus. E-mail
attachments have become a speedy and insidious way to spread
macro viruses.

To be called a virus, code must be capable of replicating or infect-
ing other host files or disks. Typically, a virus will replicate, but otherwise remain dormant until some trigger event occurs, such as a
system date or a specific user action. In addition to replication, a
computer virus typically performs some other function, usually intended to do data damage or to spread a nuisance message.

The basic virus classifications include:

◆ File viruses.

◆ Boot viruses.

◆ Multi-partite viruses.

◆ Stealth viruses.

◆ Polymorphic viruses.

◆ Macro viruses.

2.3.2 FILE VIRUSES

File viruses account for 10% of infections. The virus typically adds a jump instruction at the beginning of an executable file, which jumps to the virus code. After the virus code is executed, the virus jumps back to the original program so the user does not suspect a problem. The virus code may cause the virus to load as a TSR (terminate and stay resident) module so all future files are infected, or the code may look for a file or files to infect. File viruses spread when an infected program is executed. Figure 2-2 shows the basic format of file viruses:

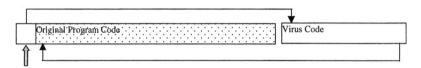

Figure 2-2: File Virus

Note that the virus adds a "jump" instruction at the beginning of the program and jumps to the beginning of the virus code.

Before the 1990's, file-infecting viruses were prevalent and were increasing substantially in number. Then, inexplicably, they experienced a significant drop. It took several years before the benevolent culprit was identified. During the early 1990's, Microsoft's Windows 3.1 became a common operating environment. Over a comparatively short period of time, many users switched from DOS to Windows 3.1. When a Windows 3.1 system is infected with a typical file virus, it won't start! Thus, the virus had to be eradicated (via software re-install, disk reformat, ...) before the system could be used. Due mostly to this phenomenon, file-infecting viruses today are fairly rare (with one exception—macro viruses) [White 96].

2.3.3 BOOT VIRUSES

Boot viruses, which account for about 5% of known PC virus strains, reside in a special part of a diskette or hard disk that is read into memory and executed when a computer first starts. As seen in Figure 2-3, the boot sector normally contains the program code for loading the rest of a computer's operating system ("bootstrap" is a reference to lifting oneself up by one's own bootstraps). Once load-ed, a boot sector virus can infect the boot sector of any diskette that is placed in the drive. Boot viruses spread when a computer is boot-ed from an infected diskette. Boot sector viruses also infect the hard disk, so that the virus will be loaded into memory whenever the sys-tem is restarted. Boot viruses are highly effective: even though there are fewer strains.

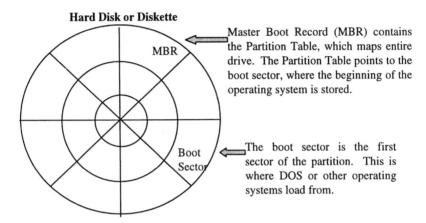

Hard Disk or Diskette

MBR

Boot Sector

Master Boot Record (MBR) contains the Partition Table, which maps entire drive. The Partition Table points to the boot sector, where the beginning of the operating system is stored.

The boot sector is the first sector of the partition. This is where DOS or other operating systems load from.

Figure 2-3: Boot Virus

The earliest IBM PCs (personal computers) did not have hard disks. Instead, they were booted from diskettes, and all programs were run from diskettes. If a bootable diskette was infected with a virus, such as the Brain virus that appeared in 1987, it was likely that more diskettes would become infected as they were used. After the mid-1980's, PCs with hard disks became almost universal. In this environment, existing boot sector viruses had a hard time spreading. As the world's computing environments change, the birth rates of boot sector viruses plummet [White96]. Unfortunately, there seems to be a fresh supply of viruses that mutate to infect the latest boot environment.

2.3.4   MULTI-PARTITE VIRUSES

Multi-partite viruses are hybrids of file and boot viruses. They can infect executable files and therefore can travel quickly over a network.

2.3.5   STEALTH VIRUSES

These hide their modifications or presence by hooking interrupts. When certain operating system functions are called, the virus "forges" the results, making everything look normal. Stealth viruses corrupt files by forging file sizes and dates, hiding changes made to the boot sector, and redirecting most read attempts.

2.3.6   POLYMORPHIC VIRUSES

These mutating viruses change form every time they infect. Each generation of infection changes the way the virus appears in the file, making traditional pattern-matching ineffective.

2.3.7   MACRO VIRUSES

Emerging in 1995, viruses such as WORD.CONCEPT were among the first to affect macros in ordinary software files, not just executable files. Macro viruses represent a new level of virus threat because, unlike stealth or polymorphic viruses, they require relatively little computer savvy or sophistication to devise. Macro viruses now account for 85% of infections (up from 49% last year). The University of Hamburg's Virus Test Center [U. of Hamburg98] reports that as of the end of 1997, there were 1,826 identified macro viruses. Joe Wells' December 1997 Wild List [Wells97] includes 73 macro viruses "in the wild"—that is, viruses reported by two or more anti-virus observers. Any application that allows a user to write scripts, or macros, to automate actions is open to the macro virus threat. Some virus payloads may simply print a message or display an image, but others will damage programs and data.

There are other kinds of destructive code, such as logic bombs, Trojan Horses, and Worms. These can steal system resources or damage data, but are not technically classed as viruses because they do not replicate. They can still be dangerous. A logic bomb in a payroll program, for example, may erase all records a couple of months after it fails to read the name of a disgruntled, terminated employee. Trojan Horses (malicious programs disguised as something innocent), a minor problem in the past, today can be downloaded from the Internet and run by thousands, heightening the potential for widespread damage. Worms (innocuous programs that send enough copies of themselves to flood networks and degrade services) also become an increasing threat as computing becomes more distributed.

We now see fourth-generation viruses. There are six to nine new viruses everyday, and most new viruses are platform-independent!

2.3.8 HOW DO VIRUSES SPREAD?

A virus infects a system by entering it at some intrusion point. Some years ago, most viruses were spread via shared floppy disks passed from workstation to workstation. On a network, potential entry points expand to include servers, e-mail attachments, files downloaded from the Internet, bulletin boards, and other shared devices.

A boot virus on a floppy diskette can enter a system when a computer attempts to boot from an infected floppy. The boot virus then infects the critical disk areas (boot sector, Partition Table, or MBR) of the computer's hard disk. Once the boot sector of the hard drive is infected, the virus installs itself in memory and infects the boot sector of any floppy diskette that is accessed by the computer—a great way to infect workstation after workstation as users swap disks.

A "multi-partite" virus can travel as a file virus and then infect a boot sector. It can also be transmitted through floppy diskettes. Executable files are a common source of spread from server to server. Servers become the central distribution points—an infection vector—for other workstations on the network. A virus on a file server becomes especially dangerous if it has infected a critical file used by all or most users, such as LOGIN.EXE.

A few years ago, computer viruses traveled around the world almost entirely on diskettes, carried from place to place. A computer virus typically took a year or more to become prevalent [White96]. The danger is no longer just from shared floppy disks. Viruses now enter the desktop more directly, through e-mail attachments, Web downloads and network servers, often without the user's knowledge until damage has already occurred. Connection to the Internet with the resulting proliferation of Java applets, Java applications, and ActiveX objects is heightening the potential of destructive Trojan Horses and Worms.

2.4 ANTI-VIRAL (AV) TECHNOLOGIES

Viruses are now affecting more aspects of a user's environment, going beyond boot sectors and executables to embedded macros in everyday word processing or spreadsheet files. The degree of destructiveness can range from total (wiping out drives and data) to annoying (consuming disk space, affecting system performance).

Detection remains a mainstay of AV defense. As the number of viruses and potential entry points grow, the process of identifying errant code strings becomes more complicated and prone to error or omission. No AV software catches every virus because new viruses are created every few hours. Virus mutations complicate detection and recovery. There are three historic types of software AV technology:

◆ Virus detection scanners.

◆ Activity monitors.

◆ Change detection systems.

2.4.1 VIRUS DETECTION SCANNERS

Virus detection scanners look for virus signatures, sections of program code that are known to be in specific virus programs but not in other programs [Slade97]. Scanning requires a search program and a database or "virus-signature-file" of known virus signatures. The scanner pattern matches for the virus signature within a file. The scanner and/or virus-signature-file must be updated each time a new virus is found. If the virus signature is not unique, the anti-virus product may produce a "false-positive", a report that a virus exists when, in fact, it does not. Corporate customers claim that dealing with a false-positive is more costly than dealing with a real virus. Virus detection scanning has evolved through first, second, and third-generation approaches as follows:

- **First-generation Virus Detection Scanners:** Pattern-matching scanners, including those that recognize wildcards in scan strings, represent the first generation of scanning technology.

- **Second-generation Virus Detection Scanners:** Second-generation scanners go beyond simple pattern-scanning, using heuristics to identify likely virus mechanisms rather than looking for complete strings of code.

- **Third-generation Virus Detection Scanners:** Third-generation scanners include virus "traps." These products wait for the virus to attempt to infect and then, by observing its activity, they trap and isolate the virus before it can complete its action. Third-generation products are a major step forward because they don't allow an infected file to open or replicate, or they clean the virus and then allow the file open to continue.

2.4.2 ACTIVITY MONITORS

Activity monitors oversee the operation of a computer and alert the user when suspicious activity takes place. For example, an activity monitor may check for calls to format a disk, or direct calls to hardware without use of the standard operating system calls. Monitoring activity is a good way to detect viral activity of new and unknown viral strains, but won't detect "all current and future" viruses [Slade97].

2.4.3 CHANGE DETECTION SYSTEMS

Change detection systems determine whether a program, file, or system has changed as compared against a previously established base. Most of these programs perform a checksum or cyclic redundancy check (CRC) that will detect changes to a file even if the length is unchanged. The change detection system considers system areas of the disk and memory. It is prone to false-positives—alerting that a change implies a virus infection when in fact the change was legal [Slade97].

2.4.4 HEURISTIC DETECTION

Anti-virus products include multiple detection methodologies, and are morphing toward fourth-generation heuristic detection where possible. Proactive heuristic scanners attempt to identify virus-like code, but suffer from false-positive alerts if not well-refined. Refinement to exclude false-positives, however, reduces effectiveness in identifying new virus strains.

"Security, of every type, is always a 'moving target,' and the virus world moves faster than most. Not only are new viral programs being written every day, but new types of viral functions are being coded all the time" [Slade 97].

2.5 VIRUS PROTECTION SOFTWARE

Computer users want and need more than virus detection and cleaning. They need virus "protection." Corporate CIOs request that viruses be identified and intercepted as they attempt to enter the LAN via the Internet, e-mail, or floppy diskette. An AV product that provides this type of protection is still not fool-proof.

Anti-virus products are the most dynamic of all software products. New viruses appear every few hours. An AV software product is never done. Engineering may complete a product and send it to Manufacturing, but before Manufacturing is complete, there are updates needed to detect new viruses. To allow for this, the most commonly updated component, the virus-signature-file, must be an independent component that can be easily and dynamically updated and deployed. Regular changes to the scanning engines must also be accommodated.

Anti-virus products interact with the computer system from the user interface (UI) to the lowest kernel level. A user, via the UI, will configure the type of protection wanted. One of the configurable options must allow selection of "real-time" scanning. Real-time (or background) scanning will scan a file for viruses before the file-open is complete, before the file-close is complete, or both. Real-time scanning implies the need for AV software to hook into kernel level zero to catch and scan the file before the system-open (or close) completes.

A customer with a virus usually needs an immediate solution. A new virus that slips through the existing AV defenses is always a threat. A major bank with international branches may get infected in

Japan during the Japanese workday, while the AV software vendor's analysts in the US are home in bed. With a worldwide economy, the AV analysts must be on-call twenty-four hours per day. Presently we see that no AV vendor dominates in multiple geographies, or in any geography other than their own. We interpret this to mean that the need for immediate response outweighs any other AV product feature. However, pioneering work is currently being done to create a super computer expert system analyst that would automatically respond to new viruses worldwide and around the clock [Kephart97].

Every computer, from a mainframe used for Internet services—to the desktop at the office—to the transportable laptop, needs AV protection. It should be noted that no viruses infect mainframes, but as file and mail servers, mainframes may store and distribute virus-infected files. Further, the variety and sophistication of new viruses imply the need for multiple layers of defense.

Anti-virus protection requires technology to identify and cure viruses, technology to intercept viruses in real-time before they spread, and technology to easily and automatically distribute updated virus protection to every computer.

2.5.1 UNIQUE NEEDS FOR VIRUS POLICY ADMINISTRATION

As noted above, detecting and resolving viruses is just one part of a complete solution against viruses. Viruses can move quickly from a single desktop to compromise data anywhere on a network. Network decision-makers need a powerful, continually active way to detect viruses and simultaneously protect valuable data from the damage viruses can cause. Virus protection should never be more burdensome than the virus threat itself. The most cost-effective and reliable network virus protection is centrally managed, easy to update, and protects both desktops and servers with little or no manual intervention.

Central management allows a system administrator to manage all multi-NOS servers and multi-OS clients in the LAN (or WAN) from a single administrator's console. This console should be able to travel to any desktop with the administrator. This central management must also provide a method for easy update of virus-signature-files and scan engines. These updates should be available via diskette, CD, BBS, and the Internet. When an administrator receives an update, he or she should be able to automatically propagate it to all computers running the AV software. This update should be done seamlessly, without the desktop users' knowledge.

2.5.2 "OLD DOG" PRODUCTS

Anti-virus technology is very specialized. In 1991, there was an urgent need for AV software to protect the desktop and the LAN. The small LANDesk team of engineers combined their efforts with those of engineers from a small company in Taiwan who focused on AV scanning technology. The relationship produced AV products for DOS and Novell NetWare in short order. These products were technology leaders and were very successful, especially in the large corporate segment.

Over the next five years, products were added for more platforms to include Windows 3.x, Windows 95, Windows NT, and Macintosh. When the LDVP team wasn't staffed to create or support translated versions for other Intel geographies, their engineers took our source code and modified it to fit their language needs. Each of the new LDVP operating system AV products arose as individual applications. Since an outside vendor produced the majority of the code (for both LANDesk and their own products), user interfaces for different LDVP products didn't look or function alike. The products were modified continually with new appendages for new virus types. There was more "patch" code than "original" code. Did we grow uncontrollably? Perhaps, but no more so than our competitors. It was difficult to balance and prioritize needs as new operating systems and new viruses leap-frogged the industry.

An old dog can't learn new tricks, so the saying goes. A new trick, macro viruses, appeared. They represented a completely new paradigm. Macro viruses were found in macros scattered throughout a data file. Previous viruses were found only in executable files, and only at the beginning or end. Further, macro viruses were easy to write and proliferated at an unbelievable rate. They required major changes to existing AV technology. The LDVP "old-dog" products had been modified to the point where they could no longer learn "new tricks" without a waterfall of side effects. This is when the Engineering Manager for LDVP joined the team.

The Marketing arm of our group had correctly identified the functionality our products needed, but it was growing harder and harder to successfully patch already over-patched code. How does a company decide when it is time to euthanize the old? Starting over is a costly proposition. We had some soul-searching to do concerning the LDVP product line.

Intel culture tells us that each employee is responsible for their own employment. The LDVP team couldn't expect to be employed with a product that didn't continue to "push the envelope" with virus detection, quality, and manageability. The strategy to rejuvenate our AV business would have to come from us. We wanted to protect our customers in an easily manageable way. We wanted to be technology leaders. We wanted to have top-notch, award-winning products.

Andy Grove, chairman of Intel, claims that "only the paranoid survive." The LDVP team had to assume that a re-architecture to create a single sustainable code base wasn't enough. We had to assume that our competitors were on the brink of releasing revolutionary new products. Our charter was to euthanize the old and start with a new puppy. But this puppy had grow fast, and had to be able to do more tricks than the old dog.

We looked to the Intel Corporation Mission Statement and Values for guidance (Figure 2-4).

OUR MISSION

Do a great job for our customers, employees and stockholders by being the preeminent building block supplier to the computing industry worldwide.

OUR VALUES

Customer Orientation
We strive to: Listen and respond to our customers, suppliers and stockholders; Clearly communicate mutual intentions and expectations; Deliver innovative and competitive products and services; Make it easy to work with us; Be vendor of choice.

Discipline
We strive to: Conduct business with uncompromising integrity and professionalism; Ensure a safe, clean and injury-free workplace; Make and meet commitments; Properly plan, fund and staff projects; Pay attention to detail.

Quality
We strive to: Achieve the highest standards of excellence; do the right things right; Continuously learn, develop and improve; Take pride in our work.

Risk Taking
We strive to: Foster innovation and creative thinking; Embrace change and challenge the status quo; Listen to all ideas and viewpoints; Learn from our successes and mistakes; Encourage and reward informed risk taking.

Great Place to Work
We strive to: Be open and direct; Promote a challenging work environment that develops our workforce; Work as a team with respect and trust for each other; Recognize and reward accomplishments; Manage performance fairly and firmly; Be an asset to our communities worldwide.

Results Orientation
We strive to: Set challenging and competitive goals; Focus on output; Assume responsibility; Constructively confront and solve problems; Execute flawlessly.

Figure 2-4: 1998 Intel Corporation Mission Statement and Values

2.6 THE REVIVAL PLAN

Based specifically on the Intel risk taking value to "foster innovation and creative thinking," we held daily think-tank meetings to air all ideas. All LDVP multi-disciplinary team members were invited to these meetings. Notes and working papers were updated daily and made available in a common repository. All opinions and viewpoints were considered.

It was clear to Engineering, and soon to all, that a completely new architecture and code base was needed. The current code was an intermingled and patched conglomeration of Intel and outside company code. It was difficult to establish accountability. This caused finger-pointing and a weakened relationship.

Based on the Intel results orientation value to "assume responsibility," a new architecture was needed to separate any outside scan
engine vendor's code from Intel code. We started the high-level architecture. It would define an API to communicate to the outside
vendor's scan engine, leaving their code distinct from our code. Assessing accountability would be simple with this design.

Motivated by the Intel customer orientation value to "deliver innovative and competitive products and services," we discussed the
peculiarity that no AV product had dominance in any geography except their own. LDVP's current corporate customers had branch offices all over the world. Our plan should comprehend the needs of
multiple geographies. The architecture was expanded to envision
multiple and changeable scan engines.

Recognizing the need to "clearly communicate mutual intentions and
expectations," our growing plan was updated daily and made available
to all think-tank participants. All relevant documents were kept on a
shared (and backed up) server that all team members had access to.

The final plan, depicted in Figure 2-5, proposed a new architecture for all LDVP products. The GUI and management functionality
would be removed and made distinct from the scanning technology.
A single API, that would service all operating systems, would be defined to interface Intel management code with scan technology. This
architecture would allow for one to many scan engines. We would
have the opportunity to always provide the current best scan en-
gine(s), and to plug in an Intel scan engine if desired.

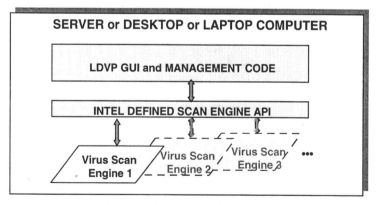

Figure 2-5: New Architecture for LANDesk Virus Protect Products

2.6.1 MANAGEMENT BUY-IN

A presentation for upper management was prepared and distributed to the team for review. We met and walked through the presentation. The Engineering Manager for the LANDesk Virus Protect (LDVP) AV products added team refinements. We met and walked through it again. Further refinements were made. The day came for the presentation to be given to three Intel General Managers. It was atypical, but the entire team was invited to attend. We wanted the General Managers to see and feel the team enthusiasm. It worked. The team aura was electrifying!

After carefully detailing the need for a change, and the plan and schedule for the change, we finalized by listing the advantages of our new architecture:

◆ **Advantage 1:** Intel can be positioned to always make the best detection scan engine available with the LDVP product.

◆ **Advantage 2:** Intel can offer the best scan engine per geography.

◆ **Advantage 3:** Intel will not need to drive the certification of a vendor's scan engine.

◆ **Advantage 4:** Intel has the option to produce a scan engine in-house.

◆ **Advantage 5:** Intel has ownership of all pieces except the scan engine.

◆ **Advantage 6:** LDVP customers can configure virus protection to meet their needs.

The risks were also enumerated.

At the end of the presentation, one General Manager said, "Is there any disadvantage to doing this?" There was silence as we pondered valid reasons not to proceed. The silence was finally broken by Ed Ekstrom's approval of the project.

The new architecture implied a contract change with our outside vendor company. Intel Legal started on the change, while Engineering started detailed design.

2.7 CULTURAL ISSUES

The existing LDVP team already knew what should be done. We had a viable business opportunity and hard-earned expertise. We had a core of extremely sharp engineers. As we entered the detailed design phase, we relied on established and accepted LDVP team goals. These goals represent specific best practices to support the Intel values and are enumerated in Figure 2-6.

LDVP team goals
Customer Orientation
We strive to:
- Integrate all customer issues into our designs—which means sampling customers, Marketing, Customer Support, rangers, PSEs, and Human Factors for input.

Discipline
We strive to:
- Minimize code.
- Create one multi-byte enabled code base for all languages.
- Never duplicate effort by re-writing code.
- Componentize via COM (Component Object Model) technology [Box98].
- Be responsive to requests for change, but manage change via the CCB (Change Control Board).
- Engineers are responsible for their own work—no separate sustaining team!

Quality
We strive to:
- Minimize code—to reduce design, code, test, localization, and sustaining time.

Risk Taking
We strive to:
- Design and document before coding starts. Put junior engineers on the critical path code – leaving senior engineers available for proof-of-concept and new technology research. If the junior engineers get behind schedule, the senior engineers can drop back to help catch up.

Great Place to Work
We strive to:
- Value and challenge "development engineers" and "test engineers" equally.
- Make time for research (i.e., have fun).
- Be pioneers in leading-edge technologies (i.e., have fun).
- "Minimize Code"?

Results Orientation
We strive to:
- Have test engineers work 24 hour days, 7 days per week via automated test scripts.
- Document to record relevant information, never just to create a document.

Figure 2-6: LDVP Team Goals

The goal to minimize code drives other goals. Minimizing code minimizes development, test, integration, and translation time. It also minimizes sustaining time.

To minimize code, we used COM technology so we coded once and re-used many times. To minimize code, we designed one NOS integrated console with 95% common code. The Novell Netware and Microsoft NT Server specific differences were treated as deltas (the weaker alternative was to code and maintain two large and distinct code chunks: one for NetWare and one for NTS). Code was to be succinct, modular, logical, and commented. The goal was not to combine multiple logical programming statements, but rather to architect wisely. This implies one multi-byte enabled source code base. Foreign language versions could never represent a different source.

2.7.1   THE PROJECT PLAN

The project, LDVP 5.0, was code-named "Newport." It was atypical because it encompassed new features as well as a rewrite of existing monolithic code. The rewrite sounds onerous. In reality, it was the opportunity to fill every programmer's dream—the chance to re-do after learning the lessons of the first-do.

> "America's quality guru, W. Edwards Deming, won the respect of American management by preaching a philosophy of commitment to quality and continuously improving the company-wide processes. His recognition that 'quality cannot be inspected in, it must be built in' raised an awareness in American businesses regarding quality... The companies that are industry leaders and retain their customer base are the ones that continuously evaluate their processes, services, and delivery mechanisms and improve them" [Jarvis97 and Crandall97].

The planning process we followed was based on the work of Alka Jarvis and Dr. Vern Crandall [Jarvis97], and on our own experience in software development. The team was motivated by Deming's idea of continuous process improvement (Intel value: "Continuously learn, develop and improve.") With the LDVP team goals in hand, we proceeded to the following Product Life Cycle (PLC) stages:

2.7.2   PLC STAGE 1: MARKETING BUSINESS PLANS

Any company, to succeed, must have a Corporate Mission Statement and a multi-year plan for how to achieve it. In our case, a three-year plan represented the sequence of products we would build and market.

Marketing, guided by our three-year plan, proposed revenue expected from the identified future products. All multi-disciplinary teams were sampled to get a preliminary estimate of development, marketing, sales, training, and support costs. With this information, staffing and financial resource needs were identified at least a year in advance. Marketing, by the way, was held accountable for the projected revenues.

Table 2-1 (page 50) shows the outputs from the Marketing Business Plans stage. This high-level planning feeds each individual product and is not product-dependent, but rather product-line-dependent.

2.7.3   PLC STAGE 2: MARKETING PRODUCT REQUIREMENTS

Once the long-range plans were established, specific product plans were addressed. The marketing team researched the specific requirements of the next product to be developed.

We strongly urge the creation of a Competition Wall [Snow97], or a wall of computers that contain competitor products. Plaster the walls with competitor's advertising and awards. Leave this wall up and running, ready for any passer-by to investigate. "The most important role of managers is to create an environment in which people are passionately dedicated to winning in the marketplace" [Grove96]. A Competition Wall will not only educate, but also motivate your team!

Marketing didn't have the hardware resources to build such a wall. We pursued the idea in Engineering. Given our team's strict and depleted budget, we put feelers out for old computers. We adopted some 'junkers', which were being replaced in a lab. We borrowed some old machines from the IE (Information Engineering) group. Our test team tore apart and rebuilt computers with spare RAM and hard drives. We bought multiplexors so one monitor, keyboard, and mouse would service three computers. The windfall came when one of our alert test engineers heard about trickle-down

Table 2-1: Outputs from PLC Stage 1

Marketing Business Plan Deliverables	Comment
Corporate Mission Statement	The Intel Corporate Mission Statement is: Do a great job for our customers, employees and stockholders by being the preeminent building block supplier to the computing industry worldwide.
LDVP Team Goals	
3-Year Marketing Plan	The marketing group identified the LDVP products to be produced in the next three years. The plan answered questions like: "What is our marketing plan for the next three years?" "What markets should we be in and what market segment share should we seek?" What sequence of products will get us there?" What new technologies do we need to master?"
Preliminary Budget	A short- and long-term budget was created for all LANDesk product teams. It included detailed plans for breakout strategies for pinpointed products.
GUI Standards Document	Each company should have a set of GUI standards. These standards should be updated as industry changes indicate, and not for each product. The standards should be followed in developing the Windows prototype.

machines at Intel Oregon. We were in a rapid hiring ramp at our site and there was never enough hardware, especially for our team. Our test lab has to be isolated—off the Intel intranet, and behind locked doors. Our virus-infected machines cannot be used or shared for other types of testing. Through a contact in Oregon, we got 16 trickle-down computers. The test team loaded competitor's products on servers in their cubes. We had to travel from cube to cube, but did get a good look at competitors' products.

Each of the products mentioned in the Three-Year Marketing Plan needed elaboration as development time approached. A Marketing Requirements Document (MRD), created by the marketing team, provided such elaboration, along with a detailed competitive analysis and the proposed behavior and functionality of the software product.

The LDVP 5 MRD was created by the marketing team. It was inspected by Quality Assurance (QA) to insure that all required information was present to include:

- Project introduction and scope.
- Project team.
- Market information, including:
  - ❑ Product objectives.
  - ❑ Market overview.
  - ❑ Competitive products.
  - ❑ Target customer.
  - ❑ Positioning imperatives.
  - ❑ Market risks.
  - ❑ Strategic issues.
  - ❑ Sales concerns.
  - ❑ International opportunities.
- Requirements, including:
  - ❑ Functional requirements.
  - ❑ Existing problems to fix.
  - ❑ Quality requirements.
  - ❑ Supported environment requirements.
  - ❑ International market requirements.
  - ❑ Installation, upgrade, migration, and serialization requirements.
  - ❑ Coexistence requirements.
  - ❑ Certification requirements.
  - ❑ Standards requirements.
- Issues, including:
  - ❑ Marketing calendar constraints.
  - ❑ Launch and channel issues.
  - ❑ Legal issues.
  - ❑ Dependencies, assumptions, and limitations.

When the inspection was complete, reviews of the MRD began. During reviews, participants pointed out areas that needed explanation or further research. Following four reviews, the MRD was finalized and signed by the Marketing PLM (Marketing Product Line Manager), Engineering and Test Managers, Documentation, Human Factors, and QA (Quality Assurance).

MRD creation to MRD approval may take months, so the multidisciplinary teams work in parallel throughout the entire Product Life Cycle. Engineering, for example, views the first pass of the MRD. We ask questions, do research, and start high-level design where applicable. We even start a prototype. Though this engineering review is informal, it serves to confirm the MRD as the formal vehicle for communication between Marketing and Engineering. Open areas are identified and driven to clarification. The MRD goes through formal inspections and reviews, but this informal first look prods the process.

Table 2-2 shows the outputs from the Marketing Requirements stage of LDVP 5 planning. Each deliverable was both inspected and reviewed before being signed by product participant teams.

2.7.4   PLC STAGE 3: ENGINEERING DESIGN

By the time the MRD was signed, the multi-disciplinary teams were well aware of what it contained. We worked in parallel to document and focus on the functionality we knew would be requested. The engineering team was not committed to complete everything in the MRD. For this very reason, every MRD prioritized requests. If a definite market window was specified, the engineering team was constrained to what could be completed in the specified time frame.

The process defined by our Program Management office indicates once the MRD is approved, Engineering should produce a Product Requirements Document (PRD, which is sometimes called the Software Requirements Document). Software Requirements Documents usually become lengthy. To provide an easy reference, we put the functional requirements from the MRD in a table, then added three columns for Engineering. The first additional column responds with a "Yes, No, or Maybe" to each item. The second additional column allows for engi-

Table 2-2: Outputs from PLC Stage 2

Marketing Product Requirements Deliverables	Comment
Competition Wall	A wall of computers loaded with competitor's software serves to educate and motivate all team members. Our wall was not implemented as a "wall." Rather, competitor products were installed and available for perusal in test engineer cubicles.
Preliminary Project Budget	This budget, considering the development time for a specific project, attempts to outline the expected costs.
Marketing Requirements Document (MRD)	This document, created by the marketing team, provides a vision of what a specific product should be. It shows how this product fits into the rest of our product line and how we differentiate our product from competitors' products. Integration between LANDesk products is defined. The MRD listed the platforms, interfaces, functionality, certifications, and international languages for LDVP 5.

neering comments. Since the MRD asks for high-level functionality, elaboration of each is needed. This can easily be added to a follow-on section of the PRD, especially if a third additional column provides a reference to where details can be found further in the document.

We should emphasize here that the MRD often represents dreams. Part of Marketing's responsibility is to be visionary. The MRD is then grounded by priorities. The TME (Technical Marketing Engineer), who is well-versed in technology, understands the current technical possibilities of what is requested and guides the setting of priorities in the MRD. The engineering team is not committed to anything in the MRD, but is obligated to respond to each requested function. Our response must be substantiated by resource availability, etc. Finalization on the product to be delivered is based on healthy negotiation between PDT (Product Development Team) members. Each member of a multidisciplinary team has a direct responsibility, but also full voice in product decision-making. In the rare case that we lack unanimity, Marketing makes the final decision—but it is a fully-informed decision.

2.7.5 PROTOTYPING

Experience in aerospace revealed that, even with extensive documentation, a communication black hole can appear. This black hole develops during coding, but is not evident until integration time. It swallows up precious time and energy, and always dictates rework. The black hole appears even if the MRD and PRD are complete. It appears even when software technical leads are part of the design team.

The Engineering Manager for LDVP had prepared an 87-page PRD for a previous project. It was deemed "very good" by QA. When coding was done, the functionality provided for server scanning didn't exactly match the functionality supported by the GUI. There was a "minor" misunderstanding that led the programmers off in different paths. In today's competitive world, however, no communication gap which requires rework is minor!

What caused this disconnect between engineers on the same team? Basically, English (or any spoken language) has communication flaws. The industry, long aware of this, has attempted various design communication methods, including pseudo-code, flowcharts, screenshots, etc...Pseudo-code, however, is not understood by everyone on a multi-disciplinary team. Flowcharts require preparation at descending degrees of detail, and even then lose effectiveness in pages and pages of traversal. Snapshots of windows with functional description are too static also. Flipping from page to page doesn't appropriately simulate usability or program flow. None of these methods has provided fool-proof (no pun intended) communication within a development team, nor even good communication across multi-disciplinary teams.

In the 1960's there was much discussion about the adoption of a worldwide language. The task appeared too politically daunting and was dropped. Today, however, much of the world reads and writes English spurred by the need/desire to use English operating systems. In like manner, "Windows" GUIs today are abundant. "Windows" has provided a new medium of communication. Windows prototypes can be used to communicate product design to almost anyone who is computer-literate. In fact, a Windows prototype is the most effective design communication tool for multi-disciplinary groups, including potential customers.

Prototypes aren't a new idea. They were created in the 1970's when code development was done with assembly language. The prototypes of this era were created as "proofs-of-concept." Prototyping took so long then that the thrown-together prototype was often used to actually create the product. The design process was absolutely necessary, but the coding needed to implement even a basic prototype was costly (manpower is still the most costly resource).

Today's 4GL tools make prototyping quick and easy. The prototypes of today, especially in the commercial arena, are used to solidify design, rather than as proof-of-concept. We have the luxury of a large and varied community familiar with GUI standards. Just as operating systems taught the computing world English, a Windows prototype today can be used to communicate design to multi-disciplinary teams.

The prototype should be created during the earliest phases of the development life cycle. A prototype that a salesperson can take to a potential customer under NDA (Non-disclosure Agreement) helps establish requirements. A prototype that Human Factors can exercise for usability testing confirms usability design before coding begins. There should be traceability from each object on the prototyped windows to the Marketing Requirements Document.

If a prototype is exercised and accepted before the development phase, development by all multi-disciplinary groups can be conducted in parallel. Marketing, Human Factors, Documentation, Test, and Development will know what the product looks like and how it functions. All can make plans for their individual pieces of the total product.

Our team went through an interesting evolution with prototyping. The idea initially met with rigid resistance. Engineers had two objections:

1. LDVP team goal: "Never duplicate effort by re-writing code." Creating a prototype violated our team goal because prototyping was to be done in Delphi or C++ Builder, and the application GUIs were to be coded with MS Visual C++.

2. Engineers wanted the freedom to design windows as they actually started coding them. After all, software development is a creative art!

Objections were neutralized by discussing real examples of re-work that a prototype would have prevented. Discussions of free agency and creativity led to the understanding that deciding where to put a button on a window was not all that creative. In fact, it is a weak substitute for the ideal. Senior developers saw the vision by re-alizing they could participate in design, which would be communi-cated via the GUI. They could participate in architecture, which would be communicated via the Architecture Document. Then they could leave the main coding to others, and tackle the high-risk proof-of-concept features. They could have time to do leading-edge research. The engineers needed to move their creativity up to the de-sign and research space.

Human Factors also got the vision. When engineers design win-dows at code time, Human Factors can only offer suggestions and critiques. Even when critiques are valid, there is resistance to code changes which don't add functionality but do impact schedules. Our Human Factors engineer recognized that a prototype forces GUI de-sign at design time. The HF engineer, thus decided to create the pro-totype! The extended team met daily to design. The HF engineer prototyped the decisions. Human Factors took the prototype to ex-isting customers and modified it to incorporate their suggestions. The finalized prototype worked as a template for developers. They no longer had to guess where to put controls, or move them after guessing wrong!

This was so successful that the HF engineer is currently teaching other Human Factors and Information Engineering (Docs) teams how to prototype with Borland's Delphi. Just imagine, documentors, who basically document the functionality of windows, will know what those windows will look like even before they are coded. Docs can thus work in parallel with coding efforts! And, engineers have no complaints because the extended team is doing the prototyping.

With a completed prototype and PRD, the requirements were doc-umented and communicated. The next step was to create the detailed architecture. The prototype illuminated where COM (Component Object Model) objects should be used. For example, when we saw the same configuration options box appearing on multiple windows, we knew it should be coded once as a COM object. Figure 2-7 shows a window from our Windows 95 Client product. Three OCX COM objects are circled.

The "Actions" OCX, for example, allows users to select primary and secondary automatic actions to take if a virus is found. This option is needed on all operating system platforms. It is needed for real-time scans (scan a file while it is being opened), scheduled scans, manual-start scans, and screen-saver scans. It was designed, coded, tested, and translated once, but appears over twenty-four times in our products. It exists as a completely independent object. This way, we could change the look and even basic functionality, compile the OCX, re-register it in every product, and the change would be implemented across the product. There was never a need to recompile any product.

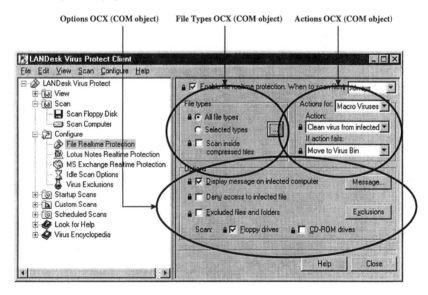

Figure 2-7: COM Object Controls

With the PRD and prototype done, and the COM objects identified, the detailed architecture could be completed. The finalized architecture pointed out all modules that needed to be coded. Remember our team goal to minimize code? An example: We architected so that one 32-bit Client source code base was used for the following products and configurations:

- Windows 95 Client.
- NT Workstation Client.
- LAN Connected Client (administered from an integrated console).
- LAN Sometimes Connected Client (requires special update when re-connected).
- LAN Never Connected Client (also called "stand-alone" client; has different default settings).
- Client TDK.
- Foreign language versions of any of the above (this is multiplicative, not additive!).

The task list was easily derived from the architecture, and was used to make the schedule. Tasks on the schedule were then staged to deliver working subsystems weekly or bi-weekly. The high-risk code was delivered first. This way, the project completed in testable units that could be passed to the test team early in the development cycle. When coding was completed, the test team had already completed most unit and some integration testing.

The engineering team then passed their PRD, architecture, test plan, and schedule to the Program Manager, who collected like plans from Human Factors, Documentation, Support, International, and Training. He compiled all into the final Project Plan. The Project Plan contained a Master Schedule as prepared by the Program Manager. This was constantly growing, and became our bible. It helped to enlarge the typical Product Development Life Cycle to become a complete Product Delivery Process.

Outputs from the Engineering Design Stage are listed in Table 2-3.

Table 2-3: Outputs from PLC Stage 3

Engineering Design Deliverables	Comment
Windows Prototype	The prototype will show all windows. All navigational objects will work (i.e., buttons which should open new windows will open new windows). This prototype of the preliminary interfaces of the proposed product is shown to all multi-disciplinary team members, and to customers and potential customers with their input being gathered for incorporation. Each requirement in the MRD should have traceability to a function in the prototype. Details of how each button, dialog, etc. should work need to be documented, preferably by the documentation team. Human Factors should start usability testing before the prototype is finalized.
Product Requirements Document (PRD)	The PRD (sometimes called a Software Requirements Specification) prepared by Engineering, serves as a response to the MRD (Marketing Requirements Document) by specifying the software product that will be built. It also points out areas of risk.
Software Architecture	The architecture can be created with one-to-one traceability to objects on the Windows prototypes (and in the PRD). It should be defined in a hierarchical structure with base unary functions appearing at the lowest level as leaf nodes. The next layer consists of modules which manage multiple functions. The architecture should eliminate duplicate modules and reduce dependencies.
Unit Test Plans	Based on the prototype and Software Architecture.
Integration Test Plans	Based on the Software Architecture.
Beta Test Plans	The number and duration of beta cycles must be identified. The type of beta support must be planned for and staffing should be identified in a schedule.
Documentation Development Plan	This plan will not only identify the type of documentation to be provided, but will include resource and development time needs. Foreign language versions should be considered and scheduled.

Table 2-3: Outputs from PLC Stage 3 *(continued)*

Engineering Design Deliverables	Comment
Customer Support Training Plan	A Customer Training Plan may also be necessary depending on the complexity of the product. If foreign language versions of the product will be produced, this plan must accommodate foreign language-speaking customer support personnel.
Support/Maintenance Plan	This plan will identify the group who will provide technical support and the support period. If foreign language versions of the product will be produced, this plan must accommodate appropriately for a lab and engineers.
Project Plan	This plan, compiled by the Program Manager, includes all design and schedule information for the entire project. It is a compilation of all documents prepared to date.

2.7.6 MANAGING CHANGE

For decades we have been telling Marketing that building a software product is like building a house—you have to architect first. Once the building begins, changes compromise the original logic and flow. Changes increase the cost. After twenty years, we truly haven't convinced even one Marketing person. They listen, smile, shake their heads in agreement, and come with proposed changes two weeks later! The AV business is even worse because there are two forces pushing constant change: Marketing AND virus writers! Software engineers can continue to evangelize, but in the meantime, we had better design a product that is tolerant of change. That is best accomplished by architecting a product that is componentized and modular, that eliminates dependencies between components, and reduces dependencies within components. (See the excellent coding suggestions in the new book, Inroads to Software Quality: A "How To" Guide with Toolkit [Jarvis97]. Componentization via COM is well-addressed in Don Box's new book Essential COM [Box98].)

Even when the architecture is tolerant of change, change must be managed so that consequences are comprehended. The CCB manages changes to requirements and functionality. Planning documents, which have been approved and signed, are updated via a BBC document if and when a change is requested and approved.

2.7.7 PLC STAGE 4: DEVELOPMENT

This paper focuses on "best practices" during the planning stage. We have already taken the liberty of discussing the design phase, so we will not pursue discussion of development and test other than to say that we followed our design and schedule. We shipped with a defect density of .8. The QA-defined minimum is 8 (8 defects per 10,000 lines of code), which we improved on by a factor of 10! The engineering team delivered the finished product as designed and on-time.

Deming says: "Cease dependence on inspection to achieve quality. The focus is on avoiding quality problems, in place of inspecting out defects after they have occurred" [Deming86].

Our planning process focuses on designing in quality, designing out errors, and controlling change.

2.8 THE RESULT—A NEW GENERATION OF AWARD-WINNING, SUSTAINABLE LDVP PRODUCTS

The LDVP team embraced change and challenged the status quo. We took a risk, but a well-understood and calculated risk. The award-winning result, LDVP 5, met our team goal to "pioneer in leading-edge technology." One highlight of our new product offering is integrated domain administration (see Figure 2-8). A system administrator can, from a single admin console, view and administer Netware and NTS servers, as well as NTW, Windows 95, Windows 3.x, and DOS clients. The administrator's console also lets the administrator configure logical domains, and view and control scan parameters for all servers and clients within those domains. Administrators can lock down client scanning parameters from the administrator's console. Client lock-down prevents users from inadvertently or intentionally modifying virus protection at the desktop.

Integrated Domain Administration Reduces Costs

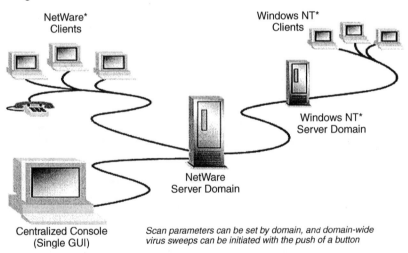

Figure 2-8: LDVP 5 Integrated Domain Administration

The most cost-effective and reliable network virus protection is centrally managed, easy to update, and protects both desktops and servers with little or no manual intervention. LDVP 5 provides easy update via automatic and invisible replacement of virus-signature-files and scan engine changes, as illustrated in Figure 2-9.

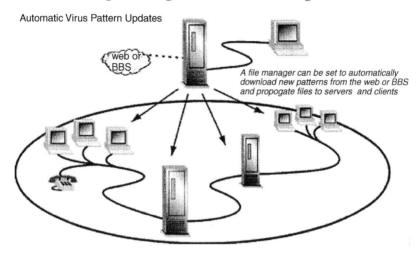

Figure 2-9: LDVP 5 Automatic Virus Signature Updates

PCWeek Magazine (October 8, 1997 issue) claims:

> "Intel Corp.'s LANDesk Virus Protect 5.0 had both the best interoperability and the lowest cost of the four packages in PC Week Labs' tests that pitted it against Computer Associates International Inc.'s InnocuLAN 4.0 Service Pack 1, McAfee Associates Inc.'s Total Virus Defense and Symantec Corp.'s Norton AntiVirus 4.0. In fact, its interoperability, low cost and stellar management of NetWare and Windows NT networks earned LANDesk Virus Protect 5.0 an Analyst's Choice award." http://www.zdnet.com/pcweek/reviews/1006/06virus.html

> Windows Magazine named LDVP 5 as the "Best network-based desktop virus protection. http://www.winmag.com/reclist/utilities.htm

2.9   LESSONS LEARNED

We find that the price paid for not spending enough time with the Marketing Plan and Sales Plan is that we end up making changes after product(s) have been installed at customer sites or when shrink-wrapped products have hit the market. If we do our homework upfront, we tend to make our deadlines with stable products, which need little change after shipping and installation. Further, we can develop user documentation, training materials, sales plans, preliminary versions of the product, etc. in parallel with the software development (which tends to take the longest time to develop). The Software Life Cycle must be based on the Parallel Life Cycle [Jarvis97 and Crandall97]. Multi-disciplinary team planning should be done in parallel. Then multi-disciplinary development/test can proceed in parallel.

Configuration control based on frozen requirements helps to synchronize parallel efforts. Any document that has been inspected, reviewed, and signed is subject to a CCB review before any change is approved. All original document signers, who must then sign a change control document, agree to necessary changes.

If the prototype is exercised and accepted before the development phase, development by all multi-disciplinary groups can be conducted in parallel. Marketing, Human Factors, Documentation, Test, and Development will know what the product looks like and how it will function. All can make plans for their individual pieces of the total product. The Project Plan will stage development in such a manner that working subsystems are delivered weekly or bi-weekly and the most high-risk code is delivered first. This will allow for early testing of subsystems. Before any code is complete, the test group will be planning and scripting automated tests.

Coding, documentation, and testing will start concurrently with development. Many of us have experienced disaster when all of the software modules are first brought together in "big-bang" integration. To avoid this, development can be scheduled so as to complete the first subsystem, then the next, and so forth. Integration is done with a "little-bang" approach: build a little, integrate a little, and test a little. This process differs from the spiral RAD model in that all of the design, including architecture, is done before coding starts. It does, however, capitalize on one of the strongest features of RAD, little-bang integration, and still conforms very closely to Deming's approach to quality.

2.10 CONCLUSIONS

Traditional software development strategies, including the waterfall and spiral life cycles, agree that requirements gathering and planning are important. Documentation of these phases provides a guideline for implementation. Such documentation should include a Software Requirements Specification, a Software Design or Architecture Specification, and a detailed schedule. Requirements should be able to be traced from a marketing research document to the tasks listed on the detailed schedule. We have had experience, however, that even with rigorous attention to these phases and documents, misinterpretations occur, not just between Marketing and Engineering, but between the engineers themselves! The problem, it is judged, lies in the inherent weakness of communicating technically precise details via an imprecise language specification. The imprecise languages we use, accompanied with the human inability to grasp hundreds of specification details from written specification, combine to cause confusion at some level in every project. The RAD methodology attempts to correct this problem by giving us prototype pieces to look at. For example, a window's functionality may be described in a specification, or it may be prototyped for users to look at and work with. The specification, geared towards engineers, won't be a standard that salespeople, for example, are familiar with. The window prototype, however, can be given to any user with Windows experience and be comprehended. With these phenomena in mind, we suggest that the prototype phase is more vital to the overall success of the project than commonly recognized. Because of its importance, the prototype should be created during the marketing phase of requirements gathering. If available at this phase, salespeople can show it to potential customers, who can have input (an effective sales strategy). Human Factors can test it for usability and standards.

If the prototype is exercised and accepted during the marketing phase, all other development phases can be conducted in parallel. Marketing, Human Factors, Documentation, Test, and Development will know what the product looks like and how it will function. All can make plans for their individual pieces of the total product.

Three astounding improvements to process still remain to be discussed. First, using the prototype, all underlying functionality can be architected and organized. If a button appears on three windows, it should be planned as one unique object and should be coded once. Second, once the functional design or architecture is complete, the components combining to make a larger component are identifiable and development can proceed component by component. Each can be passed to the test organization when completed. Third, because the design of the windows is done and because the underlying architecture is complete, average programmers can be assigned to tasks on the critical time-line, allowing advanced developers to do research and proof-of-concept work. If the critical time-line falls into jeopardy, advanced developers can drop back to catch the work up. Risk is managed with the development plan!

Software development is a creative art. Without a detailed plan, development engineers exercise their creativity when deciding how to code a loop, or where to put a button on a window. Our planning process involves senior programmers in the product design and proof-of-concept work, then sets them free to use creative thinking for new ideas, new technology, and research. Without hiring a dedicated "think-tank" group, your company can still spend time in R&D. Creativity is moved from the development phase to the design and research arena.

C H A P T E R

3

Technology Project Management Process

PKS Information Services

3.1 COMPANY PROFILE

PKS is an international company providing full-service computer outsourcing, systems integration services, and enterprise Internet services. It provides high-quality, custom-tailored solutions. The company's systems integration services help customers define, develop, and implement cost-effective information systems. Lex-iBridge, a PKS company, helps customers convert legacy COBOL applications to client/server and Internet platforms.

Headquartered in Omaha, Nebraska, PKS has built itself up quietly over the last 10 years, using its focus on quality service to differentiate itself from its larger, more established competitors. The service philosophy is inextricably embedded in the company's organization, training, procedures, and practices. The president and CEO Raul Pupo describes PKS not as a technology company, but as a service company.

After gaining a foothold in the information technology industry as a computer processing outsourcing company, PKS continued to leverage its success in the Year 2000 conversion market, establishing a reputation for itself as a top-notch systems integrator. Its strategy has been successful. PKS worldwide employee growth has increased from 500 in 1996 to 800 at the end of 1997.

3.1.1 PKS' COMPUTER OUTSOURCING SERVICES

The term "outsourcing," with respect to information technology, refers to the practice of contracting an external service provider for integrated technology (IT) services. Traditionally, companies would outsource all or a part of their IT functions with the intention of eliminating costs associated with equipment and staff. Recently, however, companies have begun to outsource more as a means of enhancing business value, rather than reducing costs. By hiring an outsourcing vendor, companies are able to take advantage of the vendor's investments in technical resources and technological expertise. This takes some of the pressure off internal IT departments to recruit and retain large staffs, perform day-to-day maintenance activities, and keep up with the dynamic developments in the IT industry. Instead, they can focus internal resources on core competencies and strategic planning.

In our computer operations outsourcing division, we replace all or a part of a firm's in-house computer department. We go into a company, study its data processing and telecommunications systems, build an identical system in our computer super-center, and seamlessly transfer the operations to our environment. In providing these services, we accept responsibility for entire mainframe and midrange computing environments, control information technology infrastructures of any size, and provide secure, dedicated computing environments.

PKS' computer super-center is a state-of-the-art facility specially designed to offer its customers a secure computer processing environment. The building houses mainframe and client/server computers that are used to process mission-critical data for PKS' customers. In this building, PKS also operates a "command center" where technicians monitor and measure computers performance 24 hours a day, 7 days a week.

With our computer outsourcing services, we help our customers reduce capital investments associated with ownership of high-priced, voluminous computing equipment; lower computer processing costs; access new resources and skills; and handle fluctuating peak requirements without running out of capacity or acquiring permanent resources. Our outsourcing engagements are generally long-term maintenance agreements, in which we manage or monitor a customer's computing environment.

We make available to all our customers a comprehensive set of computing services, referred to as "Base-Level Services." Computing services are provided without a long list of exceptions. Therefore, during the life of a contract, a customer may request various enhancements to their environments, including system upgrades or software database upgrades. These service requests are often similar for numerous customers, as many of them use the same software products. A project manager is assigned to handle the requirements of each outsourcing contract. The project manager works with a team of technicians to carry out the terms of the contract and respond to service requests within the scope of that contract.

3.2 REASONS TO IMPLEMENT

Major factors in the decision to develop a project management process included repetition among projects, planning, status reporting, and availability of information. First, technology projects often involved numerous, repeatable activities. Various technicians were continually being assigned similar projects, but were not following standardized procedures for completing those projects. Therefore, each time a particular type of project was being done, the procedure was being redeveloped over and over again. The company wanted to track the steps being followed for each project so technicians could reap the benefits of past experiences during future projects. Second, the company had consistent difficulties with planning. Project plans were not as comprehensive and well-developed as the managers wanted them to be. Third, managers were frustrated about the lack of documented status reporting during projects. They might inquire about the status of a particular project and hear things were progressing well, only to find later that inadequate resources were assigned to the project or insufficient time was allotted. Finally, managers and team members had difficulty locating and obtaining documented information regarding past or present projects partially because of the lack of documentation, but mostly because no central information repository had been set up to store the information that was being generated. Acquiring project information could prove even more difficult if the team members for a project were no longer with the company, or had been reassigned to a different area.

The successful management of technology outsourcing engagements depends on development and implementation of project plans, development of schedules, evaluation of risk, leadership, and administration. Gathering the necessary information, developing project scope, documenting the information, presenting it to management, and communicating status and developments to management of both companies require extensive documentation and coordination efforts.

In response to the short comings of current methods and increased project demands, the company developed a process to assist its technicians and project managers with customer service requests. This process is called the Technology Project Management Process (TPMP). It is used by PKS operators to meet customer quality standards. The 36-point process combines principles such as risk and impact analysis with a customer service focus. In 1997, the TPMP was recognized as the Best of the Best in Information Technology by the Quality Assurance Institute, Orlando, Florida. The process outlines the steps that should be followed for every project, no matter the size or complexity.

Whatever service is performed for a particular customer, it always requires some degree of information gathering and planning, administration of the specific project tasks, and "cleanup" tasks. Management of projects requires coordinating a team of professionals, guiding the team through the project, and communicating regularly with the customer and within our company. While we use various methodologies to complete specific project tasks (i.e., system migrations and Year 2000 conversions), the TPMP helps project managers coordinate the overall project details that apply to any technology outsourcing project. Specifically, the TPMP establishes rules for documenting procedures for repetitive tasks that can be adhered by project teams during similar projects in the future. It lists steps for information gathering and planning that should result in more detailed, accurate project plans. It draws guidelines for communication with us and customer management regarding project status, issues and concerns. And, it defines procedures for documentation throughout each project, defining a central location where that documentation is to be stored. By improving upon these areas, we are able to roll out technology changes faster, gauge progress more accurately, and improve customer communication. Each of these items contributes to the overall success of the project and satisfaction of the customer.

Project management is critical to the quality and success of projects. It is the purpose of the TPMP to define, organize, and document the required use of project management, resulting in the highest level of customer satisfaction because of high-quality project implementations. The TPMP does not introduce any ground-breaking theories of project management; many of the skills and techniques described in the manual are commonplace in projects today. The intent of the process, however, is to formalize the process in such a way that it not only ensures project success and customer satisfaction, but also facilitates continuous improvement.

Three of the most prevalent themes in the TPMP are planning, communication, and documentation, which are thoroughly addressed in the document's three main sections:

1. Project Initiation.
2. Project Administration.
3. Project Completion.

The first section defines the groundwork that is necessary to sufficiently prepare for a project. It explains that gathering appropriate information, understanding project scope, and planning the work and resources are essential steps in ensuring the success of any project. The second section defines the technician's responsibility to oversee the project and keep managers and other technicians informed about the project's progress and any issues that may arise. The third section focuses on the finishing tasks, which must be performed before a project can truly be considered complete. The finishing tasks include updating records, completing documentation, and filing all project documentation. These final tasks are essential to the success of the TPMP. If documentation about repetitive projects is not complete and available, it will not benefit future projects as expected.

The objectives of the TPMP include:

◆ Improving the quality of the product produced for customers by using a methodology that promotes the customer's involvement, awareness, and timely resolution of issues throughout the project management process.

◆ Minimizing project risk by establishing a standardized implementation process that increases the likelihood of success through early identification of the necessary tasks and steps of a project.

◆ Reducing the required effort and redundancies of project implementation by establishing a historical database of project implementations and related tasks for all customers and products that can be reviewed and applied to future projects.

◆ Identifying and establishing formal documentation for those project activities that are repetitive across all or similar projects.

◆ Improving customer satisfaction by instituting procedures which involve the customer and identify steps to help ensure that the customer's information technology environment is properly maintained, documented, and at the highest level of quality.

Several themes are prevalent in these objectives and will be repeated numerous times in this chapter:

◆ Quality.

◆ Customer involvement.

◆ Standardization/repetition.

◆ Customer satisfaction.

The following sections will show how the TPMP uses planning, communication, and documentation tasks to effect improved quality and customer service, partnership, and continuous improvement.

3.3 COMPANY PHILOSOPHY

The corporate culture at PKS fosters a professional and customer-oriented environment in which employees are given the tools they need to satisfy the customer. Our mission statement is the foundation of corporate values and beliefs, which are focused on the constant attainment of total customer satisfaction. In developing the TPMP, we did not want to stifle this environment, which encourages staff members to continually look for and implement new and improved ways of serving customers' needs. Overall, the TPMP focuses on providing the customer with a quality product, keeping in line with our customer-oriented approach. In addition, it provides for flexibility in developing processes and allows for suggested improvements or changes in procedures.

A testament to the company's customer-focused philosophy is its mission statement, which promises to provide service that will ensure the highest level of customer satisfaction, and will meet the standards of its customers. The mission statement reads as follows:

Customer Service: Customers are first. We will provide service to ensure the highest level of customer satisfaction.

Quality: To achieve customer satisfaction, the quality of our work must meet the highest standards, those of our customers.

Business Partnership: By developing a partnership with our customers we share in the responsibility for satisfying business objectives.

Ethics: We will conduct business in an ethical, legal and socially responsible fashion. Our integrity will never be compromised.

3.4 TECHNOLOGY PROJECT MANAGEMENT PROCESS

The TPMP is a tool that helps employees focus on the company's mission. By helping technicians focus on the customer, plan for projects better, and complete projects quicker, the customers are generally more satisfied, and the quality of service is higher. Using the TPMP, employees are encouraged to make decisions based on the needs of the customer, and involve the customer throughout the project. With the level of communication encouraged by the TPMP, the customer's goals are more likely to be met in the end.

3.4.1 CUSTOMER SERVICE

While the computer outsourcing industry typically has measured service in terms of efficiency criteria, we have claimed that the customer's level of satisfaction is the only valid standard of measuring service quality. The company's goal of achieving total customer satisfaction is predicated upon consistently exceeding expectations. All employees are immersed in the company's customer service philosophy from Day One. Employees are taught that:

1. Our business is driven by the company's zeal to satisfy the customer's needs.

2. Service management is proactive and preventive.

3. Service management is a company-wide concern.

With provisions for project documentation, customer status reports, and customer input, the TPMP helps achieve customer service goals by maintaining a focus on the customer's objectives throughout the project. This all translates into a project that is on schedule and focused, which in turn contributes to the customer's ultimate satisfaction.

"The Technology Project Management Process is simply one implementation of our mission to achieve the highest level of customer satisfaction," said Raul Pupo, PKS' president and CEO.

3.4.2   COMMUNICATION

One critical factor that contributes to the customer's overall satisfaction is communication. We learned this first-hand through feedback via service order report cards, customer surveys, and one-on-one communications.

Through feedback, it was discovered that some customers preferred to have more contact during their service engagements, including communication, interaction, and updates of ongoing activities. With the TPMP, procedures have been implemented to ensure ample communication with the customer throughout each project. By encouraging regular communication with the customer throughout the planning and implementation stages, the TPMP helps yield an understanding of the customer's expectations for the project and periodically gauge performance to ensure those expectations are being met.

Early in the process, the project manager is encouraged to make contact with the customer to discuss the scope and details of the project. This initial communication is intended not only to clarify details that may not be apparent, but to let the customer know their request has been acknowledged and who their contact is within our company. Reviewing the scope with the customer is crucial to the success of the project, as it is essential that the technician and customer understand and agree with the scope of work required to satisfy the request. In most cases, the technician will not have been involved in negotiations over contract terms and project scope. Therefore, this is an essential first step in ensuring the customer's objectives are understood and will be met at least to the customer's satisfaction.

The Project Administration section of the TPMP outlines the procedures the project manager should follow during the actual project tasks, and has a recurring theme of communication with the customer. The project manager is reminded throughout this section to maintain regular contact with the customer regarding current activities, outstanding questions, and relevant issues. Both written and personal communication are encouraged. The company's insistence on regularly communicating with the customer is demonstrated by the use of project management software products that aid in the production of all types of reports. Sample reports are included in the TPMP appendix.

The TPMP suggests meeting with the customer as one of the best ways to communicate any information relative to the project because it is a more personal approach compared to written updates via fax or mail. Telephone conferences are considered an appropriate, cost-effective method of personal communication, which provides the opportunity to exchange ideas, issues, and concerns regarding the project, as well as other customer-related issues. The TPMP promotes personal communication as a supplement to written communication to reduce misinterpretations regarding information provided on status reports.

3.4.3 SERVICE QUALITY

The service management process of the TPMP is founded on the Quality Assurance Institute's Quality Implementation Model and the 14 quality principles of Dr. W. Edwards Deming for service-oriented businesses. The TPMP assists in achieving two of Deming's points, which are demonstrated in this section:

1. Cease dependence on mass inspection. Eliminate the need for inspection on a mass basis by building quality into the process in the first place.

2. Continual Improvement of Process. Improve constantly and forever the system of production and service, to improve quality and productivity, and thus constantly decrease costs.

The steps in the TPMP demonstrate acceptance of these quality principles. The three phases of the TPMP work together to help the project team achieve a high-quality product the first time, and improve upon that quality during subsequent projects. The process walks the project manager through comprehensive information gathering and planning steps, which are intended to identify, as accurately as possible, the requirements of the project. The underlying principle here is that appropriate research and planning greatly increase the quality and success of the project.

"The goal is to plan your implementation strategy to increase the quality and likelihood of success while minimizing unexpected obstacles."

Various procedures in the TPMP help managers and technicians leverage their experience with current projects to improve upon future projects. Specifically, the planning and documentation steps are most helpful in fostering an environment of continuous improvement. The faster, more effective delivery of service achieved from documenting repetitive processes is one form of continuous improvement.

3.4.4   INFORMATION GATHERING/PLANNING

The section of the TPMP entitled "Project Initiation" is devoted to project research and planning, advising the project manager on matters such as understanding project scope, determining impact and risk, determining resource integration, analyzing resource requirements, and developing and approving a project plan. No matter the project's size, precise planning combined with proper management will usually result in a high-quality product. During this phase, customer interviews are critical components in gathering and understanding the project's requirements.

"This intensive customer interaction throughout the process is pivotal to every project's success," said President and CEO Raul Pupo.

Before a project plan is devised, the TPMP encourages the project manager to collect as much information as possible regarding the upcoming project. The first determination the project manager should make is whether a similar project already has been completed for the same or another customer. The TPMP requires that every project be accompanied by the proper documentation, which is stored in a central repository for future reference. If it is a repeat project, past files will be helpful in identifying the information needed and subsequent steps that should be taken.

Evaluations of risks, impacts, and resource integration are also essential initial research steps of a project. The TPMP helps the project manager calculate impact and risks (both pre- and post-implementation) based on project complexity, time, and people or departments affected. Projects with a short schedule or numerous steps to complete have increased risks. With this evaluation of risk and impact, the project manager can plan accordingly. With an analysis of resource requirements, the project manager determines how many people and what kind of hardware and software resources will be needed throughout the project.

Through this fact-finding mission, project managers are able to anticipate potential obstacles to a successful project and resolve those issues or plan accordingly before they impact the success of the project. Using this information, the project manager can devise a plan that has a good chance of leading to a successful project. Also, the background work will help in the plan's approval process. A well-researched, thought-out plan has a better chance of surviving management's scrutiny. This planning and approval process helps technicians understand where they are going and how they are getting there. It forces them to examine all the details of the project, rather than jump headlong into an unknown abyss, which ultimately will translate into a higher quality product. At the same time, managers can see the benefits of this planning exercise when they are asked to approve a plan and assign resources. With a detailed, accurate plan, managers can easily determine the resource requirements for the project, with the result that the project is not rushed due to lack of time or people.

3.4.5   CUSTOMER INVOLVEMENT

Regularly consulting with customers regarding matters of scope definition, objectives, and progress demonstrates a willingness to work with the customer toward a common goal. It ensures the project team uses its technological expertise in concert with the customer's vision for a successful project. The TPMP encourages customer involvement from initial information gathering stages through project completion. In fact, in two of the stated objectives of the TPMP process, customer involvement is mentioned outright:

1. The first of five objectives is to improve quality by using a methodology that "promotes the customer's involvement, awareness and concern."

2. The last objective is to increase the customer's satisfaction using procedures that "involve the customer."

Although the topic of communication has already been discussed in this chapter, it is necessary to briefly revisit the discussion to demonstrate how the TPMP promotes customer involvement. During one of the first steps of the project management process, the technician is encouraged to call the customer to discuss various aspects of the project, specifically the level of involvement the customer wishes to maintain during the project. Establishing the customer's desired level of involvement at the onset eliminates guessing games. It gives the project team a specific goal for involving the customer in project decisions, implementations, and status reports. Later in the process, guidelines are developed in the form of status reports and regular phone meetings to help maintain the desired goals for customer involvement. Finally, the TPMP states that the project cannot be considered complete until PKS and the customer both agree as such. Usually this will be signified by the customer signing off on a customer service order.

3.4.6   RISK EVALUATION

The TPMP section entitled "Determining Impact and Risk" explains that improper planning could result in a failed project or task, and consequently put the customer at unnecessary risk. Services provided to customers involve sensitive, mission-critical information systems, and therefore carry the potential for negative impacts for the customer, such as disabled or dysfunctional systems. Such a failure could strain the partnership. That is why planning the project or task, no matter how small or complex, is critical. To protect the customer from such risks, risk and impact evaluations are implemented into the TPMP.

The risk evaluation suggests a careful review of the system areas that will be affected by the project, and identification of areas where risk is the greatest. Typically, but not always, the risk level will increase with the size and complexity of the project. Larger projects involve a greater number of tasks, and an increased likelihood that errors could occur. Also, when projects are rushed, the risk factor increases. Checkpoints might be bypassed for the sake of meeting the deadline. The risk evaluation assists technicians first in determining the level of risk a particular project carries, and second in planning accordingly.

The manual includes a "risk table" to help in the evaluation. The table defines low-, medium- and high-risk projects and gives examples of each. A low-risk project includes changes that are very straight-forward and does not require an outage of the customer's system, while a high-risk project includes a major, usually system-wide, level of outage. Technicians may not necessarily be able to eliminate risks by identifying them beforehand, but they can prepare for them in advance, which can reduce the impact the risk carries.

The TPMP's discussion of impact evaluations, is intended to determine the potential impact to the organization as a result of the risks already identified. Impact evaluations take into account the scope of the project, the number of people in the organization impacted by the change, and the change to the environment. An increase in the number of people affected by the project plays a direct role in the potential impact to the customer. Impact evaluations are executed in much the same way as risk evaluations, including an impact table that defines low-, medium- and high-impact projects and lists requirements for each. Low-impact projects do not impact the production environment and customers will be able to operate in a business-as-usual fashion. The change does not require direct customer approval to implement. A high-impact project affects production in a significant manner, typically system-wide. Customer approval, peer review and back-out procedures are required.

Once risk and impact levels have been determined, the TPMP suggests combining the results to determine an "overall risk level," generally the highest level between the two. By including risk evaluations as a standard procedure in the TPMP, PKS has demonstrated its commitment to the customer's success.

3.4.7   DOCUMENTATION

The Project Completion section of the TPMP addresses documentation as a critical element of each project. Documentation is touted in the TPMP as "one of the more important aspects of any project or task." So much is learned throughout a project, and the transfer of this knowledge to written form can benefit many projects for years to come. A detailed record of changes made for a customer is an excellent resource for other technicians to consult during future projects for this or another customer. If the TPMP is followed correctly, documented information will identify any changes that affect operations or help desk services and any changes to the customer's software inventory. Therefore, when front-line employees working at the help desk receive a call from a customer, they are more able to administer quality service if they are working from accurate, up-to-date information about that customer's system.

Documentation is essential both during the administration of a service, and once the service request has been completed. Discussions to this point have examined the importance of documentation during the execution of a service to speed up service delivery for future projects. While rapid implementation of a service adds to the customer's satisfaction and consequently adds value to the partnership, it also goes beyond that. Having a file of documentation for each customer ensures that down the line in the service engagement, any technician or project manager can look back to see what has been done for that customer and accurately answer any questions the customer may have.

A particular technician, responsible for a customer's service request at one point in time, may not be the responsible technician for that customer's subsequent service request. Conversely, the customer's contact for a particular service may no longer be with the company when another service is requested. With PKS' documentation library, a technician knows exactly where to find information regarding any customer's previous service requests. These documents could provide valuable information in that they contain all research, customer correspondence, and working documents. This information will define the steps taken, as well as issues that may have surfaced during implementation and how they were resolved.

The results of an implemented service request often require revisions to manuals and other documentation. For instance, a service may affect operational and help desk areas and might change console messages or hardware status codes. Unfortunately, many technology professionals consider a project to be complete upon successful implementation. The TPMP helps technology staff look beyond the present engagement and consider the future welfare of the customer. The TPMP emphasizes the importance of "finishing tasks," which are to be completed after the service has been implemented. These tasks are intended to create an accurate record of the project that can help the customer work through the change seamlessly. According to the TPMP, a project is not considered complete until these steps have been followed. Changes must be noted in the appropriate documentation and distributed to the customer's affected areas, as they are ultimately the users of the product.

3.4.8 REPETITION AND STANDARDIZATION

The TPMP is one way in which PKS is trying to ensure the goals of its mission are achieved. By combining comprehensive planning steps, communication procedures, and project documentation, we have developed a process that ensures each project is completed reliably and as quickly as possible. When implemented correctly and consistently, the TPMP contributes to overall high-quality service, which consequently results in increased customer satisfaction.

Repetition and standardization are two issues which have been briefly addressed in this chapter. The company chose standardization as a means of achieving service goals. However, the company first had to identify projects and tasks that were repeated for numerous customers before standardized procedures could be developed.

Repetition is one of the first topics addressed in the TPMP. The Preface to the document states:

> "Some of the work performed during a technology implementation can be turned into repetitive procedures. These procedures, when properly documented, allows to implement the technology faster and more effectively to customers in the future."

Service requests can be classified in one of two ways: projects or tasks. A task is defined as an assigned piece of work limited in time and scope. Normally it is assigned to an individual and has a focused purpose, a relatively short duration, and a single work element. A project, on the other hand, is defined as multiple work elements, the size and effort of which are limitless. Both tasks and projects can have repetitive elements that, if documented for future use, can help reduce the time and effort involved in the service.

One step in the Project Initiation section of the TPMP is to determine if a project has been previously performed and documented. To do this, the technician should review the Project History list and Repetitive Task List for the same or similar project. These lists are contained in the project documentation library. If a similar project is found in the Project History List, the technician is encouraged to use the documentation for the past project in planning the current project. However, documentation specific to the current project still must be produced according to the steps in the TPMP. If the request is found to be a repetitive task that has already been documented, the technician simply has to obtain a copy of the established procedures and follow them accordingly. At this point, no further planning is required.

If the history of a similar request cannot be found, the technician has the responsibility to develop the procedure following the guidelines in the TPMP. The last steps in the TPMP are to determine whether the project completed was a repetitive task and if so, write the formalized procedures. The manual provides a list of questions that help determine whether a service falls under the project or task category:

◆ Did the task or project take longer to perform the work than it did to fill out the paperwork?

◆ Was more than one staff member involved in the task or project?

◆ Did the task or project take more than two weeks to implement?

◆ To implement the task or project, was it necessary to develop a project plan?

◆ Do you believe this should be called a project versus a task?

◆ Was it necessary to directly involve the customer?

♦ Was this project or task high-profile (did it require significant PKS/customer interaction)?

Negative answers to each of these questions implies that the service was a repetitive task and formalized procedures should be written. According to the TPMP, if the required steps have been followed throughout the project, most documentation should already have been prepared. Therefore, documenting the procedure should be a relatively quick and simple job.

Not only has the TPMP provided the staff with a standard procedure for approaching technology projects in general, it has helped harness the knowledge gained from specific experiences and apply that knowledge to future projects in the form of proven, standardized processes. The process ensures new projects are approached in the same, methodical manner, considering all the necessary planning, communication, and documentation steps. It also ensures repeated services are performed according to processes that are known to have worked in the past.

Documenting plans and procedures for projects and tasks, and storing them in a central library, has assisted in standardizing procedures for specific services. The libraries in which documented procedures are stored constitute a comprehensive, growing resource that technicians and managers can refer to during future projects.

The TPMP provides for a Technology Project Management Workbook, which was designed exclusively to support technology implementation projects and is the primary location for all documentation relevant to the implementation of a service request. The workbook standardizes forms, documentation, and project administration techniques. It contains all required forms along with completed examples. This standardization of documentation ensures the quality and completeness of all project information distributed to the customer. While not restricting the ability of the technician and his/her team to be creative, the workbook standardizes those areas where inventiveness is less desired.

One example of a standard document provided in the workbook is the checklist that technicians complete during a project. The checklist acts as a quick reference that walks the technician through the planning, administration, and cleanup steps defined throughout the process. Other documents contained in the workbook include customer communications, project plans, and any other pertinent project documentation. Workbooks for all projects are stored in a central location and maintained by the administrative staff.

The benefits of standardizing the project management process include:

♦ Technicians managing future projects can refer to standardized documentation for guidance during similar projects, resulting in less time spent gathering information and planning.

♦ Managers know where to find information relating to a project, and what type of information is available.

The TPMP promotes ethical standards in that it helps keep the project manager focused on the customer—making decisions based on the customer's expectations. One theme that is pervasive throughout the TPMP and has been mentioned repeatedly throughout this chapter is open communication with the customer during the project. If the project team maintains contact with the customer as suggested in the TPMP, the customer's interests are sure to be at the forefront of any decisions made. Another more isolated theme involves the risk and impact evaluations described previously. Once a risk evaluation has been completed, the TPMP recommends notifying the management and/or the customer of any potential risks. Based on this knowledge, the customer may alter the request or decide to continue as originally planned. Either way, the customer's best interest is at hand.

3.4.9   FLEXIBILITY WITHIN THE TPMP

Because the service requests we receive require varying degrees of planning and effort, the developers of the TPMP attempted to incorporate a degree of flexibility in the document. This flexibility allows the process to maintain applicability to all service requests. The process is valid for both repetitive tasks and full-blown projects. Tasks are generally much smaller in scope than projects, and require fewer resources and time to complete. When defining "management," the TPMP explains that the amount of management activity will vary with the size of the project. A software upgrade will not require the same project management activities as an operating system upgrade, but the TPMP will apply to both projects. These projects will require much of the same information, but varying amounts of effort are necessary to address the requests.

Both projects and tasks require information such as targeted start and end dates, critical tasks, milestones, dependencies, and resources. Software upgrades are repetitive services requested by numerous customers. Therefore, by using documents from past projects, planning and information gathering efforts will be limited and administration will already be defined. An operating system upgrade, on the other hand, requires substantial knowledge about the customer's environment, which in turn demands extensive information gathering, as well as comprehensive planning based on that knowledge.

An added bonus to the document's adaptability is that it creates a degree of freedom for technicians and managers to alter processes as needed to fit a particular project. This gives a sense of standardization to a project, while allowing for customized features.

3.5 CULTURE CHANGE

Development of an official project management procedure did not stifle the creativity of PKS employees. Input from all employees is constantly sought to stay ahead of the competition. No policy or procedure is considered final, or static. In fact, the TPMP itself is not even considered a final document at one point, it requests suggestions that might help make guidelines valid and applicable across additional functional boundaries.

All employees are uniquely positioned to influence the company's direction through new ideas and suggestions. When developing the TPMP, managers wanted to maintain this quality, so while the process was designed to standardize tasks that are repeatable across projects and customers, it was also designed to be flexible. It tells technicians the tasks that are necessary for a successful project, but does not mandate how to execute those tasks. By following the TPMP, technicians are able to influence future projects by creating and revising procedures for repeatable tasks and full-scale projects. The tasks outlined in the TPMP range from initial research and planning steps, through project administration, and final cleanup and documentation stages. Many factors are left up to the technician's discretion, calling for consultation with management only when unsure about a particular issue.

Gaining management's acceptance for the TPMP was simple. The process was initiated at the vice presidential level and several managers were involved in the development process. Acceptance of the document at the middle management level has been somewhat varied. Some directors have embraced the process wholeheartedly, requiring their teams to use it for all projects, while others have made using the TPMP voluntary.

For those groups in which using the TPMP is required, buy-in at the technician level was difficult. Those who, at first sight, could see the benefits in both the short and long term found value in the TPMP. Others were a little skeptical of the TPMP at first. Many thought the emphasis on documentation would streamline their work. The extensive planning was also an issue. One top manager said it was a challenge for the technicians to accept the process because "technicians are doers, not planners." Indeed, the process does place a great emphasis on documentation and planning. Earlier sections in this chapter described the TPMP checklist that is to be followed for step-by-step planning, communication, and documentation tasks. The first impression of the document was that it would stifle creativity, create extra work, and add time to projects. Once the technicians worked with the process and saw what it did for them, they realized the value of using it and have had substantial success with it.

3.6 IMPLEMENTATION

Once the TPMP was complete, the Vice President of Technology and the Director of Project Management formally introduced it to each group during weekly team meetings. Each employee was supplied a copy of the process, with the expectation that it would be used for all future project implementations. No specific person was tasked with implementing the process. Rather, it was the responsibility of each director to manage implementation within his or her staff. Some directors allowed their technicians to finish projects that were in process at the time and use the TPMP for all new projects. Other directors required their groups to go back and document projects in process according to the TPMP. At this point, some directors have not required their teams to use the TPMP at all; however, it continues to gain acceptance. As new employees are hired into the groups that use the TPMP, the document is introduced to them as a procedure they are required to follow.

On a broader spectrum, the TPMP is beginning to take hold in other areas of the company. Although currently the process is mainly used in the company's Computer Operations division, it is gaining appreciation in Systems Integration as well. Managers in that division have reviewed the process and believe that, with a few alterations, it can be applied to their projects as well.

3.7 FINAL RESULTS

We are currently in the process of measuring the success of projects in which the TPMP was used, so it is difficult to cite quantitative benefits of using the process. There is little doubt, however, that the process benefits the technician (and ultimately our company), the customer, and project managers. Those who have used the process have expressed favorable comments regarding their projects. Groups that have implemented the TPMP are starting to realize benefits from ongoing utilization of the process. For example, advantages to documentation described earlier, such as quicker implementation of repeatable tasks, are now being realized.

The Vice President of Technology Center Services has used the TPMP in three capacities: as a technician, as a project manager and as a vice president. His impression is that the TPMP has merit and can add value to a project. He has used the TPMP for varying purposes. As a technician, he found it helpful in requesting appropriate resources for a project. By using the checklist to determine whether a service request was a full-blown project or a repeatable task, he was able to make more accurate estimates regarding the timeframe for completion and human resources needed to achieve the service goal. As a director, he found it useful in managing his staff. By requiring his staff to use the TPMP, he was better able to keep abreast of their projects, as well as secure for them the appropriate resources for each service request, again using the checklist. Presently, he focuses his time on full-blown projects and uses the TPMP a little differently. Specifically, he finds the risk evaluations useful.

3.8 LESSONS LEARNED

The biggest lesson learned in developing the TPMP was in the implementation of the process throughout the targeted groups. As stated previously, acceptance of the TPMP in the various groups within PKS was mixed at first. Some quickly adopted its use, while others used only portions of it, and others waited to see the results other groups experienced. One vice president has said of the TPMP, " you can lead a horse to water, but you can't make it drink," meaning simply introducing the TPMP during a weekly meeting and leaving implementation up to the various group leaders may not be the most effective means of implementation. A more formal roll-out would have made implementing the process easier and clearer.

3.9 CONCLUSIONS

Presently, the document is being revised based on observations by its users. PKS' management realizes that once the new version is released, it will be necessary to create an environment that more clearly informs its technicians, management, and customers on the use of its process. This release is expected to be completed in 1998 and will encompass other lines of business not covered by the first TPMP. We have learned that establishing quality processes is an ongoing process in itself.

3.10 TPMP SAMPLE

This section presents a sample of PKS Information Services's TPMP document.

**PKS INFORMATION SERVICES
PROJECT MANAGEMENT PROCESS (SAMPLE)**

TABLE OF CONTENTS

TABLE OF CONTENTS. 52
PREFACE 54
I. TECHNOLOGY PROJECT MANAGEMENT PROCESS. . . 55
Purpose. 55
Objectives. 55
Introduction 55
Definitions 55
Task 55
Project 55
Management. 55
Requirements 56
Technology Project Management Workbooks. 56
Summary 57
II. PROJECT INITIATION 57
Introduction . . . . :. . 57
CSO Review. 57
1. Review CSO to understand the requirements as defined by
    the requester. 57
2. Determine if the project has been previously performed. 57
3. Determine if an established repetitive task has been requested 58
Gathering and Understanding the Requirements 58
4. Call requester to discuss CSO requirements. 58
5. Discuss the project with your supervisor. 59
6. Discuss the project with the customer account manager. 59
Addressing the scope of the project. 59
7. Define the scope of the project. 59
8. Review the project scope with the customer or requester. 59
Assessing Impact and Risk 60
9. Evaluate the risk factor(s) of the project. 60
10. Evaluate the impact of the project to both the customer
    and PKS. 61
Determining Resource Integration. 62
11. Research for changes: procedural-related or other system
    components. 62
12. Contact vendor(s) for applicable component information. . . 63
Analyzing Resource Requirements 63
13. Determine the people resources required to accomplish
    the project.. 63

14. Determine the hardware resources required to accomplish
     the project. 63
15. Determine the software resources required to accomplish
     the project. 63
16. Develop a benchmark to determine the impact of the
     change. 63
Putting the Plan Together. 64
17. Produce the project plan from the information previously
     gathered. 64
Getting a Plan Approved 64
18. Submit the project plan to management for approval. 64
Summary 65
III. PROJECT ADMINISTRATION 65
Introduction 65
Definition 66
Administer 66
Update Activities 66
Updating the Project Plan 66
19. Update the project plan with as much detail as is currently
     available. 66
Stay Apprised of Task Activity 66
20. Monitor the progress of the project. 66
Project Support. 67
21. Produce a testing plan or schedule. 67
22. Conduct a peer review at strategic points in high-risk
     projects. 67
23. Communicate milestone activity to a project's interested
     parties. 67
Project Status Reporting. 67
24. Produce project status reporting for internal and external
     communication. 67
Frequency: Updates and Reporting 68
25. Produce the updates and status reports at the appropriate
     frequency. 68
Customer Meetings 68
26. Provide an agenda for each meeting to optimize the allotted
     time. 69
Summary 69
IV. PROJECT COMPLETION 70
Introduction 70
Finishing the Project 70
27. Perform the benchmark to determine change impact. 70

Product Cleanup. 70
28. Clean up the old libraries after product upgrade or
    maintenance. 71
DASD Cleanup 71
29. Clean and release any DASD utilized throughout the
    project's duration. 71
Product Manual Updates 71
30. Ensure the customer is provided or informed of any
    updated manuals. 72
Documentation. 72
Operational and Help Desk Documentation 72
31. Review or update any applicable operational or help desk
    documentation. 72
32. Update Software Inventory with the appropriate information.72
Workbook Documentation. 72
33. Finalize the Technology Project Management Workbook
    documentation. 73
CSO and INFO Management. 73
34. Update the INFO Management change request and CSO
    work order. 73
Turning the Project into a Repetitive Task 73
35. Determine if the project you just completed is really a
    repetitive task. 74
36. Write formalized procedures for the repetitive task. 74
Summary 74
V. TECHNOLOGY PROJECT MANAGEMENT PROCESS
    SUMMARY 75

PREFACE

Managing a project of any magnitude can be a difficult feat. Have the project be the implementation of new technology and the difficulty can increase exponentially. PKS Information Services, Inc., (PKS), has developed a Technology Project Management Process (TPMP) to assist project managers and technicians with technology-related projects. PKS' Information Services Project Management Process, coupled with expert information technology knowledge, ensures success regardless of the size or complexity of the task.

PKS designed TPMP to be flexible yet complete. This manual begins with an introduction of TPMP that establishes some of the basic ground rules for using the process. The manual then steps through the three basic phases of a project: Project Initiation, Project Administration, and Project Completion.

Initiating a project requires that sufficient preparatory groundwork be performed prior to execution. Gathering appropriate information, understanding the project scope, and planning the work and resources are essential steps in ensuring the success of any project.

Effective administration of a project requires that project managers and technicians keep others informed about the project's progress and any issues that may arise. Communication to peers, management, and the customer keeps the project on schedule and focused.

A project is considered complete only after the customer is satisfied with the work performed, and all documentation and housekeeping tasks are completed—not when the technology is implemented. These project completion tasks not only ensure customer satisfaction, but also help keep the new technology viable and maintainable in the future.

Some of the work performed during a technology implementation project can be turned into repetitive procedures. These procedures, when properly documented, allow PKS to implement technology faster and more effectively to customers in the future. This critical component of TPMP is specifically addressed in the "Project Completion" phase where guidelines for determining if a task is repetitive are outlined, and formalized procedures for documenting repetitive procedures are discussed.

I. TECHNOLOGY PROJECT MANAGEMENT PROCESS

Purpose

To define, organize, and document the required project management process for technology implementation projects at PKS Information Services, Inc., with the overarching goal of ensuring the highest level of customer satisfaction with the services we provide.

Objectives

- Improve the quality of technology implementation services to customers by utilizing a methodology that promotes customer involvement, awareness, and timely resolution of issues throughout the project management process.
- Minimize project risk by establishing a standardized implementation process that increases the likelihood of success through early identification of the necessary tasks and steps of a project.
- Reduce the required effort and redundancies of project implementation by establishing a historical database of project implementations and related tasks for all customers and products that can be reviewed and applied to future projects.
- Identify and establish formal documentation for those project activities that are repetitive across all or similar projects.
- Improve customer satisfaction by instituting procedures which involve the customer and identify steps to help ensure the customer's information technology environment is properly maintained, documented, and at the highest level of quality.

Introduction

Project plans; implementation schedules; milestones and deadlines; communication; project leadership; and documentation all are important elements of project management. It is the purpose of this manual to define, organize, and document the required use of project management at PKS Information Services, Inc., with a primary focus on ensuring the highest level of customer satisfaction with the implementation of new technology.

Throughout this manual, the terms task, project, and project management will be frequently put to use. To ensure that all PKS personnel work with the same basic understanding, it is important that we take a few moments to define these terms as they apply to the technology project management activities at PKS.

Definitions

Task A task is defined as an assigned piece of work limited in time and scope. Normally a task is assigned to an individual versus a group of people. It has a focused purpose versus being all- encompassing, typically having a relatively short duration and a single work element.

Project A project, on the other hand, is defined as multiple work elements or tasks. At PKS, a project is typically requested utilizing a Customer Service Order (CSO). The CSO defines, in the customer's terms, the nature of the technology implementation project. The size of a project and the effort necessary to carry out a project are without limits. However, at a practical level, not all projects require the same effort to implement or manage. Therefore, guidelines must be established to help ensure a balanced approach to the execution and management of a project. These guidelines are defined later in this manual.

Management Management, as the word implies, is the administration of collective work elements or tasks to ensure a concise delivery of service from inception to completion. Management activities include performing research, communicating to both internal and external personnel, planning of tasks, coordinating the efforts of individual personnel, and keeping management at various levels informed through timely status reports. As previously implied, the amount of management activity required will vary with the size and scope of the project. A two-hour task will not require the same project management activities as a large project spanning multiple months. However, in either instance, a requisite level of project management and planning must be performed. Precise planning of a project coupled with an appropriate level of project management will almost always result in a high quality, low maintenance end product.

Project management is certainly not a new concept. In fact, many of the project management skills and techniques described in this manual are commonplace in projects today. The intent here, however, is to formalize the process in such a way that it not only ensures project success and customer satisfaction, but also facilitates continuous improvement.

Requirements

The PKS Information Services Project Management Process has been designed for ease of use by way of a "fill-in-the-blanks" Technology Project Management Workbook. These workbooks are provided on all projects and, based on the size and scope of a project, can be completed in pencil, using secretarial assistance, or on a personal computer. For all major projects, detailed project plans and other information will be required as a supplement to the workbooks. Specialized software, a local area network (LAN), and personal computers are provided by PKS for this purpose. This standardization of documentation ensures the quality and completeness of all project information distributed to PKS and customer management.

Project status reporting is required on a monthly basis as a minimum. The customer or PKS management may impose more frequent status reporting depending on the size and scope of the project. Status reports are due by the 17th of each month. The format for reporting project status has also been standardized, and can be found in Appendix E. Additional information regarding status reporting is discussed in a later section.

Technology Project Management Workbooks

The Technology Project Management Workbook has been designed exclusively to support technology implementation projects, and provides two key benefits. First, the workbook provides standardization of forms, documentation, and project administration techniques. While not restricting the ability of the project manager and his/her staff to be creative, the workbook standardizes those areas where inventiveness is less important or desired. For example, a checklist is provided that helps identify "What tasks need to be done", but not "How to get the tasks done." The checklist, which is required for use on all projects, can be found in Appendix A. In addition, Appendix B provides the location of the "softcopy" of the checklist on the PKS LAN.

The second benefit of the workbook is that it consolidates all project-related documentation. There may be instances when resources need to be transferred from one project to another. The impact of bringing new people onto a project is greatly minimized when all project documentation is in order and maintained in one location.

The Technology Project Management Workbook includes all required forms with completed examples. Each form and the software that created it are maintained on the PKS LAN. These documents and their LAN location are identified in Appendix B of this manual. Any updates to these documents must be made using the software identified in Appendix B. Use of any software product other than those specified requires PKS management approval.

Upon completion of a project, the Technology Project Management Workbooks and any supporting documentation should be finalized and turned over to the administrative support staff. The administrative staff will ensure that the workbook and its associated documentation are stored in both hard copy and diskette format. Storage areas have been made available in each workroom for long-term storage.

Summary

This introduction presented the basic concepts of the Technology Project Management Process at PKS, and the critical role it plays in ensuring project quality and the attainment of customer satisfaction. Customers are first and foremost at PKS. The quality of our work on their behalf should reflect this belief.

This section also provided definitions for the most used terms in this manual: task, project, and management. Task was identified as an individual work element or activity that can be carried out by a single person, whereas project is a group of related tasks or work elements. Management is the administrative activity that plans and oversees a project and its associated tasks to ensure they are appropriately followed from beginning to end.

Last but not least, this section identified the key requirements of the process, namely the importance of timely status reporting and the major role played by the Technology Project Management Workbook. Emphasis was placed on the value of the workbook as a single location where all information relative to a project including the project checklist, customer communications, project plans, and any other pertinent project documentation is maintained.

The following sections of this manual describe, in detail, the recommended process that should be followed on any technology implementation project. It is a road map of sorts, providing points of interest along the way. It is the intent of this "road map" to help lead you to your destination: the successful implementation of technology on behalf of our customers.

II. PROJECT INITIATION

Introduction

Oftentimes, the most difficult part of a new project is getting started. For any project, large or small, the best place to start is developing a complete understanding of the customer's requirements as documented in the customer service order; better known as the CSO.

CSO Review

1. Review CSO to understand the requirements as defined by the requester.

By reviewing the CSO you should get a general idea of what the customer is requesting. The information presented in the CSO will vary from vague to detailed depending on factors such as the scope of the request, the requester, and the requester's understanding of the need. For example, a CSO might contain a request for the implementation or upgrade of a software product. This type of request is often very straightforward, identifying the who, what, and when details of the project: who wants it; what do they want; and when do they want it done.

Another example of a less typical but very possible request might be a major software enhancement or an operating system upgrade. While this type of request contains the same who, what, and when, the project scope and the effort required to develop an understanding of all the issues and ramifications of the request is significantly greater. The point being made regarding these two examples is that regardless of the nature of the request, much of the same information is required. What differentiates each request is the varying amount of effort necessary to fully investigate and understand their specific requirements and associated issues.

2. Determine if the project has been previously performed.

Before jumping right into planning the project, you should determine if the CSO is requesting a project that may have already been performed and documented by someone else within the organization. To determine this, you should obtain and review the project history list for the same or similar project. This information is contained in the Project Documentation Library or DOCLIB.

The best possible match is one on both software product and customer. If a match of this type cannot be found, a match on software product alone is next best option. If either match is found, you have a planning document which can assist you in the execution of your specific project. Nevertheless, it is important to understand that you are still expected to follow the remaining steps in producing your own project documentation, and plagiarism is encouraged to reduce the effort and improve the quality of your project plan.

3. Determine if an established repetitive task has been requested.

If you were unsuccessful in finding the same or similar project on the historical project list, you should then determine if the CSO is requesting an established repetitive task. A "repetitive" task is work that already has an established procedure that simply needs to be re-executed. The list of established repetitive tasks is also located in the DOCLIB. If you find the project or task on this list, you are through with the planning process. Simply obtain a copy of the established procedures for the task from the DOCLIB and follow them accordingly. Refer to Appendix B for more information regarding the DOCLIB.

Whether or not a CSO is requesting a project that has been previously performed, a repetitive task, or a completely new project, it is ultimately the project manager's responsibility to ensure the accuracy and completeness of the project plans and procedures, and you should continue to progress through this manual. The last section of this manual outlines the specific activities required by PKS for project documentation and procedure preparation, both for repetitive tasks and new projects. Each project manager must ensure that there are established procedures that can be reused on any subsequent repetitive requests.

Gathering and Understanding the Requirements

4. Call requester to discuss CSO requirements.

The best place to start in gathering additional information about a specific request is at the source. Discussing the CSO with the requester can enlighten you, providing the project manager with additional insight to the request that cannot normally be obtained by simply reading the CSO. This discussion also provides the requester with awareness that his or her request is being addressed and who is their point of contact at PKS.

There are numerous issues that should be confirmed with the requester to ensure a clear understanding of the project. These issues include, but are not limited to:

- the project's desired start and completion dates,
- who will be the primary customer contact for the project,
- what is the project's priority relative to other work performed for the customer,
- identify any possible project prerequisites,
- discuss the level of required customer involvement, and
- clarify any aspect of the project that is not readily apparent.

When discussing dates with the CSO requester it is important to be aware of any issues that may have an impact on the project implementation date. While the date may be ideal for the requester, it may have a profound impact on the customer's environment and available staff resources. For example, it could be problematic to schedule multiple software or system upgrades to occur on the same weekend. This could stretch available resources and position one or both projects for failure. Project managers should discuss this issue further with appropriate supervision if unsure as to how any other major project activity might impact their project implementation dates.

5. Discuss the project with your supervisor.

After discussing the project with the requester, it may be necessary to discuss the project further with your supervisor. This will depend upon any number of factors such as project scope, current project workload, and cross-departmental involvement, just to name a few. Use discretion in determining whether a conference with your supervisor is necessary. However, when in doubt, always take the time to discuss it with your supervisor. Too much communication is better than not enough.

6. Discuss the project with the customer account manager.

Another excellent resource for gathering information about a project is the customer's account manager. The account manager is in constant contact with the customer and is often aware of the customer's ongoing needs. The account manager may be able to provide information or an additional perspective regarding the project request that cannot be obtained through customer discussions. This also keeps the account manager informed of pending actions on behalf of their account.

Addressing the Scope of the Project

Up to this point you have taken the time to gather, discuss, and evaluate the general project requirements based on your current level of understanding. Now is the ideal time to document the full scope of the project and define the specific project activities to be performed.

7. Define the scope of the project.

The purpose of defining and documenting the full scope of a project is to lay out what exactly is to be accomplished and the activities that are required. Based on the information that has been gathered, it is the project manager's responsibility to identify the work to be performed and the expected results. This is perhaps the most important part of developing the project plan and procedures, since it is imperative that the project manager's goal and the requester's goal are the same.

Documenting the scope of a project identifies and helps validate any assumptions the project manager may have made regarding the project. During this process it is extremely important to articulate any variables or factors which may have an impact on the success of the project. For example, the request may simply identify the need to upgrade a particular software product to a new release. However, the true scope of the project may also require that a number of related or prerequisite tasks be performed to complete the upgrade. Therefore, the scope must include these additional tasks, even though they were not identified on the project request. In all instances, the project scope is a definition of all the major tasks, at a high level, that are required to complete the customer's request. Only after the scope of the project has been clearly defined should the project manager proceed to the next step.

8. Review the project scope with the customer or requester.

Before delving into the project any further, the project manager should review and discuss the defined project scope with the customer. This review process is crucial to the success of the project, as it is essential that the project manager and the customer understand and agree on the scope of work required to satisfy the initial request. This is particularly true when a single request may require that multiple tasks be performed.

The final scope document should contain an agreed upon description of the purpose or reason(s) for the request, a definition of the tasks to be performed, and any issues or assumptions that may have an impact on the success of the project. This information helps provide others with a clear understanding of the purpose and activities of the project.

The following analogy is offered to aid in the understanding of this point. If the customer has requested that you produce a peg that fits into some type of hole, it is essential that you, the project manager, understand the shape and dimensions of the hole. You and the customer must then agree on the size and shape of the peg to be produced. Failure to adequately understand the details of the customer's request, or to jointly agree upon the specifications for the peg, will ultimately lead to a peg that does not fit in the hole and a dissatisfied customer. While this is obviously an oversimplification of the problem, it points out that understanding the customer's requirements and agreeing on the work to be performed are crucial to the success of any project.

Assessing Impact and Risk

Now that the scope of the project and its related tasks have been defined, and both the project manager and the customer are in agreement, both parties should have a clear and thorough understanding of what the expectations are for the project. It is now equally important to identify and assess the potential risk and impact the project may have on both organizations.

9. Evaluate the risk factor(s) of the project.

Any project brings some level of risk to the organization. Without proper planning, a project could place the customer at risk if the task fails during or after implementation. Such a failure can also place strain on the business partnership PKS continually strives to develop and maintain. For these reasons, project managers are expected to identify and evaluate the potential areas of risk on all projects.

Typically, but not always, the potential for risk increases with the size and complexity of a project. The greater the project scope, the greater the number of tasks, and the increased likelihood that an error or omission can occur. As such, you should carefully review all customer system areas the project will affect, focusing on those areas where the potential for risk is greatest. Each potential area of risk should be noted for future discussions with the customer and PKS management. These areas include (but are not limited to) any version changes to the operating system and related software, critical applications, databases, and the network. Various OEM software changes can carry the same exposures and should also be evaluated accordingly.

Another factor that increases risk is time. When a project is rushed, the element of risk increases. Checkpoints are oftentimes bypassed for the sake of meeting a deadline. The saying "the faster I go, the further I get behind" is very appropriate here. Therefore, it is the project manager's responsibility to take exception when an inappropriate amount of time is allotted to accomplish the project or a particular task. Should you be instructed to perform a task within a restrictive or inappropriate timeframe, it is essential that the appropriate individuals are aware of, and have indicated a willingness to accept, the associated risks.

Complexity also plays a role in the risk factor. Complexity can be a major issue, both before and after implementation of new technology. On the pre-implementation side, the greater the effort necessary to prepare for and implement a requested change, the greater the complexity and risk. Relative to post- implementation, if the implementation of new technology has the potential to render a function or system inoperable, you must also evaluate the effort necessary to remove the change to fully determine how simple or complex the work.

To assist in identifying the level of risk associated with a project, the chart below has been provided. It is important to understand that determining risk is oftentimes very subjective, and is not always black and white. Management may view the level of risk differently and should be consulted whenever there is an element of uncertainty in your decision.

The table below centers on complexity as a major factor in determining risk. Three levels of risk are identified with brief definitions and examples of each one.

Risk Table

The risk table may not have all the information you need to accurately evaluate the risk level of the project or task you are performing. If this is the case, please see your supervisor for additional direction. If you believe the project is borderline between two risk levels, always choose the risk level which is higher, erring on the side of caution.

When complexity of change is considered, it may not provide the

Risk Level	Definition	Examples of Risk at this Level
Low	Changes at this level are very straight-forward. Change implementation or reversal does not require an outage.	Performance parameters (IEAICSxx, IEAIPSxx, or IEAOPTxx) change. Implemented or removed using MVS SET console command.
Medium	Changes at this level require some form of outage, usually by function, for either implementation or reversal.	CICS or DB2 release-level changes, various software or hardware upgrades.
High	Changes at this level require a major level of outage, usually system-wide, for implementation or reversal.	System IPL, various software and/or hardware changes, new operating system.

ability to reduce the level of risk for a given change. However, identifying other risks and preparing for them in advance should reduce the impact the risk carries. But how about the impact of the project itself? Let us take a further look at this.

10. Evaluate the impact of the project to both the customer and PKS.

Along with risk, a project will also have different degrees of impact to both organizations. To the customer, an intense project could have a considerable impact to the organization. However, as with risk, even the smallest project can have a major impact to the business. As with risk, each project will have to be evaluated to determine its placement on the impact scale.

To determine the impact of a project, many of the same evaluations used with risk should be considered. Take into account the scope of the project; the number of people within the organization impacted by the change along with the change to the environment. The increase in the number of those affected by the project plays a direct role in the potential impact to the customer. Communication of the environmental change to those impacted will elongate as the impact increases. Therefore, communication and people play an important role in the evaluation. However, communication takes time which makes it a consideration as well.

As was just mentioned, time also plays a role in the impact of a project. A project with a limited timeframe to complete also limits the ability to roll the change out to the customer, thereby reducing the customer's ability to prepare and plan. Therefore, consider the time factor. Let the customer or management know if you believe there is an insufficient amount of time allocated for implementing the project. This is to be done for the good of both organizations.

To assist you in your attempt to identify the impact level of a project, the following chart has been provided to help guide your decision. As was stated with the previous table, please understand that this process is very subjective. Determining the correct level is not always black and white and, therefore, should be considered accordingly. Management may view it differently and should be consulted whenever you are unsure of your decision.

Please note that there are three levels of impact identified with brief definitions and examples of each one.

Impact Table

The impact table may not have all the information you need to accurately evaluate the impact of this project or task. If this is the case, please see your supervisor for additional direction. If you believe your project is borderline between two impact levels, always choose the impact level which is higher, erring on the side of caution.

The last step of determining impact and risk is combining the selected risk and impact levels to derive the overall risk level. The approach to be used is to select the highest level between the two, adopting this as the overall project risk level. For example, let us assume the project involves performance enhancements. And, for the sake of example, the complexity level for this change is low and the impact level is high. Given these assumptions, the resulting risk level would be high because of the level of impact.

Determining Resource Integration

It is seldom anymore when a project does not impact existing software components or procedures. Software, both IBM and OEM, along with hardware work in concert to perform the various functions required in data processing. Accordingly, you must determine if and how this project will impact any customer or PKS procedures or associated components.

11. Research for changes: procedural-related or other system components.

Each functional area may have procedures which must be reviewed. This is done to ensure procedures remain accurate once the project is imple-

Impact Level	Definition and Requirements	Examples of Impact at this Level
Low	Changes at this level do not impact the production environment. Customer will be able to operate in a business-as-usual fashion. Change does not require direct customer approval to implement.	Test CICS table changes, documentation changes, non-production user-ID additions.
Medium	Changes at this level impact isolated areas of the production environment. The change requires direct customer approval. Backout plan is required. Peer review may be appropriate.	Production CICS table maintenance, various software or hardware changes, production STC or batch JCL changes.
High	Changes at this level impact production in a significant manner, typically system-wide. Customer approval is required as is peer review and backout procedures.	Operating system upgrades, system performance parameters, various software or hardware upgrades.

mented. This may also assist in determining the level of involvement of the affected department, both from an implementation aspect as well as documentation. Involving each applicable functional area helps keep them abreast of ongoing changes. It also provides them with a vehicle for providing input to the pending change. Involvement level will vary based upon the complexity, impact, and size of the change.

Hardware and software components are self defining. Some software upgrades occur in order to take advantage of new hardware or software features. Hardware needs to be at the appropriate microcode level. Software may require a specific level of operating system to be functional. Each issue must be considered and researched to determine the applicable impact.

12. Contact vendor(s) for applicable component information.

Some of the research should include discussions with the vendor or vendors to ascertain the latest release information relative to the components. This includes any hyper fixes, special zaps, CPU dependent zaps, and documentation changes that could impact your implementation of the project. When considering the software release information, include in your review the Software Inventory list which is maintained for each customer. An example of this list is included in Appendix I.

Analyzing Resource Requirements

Every project requires a certain amount of resources in order to accomplish each task. There are a number of different types of resources. Three discussed here include:

- people: includes cross departmental and external such as the customer
- hardware: includes additional CPU, memory, DASD, and other peripherals
- software: programs above and beyond that which is a direct part of the task

13. Determine the people resources required to accomplish the project.

Regardless of project size, individuals from multiple departments are likely to get involved with your project, either directly or indirectly. Previous topics have already identified the account manager, the customer, the vendor, and management as resources for the project. Other individuals from various departments may get involved as your project develops. The sooner you can involve them, the better those individuals can prepare for their part of the project and increase the likelihood of success.

14. Determine the hardware resources required to accomplish the project.

Hardware requirements may or may not be readily apparent. Determining any additional hardware requirements may require statistical analysis. The requirements may be very clear, as in the case of implementing expanded storage. Or in the case of a merger project, projections play a critical role in determining hardware needs. The point being made is this: The project should be evaluated to determine if the implementation of this project will have enough effect on the existing hardware environment to place the sustaining of contractual service levels in jeopardy. If this is the case, additional hardware may be required and should be considered accordingly.

15. Determine the software resources required to accomplish the project.

Software is probably the greatest percentage of the changes that take place in our environment today. It was previously mentioned that software levels and their integration must be considered during the project. While that is an important aspect of the project, it is not the point of discussing software here. The point here is to consider if there is any new or additional software which may be required as a result of this project. This may include new releases as mentioned earlier. But it may also mean software not previously utilized within the customer's environment. In one instance, the requirement of a corporate merger necessitated the installation of a new software product not previously implemented on their system. It is an area that does not happen frequently but should be considered and not overlooked.

16. Develop a benchmark to determine the impact of the change.

One final consideration before putting the plan together is to establish a benchmark prior to the change. This assumes the change will take place and is capable of being benchmarked. The purpose of the benchmark is to validate the impact of the change made to the environment as well as raise a flag if something does not appear to be correct. It will be necessary to execute the benchmark prior to and after the change. The results should be compared, evaluated, and disseminated to management and the customer, especially if the change is significant.

An example where having performed a benchmark could have been revealing has to do with CPU swapping. When an MVS environment is moved from one CPU model to another CPU model, leaving all other variables unchanged, there have been instances of a noticeable change in the performance of the environment. This has been contributed to the processor itself. A benchmark which tested both CPU time and I/O time may have brought this information to light and provided the opportunity to investigate the situation prior to the problem presenting itself. While a benchmark cannot guarantee to find all situations, it has a better chance of finding potential problems than performing no benchmark test at all.

Putting the Plan Together

At this point you should have completed the information gathering process. The amount of data you have collected will vary depending on the extent of the project. You will have spoken with a varying number of people about the project. You should have a general feel for what it is going to take to accomplish the task. It is time to begin putting together a project plan, a strategic itinerary for your project. The goal is to plan your implementation strategy to increase the quality and likelihood of success while minimizing unexpected obstacles.

17. Produce the project plan from the information previously gathered.

Before sitting down and formalizing your project plan, there are key components you must identify and have available to "plug in" to the plan. These components include:

- **Targeted Start Date:** when the project is scheduled to begin
- **Targeted End Date:** when the project is scheduled to complete
- **Critical Tasks:** tasks crucial to the success and completion of the project
- **Task Start Date:** when individual tasks are scheduled to begin
- **Task End Date**: when individual tasks are scheduled to complete
- **Milestones:** points in the project that identify key completion points
- **Dependencies:** tasks which require other tasks to be completed prior to starting
- **Resources:** people or facilities critical to the implementation of the project

The components identified above are necessary for the successful completion of the project plan. Understand that a project plan is not a one-time document. It is a working document; a document that is dynamic in nature, evolving throughout the duration of the project. You are at the initial phase of the plan. During this phase the higher level tasks are identified without describing all of the necessary details.

This phase shows the implementation path of the project at its highest level. Key dates, critical tasks, milestones, and dependencies need to be identified within the plan where, at a glance, one can view the overall scope of the project and its critical components. This phase will be presented to management for approval.

An example of a project plan can be found in Appendix C. The example shows the project plan with most of the tasks identified. The PC file of this example is contained on the network. The location of the project plan example and the tool it was developed with can be found in Appendix B.

Getting a Plan Approved

The last step in the Project Initiation process is getting your project plan approved. If you have done your homework, the approval process should be quite painless. On the other hand, if you have not adequately researched the project, documented it well, and are unable to respond to specific queries, you will be sent back to retrieve this information. Be certain your research and documentation is thorough. This will save everyone time and effort in the long run.

18. Submit the project plan to management for approval.

The goal of this step is to raise the awareness of management relative to the scope of a project previously agreed upon with the customer. Any project, on the surface, may appear simpler or more difficult than it really is. Management cannot properly allocate resources without having the correct information your research will provide. Departmental resource and workload appropriation ultimately depends on the accuracy and completeness of your research.

Another goal of this step is to assure management that you are aware of the project's scope. It is safe to say that people occasionally jump headlong into a project without fully understanding the impact of what they are about to take on. Certain assumptions are made only to find they were wrong. And, at this juncture, they are too far in to back out. The planning and approval process increases the level of assurance that you know where you are going and what you are getting into.

Summary

To this point, project planning has been covered in a great amount of detail. Outside of actually executing the project, planning for its implementation is its most intensive process. As you have seen, it takes a great amount of time and effort to properly complete this part of the task. It starts with a review of the request or CSO to determine the general scope of the project. Once determining if it is a repetitive task or full-blown project, the appropriate path is selected.

Continuing down the project path, the next step leads to people involvement. This includes the customer: the user community, the project leader (when applicable), and other management types when and where the project or reporting dictates. It also includes PKS: the account manager, your supervisor, and people from other functional areas. The key here is communication, both internally and externally.

Other key factors identified in this section included complexity, risk, impact, and resources. Risk is not limited to the customer but also PKS.

Identifying this element can play a major role on the project's implementation. As with risk, impact was also critical. The smallest change can have a significant impact on all parties. Therefore, it should be handled accordingly. And last was resources. Resources included people, hardware, and software. The level of the project could affect any one of these in a significant way and should be measured carefully.

Having discussed, measured, and gathered significant amounts of information, it was then time to mix all this data together, producing a finished product identified as the project plan. The plan was to identify the targeted start and end dates, the critical tasks and milestones, any dependencies, and the resources necessary to accomplish the project. The plan would then be passed on to management for their review and approval.

Again, it cannot be stressed enough that the quality and success of any project can be greatly increased when it is appropriately researched and planned. It is a significant effort to properly gather this information. However, the dividends it can provide in the end will make it well worth the time investment.

III. PROJECT ADMINISTRATION

Introduction

Congratulations on reaching this point in the Project Management Process. This indicates your research, documentation, and understanding of the project's scope has been successfully conveyed to and approved by management. The project has received the necessary green light to proceed towards the goal of successful implementation. But, as you know, the fun is just beginning. You have the responsibility to administer the project now that it is moving forward. Before identifying some of the specific administrative activities, let us take a moment to understand this paper's meaning of project administration.

Definition

Administer

You may remember that project was previously defined as multiple work elements or tasks, requested via a CSO which is necessary to implement a change requested by, or on behalf of, the customer. Administer, as the word implies, is to manage or direct. In this case, the managing or directing applies to the project or task. As project administrator, it is your responsibility to oversee the work and communicate its progress to the appropriate authorities, both internally and externally.

Additional responsibilities include updating the project plan, staying apprised of task activity, project upkeep, project status reporting, determining update frequencies, and conducting customer meetings which are necessary to brief the customer regarding current activities, outstanding questions, and relevant issues. These activities are done throughout the life of the project. The project's conclusion is reached when you and the customer agree that the project is complete. The customer will usually signify this agreement with a signed-off CSO.

Update Activities

Now that the definition of project administration has been identified, let us describe some of the activities identified above which are necessary to properly administer the project.

Updating the Project Plan

One of the previously identified key components to the project is the project plan. If the project is of any size, you created a project plan identifying the required tasks to successfully complete the project. At this time, you may or may not have identified the specific details or all of the individual tasks of the project. Now would be a good time, if you have not done so already, to identify and record the necessary details of your plan.

19. Update the project plan with as much detail as is currently available.

Again, as previously mentioned, the project plan typically is a very dynamic document. Experience has shown that larger projects covering a greater number of tasks and a vast period of time tend to be more dynamic than smaller, less involved projects. Depending on the project, you may need to frequently update your plan to add, delete, or alter task information such as dates, duration, resources, etc. How frequently one should apply updates will be discussed in greater detail in a separate topic later in this section.

Another reason for updating the plan has to do with the individual tasks contained within. As the project progresses, not only will you apply any pertinent changes mentioned above, but you will also identify individual task progress which includes the percentage complete. This requires you to stay on top of any task-related changes to the project and its current activities.

Stay Apprised of Task Activity

20. Monitor the progress of the project.

You are responsible for ensuring the project activity progresses in a timely fashion, meeting or preceding the stated implementation target dates. However, issues may arise that cause a delay of a project. These issues should be carefully considered and communicated back to management. Any changes that may occur as a result of delays would be applied to the plan.

Another aspect you must administer has to do with change activity. This includes any activity coordination necessary to ensure too many changes are not implemented simultaneously. This applies to this project as well as other non-related projects where you may be a participant. An abundance of simultaneous changes can overburden you, impeding your ability to perform quality work for any of your individual tasks.

For some projects, keeping in touch with task activity should be easy. Obtaining the necessary update information is effortless if you are the only individual directly involved with the implementation activities. However, you will need to interact and solicit update information from others if there are individuals who are performing activities on behalf of the project. You may need to produce additional documentation for testing or peer reviews as well. Collectively, this can be called project support. Let us consider a few of the options.

Project Support

As a project progresses, it will go through a number of tasks as outlined in the project plan. One step included in the project plan is testing.

21. Produce a testing plan or schedule.

It is possible that a distinct test plan or schedule document would be appropriate to proceduralize the testing process. It would be your responsibility to coordinate the generation of this document. An example of a testing schedule or checklist is included in Appendix H. This document should be used for planning purposes. You could also use it for the actual production implementation. This document may be appropriate to use during the peer reviews which is the next topic of discussion.

22. Conduct a peer review at strategic points in high risk projects.

Peer reviews are not necessary for all projects. However, peer reviews are required with projects that are high impact or high risk. Peer reviews are held to provide the opportunity for others to scrutinize the activities, ensuring all of the bases are covered. Questions are to be asked of the individual(s) performing the work. Backout procedures should be reviewed to determine validity and reliability. A sample peer review agenda document can be found in Appendix K. Peer reviews may occur more than once during the project if the project has a number of significant tasks occurring throughout the implementation process.

As major activities or specific milestones (testing or otherwise) are completed, you should communicate this information to the customer as well as PKS internal management.

23. Communicate milestone activity to a project's interested parties.

The communication is to be specific and concise, addressing the milestone achieved. An example of a customer communique, is included in Appendix G. This example was sent as an informal e-mail. Formality is less important than the need to send the information.

The testing and milestone achievement should also be included in the updates you apply to the project plan. These updates are then applied and communicated back to PKS management as well as the customer in a general form using project status reports. To determine how this information is communicated, let us discuss reporting in greater detail.

Project Status Reporting

Project status reporting can be done in a variety of ways. Producing a report from the project management software is an option. There is also a standardized status report produced for the executives which may be an alternative. Either way, reporting the ongoing status of the project is essential.

24. Produce project status reporting for internal and external communication.

The selected project management software product is identified in Appendix B. This software provides the flexibility of producing reports of all types including Gantt and PERT charts, resource utilization and graphs, and other reports too numerous to mention. The common or standard report example is included in Appendix D. It is recommended to use one of these reports during your status meetings with the customer.

You can also produce a separate status report utilized by PKS for executive reporting. An example of this report is included in Appendix E. This report is included in a monthly status report distributed among PKS executives identifying the status of major I/S projects. Check with your manager to determine if you are required to produce this report.

You may be required to provide both of the above reports depending on the scope of the project. The report choices will vary based upon what agreement you have made with the principals of the project. Regardless, the important thing to remember is to communicate this information, especially to the customer. In the past, PKS has been chastised by our customers for not communicating enough with them. This includes both the frequency and quantity of information. Therefore, provide the customer with as much information as it takes to meet or exceed their need. The customer should never be left wanting for project-related data.

Frequency: Updates and Reporting

We have discussed updating and reporting on the project plan. But how frequently should this activity be done? As with many other issues throughout this process, reporting frequency will vary as well. And, reporting frequency may or may not coincide with the update frequency. Let us consider both aspects, frequency of updates and reporting.

25. Produce the updates and status reports at the appropriate frequency.

How frequently the plan is updated depends upon a couple of factors. The first is the amount of activity within the project. Infrequent updates are likely for projects with a short, well defined path, having little activity that crosses departmental and customer boundaries. However, projects with increased activity or customer exposure will likely require more frequent updating.

Another factor which may drive the frequency of updates is the exposure of the project. If the project happens to be high profile, management may drive the update or reporting frequency to ensure executives on both sides are well informed of the current project activity. Consequently, this will also drive the frequency for which the project is reported. Report frequency is the final factor discussed in this section.

Reporting may play an important role in how frequently the plan is updated. The minimal frequency period for reporting is once a month. This coincides with the frequency of the executive reporting which occurs on a once a month basis. The previous example of a high profile project may drive the reporting to occur once a week. Reporting is something that has to be worked out between you, management, and the customer. The key thing to remember is to keep the customer well informed of any project-related activity.

Customer Meetings

Meeting with the customer is one of the best ways to communicate any information relative to the project. It is a more personal approach compared to simply sending the updates via fax or mail. It provides the opportunity to exchange ideas, issues, and concerns regarding the project as well as other customer-related issues. It helps to ensure there is little room for misinterpreting any information provided on the status report or project plan.

Meeting with the customer can be done in a few different ways. The simplest is via a conference call. Many of the PKS and customer-related issues are addressed in this manner. It provides a cost effective means of keeping connected with the customer. This should be the primary approach for communicating a project with the customer.

Another means is to meet with the customer directly. This could be done on-site either at PKS or the customer's location. Again, this provides a very personal approach and provides greater exposure to both organizations. Keep in mind, on-site visits are not something for all projects. Typically, this will be more appropriate for high profile or larger, more involved projects such as operating system or major component upgrades. Any travel considerations for a given project, either to the customer or customer to PKS, must be authorized by your supervisor.

26. Provide an agenda for each meeting to optimize the allotted time.

Before you meet with the customer, be sure to prepare an agenda which outlines the topics of discussion. Provide the agenda in advance of the meeting. This provides each individual with the ability to properly prepare for the meeting. This should enhance the efficiency of the meeting and show everyone that, most importantly, you are ready for the meeting as well. An example of an agenda used for a meeting is provided in Appendix F.

Summary

As you have seen, administering the project is certainly an involved process. And, if you happen to be the one who is also implementing the project, it becomes an additional task to an already busy process. However, properly executed, project administration can raise the awareness of all involved parties while reducing the communication gap that customers have repeatedly identified.

This chapter began by defining project administration as managing or directing the project. It was identified as your responsibility to oversee the work and communicate its progress to the appropriate authorities, both internally and externally. This is to be done throughout the life of the project. A signed-off CSO is the typical instrument used to close a project or request.

The next step after defining project administration was update activities. The first update activity was revising the project plan. This aspect was geared towards supplementing the project plan with information which detailed those tasks necessary to implement the project. This would also include future changes due to dynamic changes to the project.

The second update activity in administering your project was staying apprised of task activity. As project administrator, you are responsible for ensuring project activities progress in a timely fashion. Activity coordination is necessary to help balance resource requirements and availability. Also, you need to stay in contact with those involved in the project in order to remain knowledgeable of current project activities. This assists you in the step which follows, project status reporting.

Project status reporting consists of producing reports from the project management software or using standardized reporting already found in-house. The whole point of reporting was keeping management, both PKS and the customer, informed of the ongoing progress of the project. The customer has indicated the need for greater communication. This is a key means for fulfilling their request.

Having identified the need to update the project and produce the reports, we then discussed how frequently this should occur. It was determined that there is no hard and fast rule. The minimal period of time was determined to be monthly. This coincides with the executive reports which are also produced on a monthly basis. It was noted that project visibility or complexity may also play a role in the overall frequency. Either way, the customer should be provided the opportunity to provide input into how frequently updates and reporting should occur.

The final topic of discussion was customer meetings. While much of the information provided could be applied to any customer meeting, this topic was geared more towards project-related meetings.

Meeting with the customer is one of the best ways to communicate information regarding the project. It was identified as more personal, providing a means to exchange ideas, issues, and concerns regarding the project. Conference calls were identified as the best overall way to conduct these meetings. However, it was noted that direct customer contact, either on-site locally or at the customer site, may be appropriate depending on project scope and visibility. Any travel must be approved by your manager.

Administering the project can be a very beneficial and rewarding task. It can be gratifying to watch your project grow from inception through conclusion, knowing you played a vital role in its successful completion. To that end, let us move on to the next topic of discussion, Project Completion.

IV. PROJECT COMPLETION

Introduction

You have reached the place in the Technology Project Management Process where most or all of the project implementation is complete. This section should be viewed as a wrap-up section, the final steps one takes while implementing a project. However, this section may be viewed as the most difficult section of the whole manual. This is simply due to the fact that it will identify much of the documentation required at the close of any project. This documentation is a part of the foundation that makes this whole process valuable to those who utilize its information. Unfortunately, for a variety of reasons, documentation is an area where many people fail to complete the work.

This section will focus in on the finishing tasks, those tasks which need to be performed before a project can truly be considered "completed". Some of the finishing tasks include: updating the CSO and INFO records; completion of the appropriate documentation; determining if the task is repetitive; product cleanup; and filing all project-related materials. While this list is not all-inclusive, it is indicative that there is plenty of work yet to be accomplished.

Without further ado, let us move right into the heart of this section, Finishing the Project.

Finishing the Project

A recurring theme throughout this manual has been the idea that the amount of work will vary depending upon the size of the project. As one should expect, this is true in this section as well. Larger projects are going to require a significant allocation of time to ensure all of the finishing tasks have been thoroughly completed.

There are many areas which can be identified as finishing work. The following sections will identify many of those tasks required to sufficiently finalize a project. These tasks are not listed in any order of importance. Each task has a level of importance all its own. Therefore, look at each task equally knowing your dedication to completing each one will bring an overall benefit to the project management process.

27. Perform the benchmark to determine change impact.

As discussed earlier in the manual, you were to develop a benchmark to help determine the impact of the project on the environment. If a benchmark was developed, this would be the appropriate time to execute. Review the results and report any significant change to the appropriate management levels.

Product Cleanup

One area which has been neglected is cleaning up after a product upgrade or application of maintenance. This leads to wasted DASD space and confusion when it comes to addressing these data sets sometime in the future. It forces the next individual (maybe that is you) to investigate the reasons behind multiple versions of the software. This time wasting element needs to be eliminated.

There are a number of reasons cleanup does not occur. Some of the frequently used rationale include: change backout or recovery, unchanged JCL which still points to old libraries, and "I plan to do that later..." Each rationale has its merits. However, if the effort is not completed, the lack of follow-through is inexcusable.

28. Clean up the old libraries after product upgrade or maintenance.

There are alternatives to leaving the libraries spinning on DASD. Given any alternatives, however, the primary goal should be the elimination of any libraries which can be specifically identified as part of the older release. This would include product libraries such as LINKLST, LOADLIB, and PARMLIB.

One alternative to leaving older release data sets on DASD would be to migrate them to tape. A benefit is the data sets remain cataloged and available if a job came along and requested one of the data sets. The hope would be that sufficient research was performed to eliminate this possibility. After a brief period, the catalog could be reviewed to determine if any of the data sets were recalled. Appropriate action could be taken once this is reviewed.

Another alternative would be to back up the data sets using the appropriate utility, then scratching the data sets residing on DASD. The benefit here is the availability to restore the data sets if a situation requires. Another benefit is that all the work is complete. The data sets are deleted, yet available if required. No other cleanup is necessary unless a problem occurs which should be handled on an exception basis.

DASD Cleanup

Similar to product cleanup, DASD cleanup goes a step further. Some projects will require additional DASD to be allocated for testing or development. For example, applying operating system maintenance may require the duplication of the resident (RES) volume. The concept of OLDRES/NEWRES helps provide the ability of backout if the maintenance were to fail. On the other hand, the old RES volume becomes the residue once the maintenance is successfully implemented.

29. Clean and release any DASD utilized throughout the project's duration.

There are a number of ways you could "clean" DASD in preparation to returning it back to the available pool. A simplistic way would be to re-initialize the volume. This approach may be problematic depending upon how the DASD was utilized. The main caution to consider is leaving residual catalog entries from the volume that was initialized.

Using the example identified above, there is a greater likelihood that OLDRES and NEWRES will be identical volumes containing identical data sets. The essential difference would be the maintenance applied to the NEWRES volume. In this case, assuming the catalog entries have been redirected from OLDRES to NEWRES, initializing the volume is not an issue. The catalog should correctly reflect the change, especially if all of the RES data sets are generically cataloged.

However, in the case where a scratch volume was utilized to build a temporary environment to test a product upgrade or operating system upgrade, initializing the volume could be a problem. One has to consider if data sets on this scratch volume were cataloged in the production catalog structure. If this is the case, you want to ensure these entries are removed from the catalog. The best approach may be to actually delete the data sets from the scratch volume versus initializing the volume. The bottom line is to leave a clean, garbage-free environment once the DASD is returned.

Product Manual Updates

One item frequently heard about from the customer is the issue of manuals. As upgrades are implemented, a frequently forgotten issue is to inform or provide the customer with updated manuals. This is important for one obvious reason: the customer is typically the user of the product.

30. Ensure the customer is provided or informed of any updated manuals.

You should clarify who is the license holder for the product. This helps to identify who pays for any extra copies of the manuals if they are requested. For example, the customer is typically the license holder for non-IBM software. They would be responsible for the purchase of additional copies of the product manuals. Ultimately, this should be addressed with your supervisor. However, you should make additional copies available to the customer if the product provides them.

Documentation

The final segment in this section addresses the topic of documentation. As mentioned previously, documentation is an area of deficiency for many in the technical area. Yet, it is probably one of the more important aspects of any project or task. There is so much that has been learned as you proceed through a project. Transferring this knowledge and experience to written form can benefit many for years to come.

Documentation can identify critical pieces of a project which may not be inherently known or obvious. Documentation can provide the "road map" to assist others, even yourself, as the route is followed during a future execution of a similar project or task. This is one of the primary benefits of thorough documentation.

In this section, documentation is going to be broken down into multiple categories. The remaining segments identify various aspects of documentation which may be required for any project assigned within the PKS Information Services, Inc. environment.

Operational and Help Desk Documentation

Oftentimes, changes that are implemented will have some level of impact upon the operational or help desk area of the organization. It may have to do with IPL or task startup procedures, new console messages, or hardware status codes, just to name a few. Unfortunately, it is all too often that updated documentation related to these types of changes never work their way down to these two critical areas. Unfortunately, the old documentation ends up going unaltered.

31. Review or update any applicable operational or help desk documentation.

Documentation is critical in many areas, but especially in Operations and the Help Desk. These people are the front liners. They are the people fielding the calls when the customer has a problem or question. They hear the alarms regardless of whether the alarm is hardware or software driven. They cannot effectively perform their task when they are working with outdated documentation. For these and numerous other reasons it is imperative that any and all updated documentation make its way to all affected areas. People's ability to perform their function depends on it being completed.

32. Update Software Inventory with the appropriate information.

As noted earlier in the manual, the Software Inventory list is available as research information for the project. Now that you have implemented the project or task, if applicable, update the customer's Software Inventory list with the appropriate changes. This includes software and customer name information, release and maintenance levels, and CPU zap data. This will be a significant benefit to yourself and others when you depend upon this information during future projects. As a reminder, an example is included in Appendix I. File location information is included in Appendix B.

Workbook Documentation

The next piece in the area of documentation is the workbook. As mentioned in the beginning of this manual, the workbook is to be the primary location for all documentation relevant to the implementation of the project. This helps consolidate all research, customer correspondence, and working documents into one place. This is beneficial when the need arises to look back on something regarding the project. It also provides a nice packet for the individual who deals with a similar project in the future.

33. Finalize the Technology Project Management Workbook documentation.

There are multiple steps requiring completion in order to finalize the workbook documentation. The following points identify those steps:

1. Ensure all documents are properly filed within the workbook. This would include all documents such as memos, e-mails, project plans, status reports, etc. that were developed for the purpose of this particular project. The documents should be positioned in the proper sections of the workbook.
2. All electronic files related to the project should be copied and stored on diskette. This is done for archival purposes. This frees up costly LAN disk space. It also keeps any project-related files with the paper documents, consolidating all information into one area.
3. Label the workbook with the information contained in Appendix J. The information sheet in Appendix J identifies the who, what, where, etc. of the project. This is the cover sheet for the workbook.
4. Deliver all materials to your supervisor for review. The purpose for this is to validate the closure of a project. The supervisor will be responsible for verifying all steps are completed along with reviewing and approving the documentation.
5. Once receiving the necessary approval, have all the materials properly filed by the department secretary. The secretary will be responsible for filing the documentation in the appropriate location.

The primary documentation process has been completed once you have performed the steps mentioned above. The next documentation step is closing the change request and CSO.

CSO and INFO Management

As previously mentioned, all changes performed by PKS Information Services, Inc. should have an associated CSO and/or work order along with an INFO Management change number when implemented. Each of these change management tools require an update which indicates the results of the implementation.

Since this section is addressing those tasks to be performed when finishing a project, at this point, we shall assume the change was successfully implemented. Now that the documentation has been completed, it would be time to close both the change request and the work order.

34. Update the INFO Management change request and CSO work order.

There may be fields for which a description identifying the conclusion of the change may be required. Any appropriate text should be added at this time. There are also fields which are status indicators. The appropriate status fields should be updated accordingly to show the project is completed. Please refer to the appropriate change management documentation for complete instructions on how to correctly close or complete the change or CSO.

Turning the Project into a Repetitive Task

This is the final segment in the Project Completion section. Having gone completely through the Technology Project Management Process, you should have a pretty good idea whether the project you just completed is truly a project, or really a task. This is your challenge:

35. Determine if the project you just completed is really a repetitive task.

There are a number of questions you could pose against the project to help determine which category it falls into. Please consider the following:

1. Did it take you longer to perform the work than it did to fill out the paperwork?
2. Was there more than one staff member involved in the task or project?
3. Did the task or project take more than two weeks to implement?
4. To implement the task or project, was it necessary to develop a project plan?
5. Do you believe this should be called a project versus a task?
6. Was it essential to directly involve the customer during the life of the project?
7. Was this project or task high profile (significant customer/PKS interaction?)

If you can answer NO to each one of these questions, it is likely that this project was really a repetitive task. While this test is neither scientific or definitive, it should be a fair judge in making that determination. Certainly, if you have any question as to whether this is a repetitive task or project, please see your supervisor.

If it has been determined that this a repetitive task, the next step would be to establish formalized procedures.

36. Write formalized procedures for the repetitive task.

Writing formalized procedures for this task should be a relatively elementary process. First of all, you have just gone through this procedure and implemented the change. Therefore, this process should be fresh in your mind. Secondly, you should already have most of the documentation prepared because this process required you to document much of the procedure. Accordingly, it may be nothing more than identifying this as a repetitive task when turning in the documentation to the secretary. Much of it will depend on the clarity of the procedures you established while executing this task.

As implied above, producing formalized procedures for repetitive tasks should not be a step that consumes a significant amount of time. If properly performed from the start, much of the work will already be done. Remember, the idea here is to improve the quality and save time in the long run. It is not to increase the amount of effort necessary to accomplish the task. Ultimately, everyone should benefit from these procedures in the future.

Summary

Completing the project is as critical as executing the plan to implement. Moreover, the work required to perform this part of the project should be scheduled with the same level of importance as the implementation itself. The significance of completing this work should not be overlooked. Let us take a moment and review the critical aspects of this section.

This section had two main sections: Finishing the Project and Turning the Project into a Repetitive Task. The section started out by identifying the need to finish the project. This is an area frequently neglected throughout the MIS community. Hence, we are not alone when it comes to this dilemma. One of the reasons for this manual is to overcome this problem by instituting mechanisms which instruct, provoke, and even force the individual to perform the duty and take ownership for its completion.

The first step in Finishing the Project was product cleanup. This entails the removal of residual libraries resulting from release upgrades or maintenance. On a frequent basis, this data is made available in case the need for recovery is necessary. Two alternatives provided were migrating older data sets or backing them up to tape using the appropriate utility. Regardless of the method, the obligation is to remove these data sets from the environment.

The next subject was DASD cleanup. Depending on the project, additional DASD may have been required to satisfy testing or development. Once a project reaches the point where the additional DASD is no longer required, it should be cleared of residual data and returned to the Data

Services group. Effort should be made to ensure the DASD is cleared of data in order to reduce the likelihood of residual ghost catalog entries.

The third topic had to do with updating product manuals. This is an area popular with our customers. It is important to provide the customer with the current version of the manuals once the change is implemented. This may require ordering additional copies on their behalf. Product licensing will dictate who pays for the extra copies if there is a cost involved.

The final subject of the section revolved around documentation. Documentation, as explained during this lengthy section, is extremely critical to the success of the project. Documentation is the part that lingers on and people deal with after the implementation.

There were three areas addressed within documentation. These included:

- **Operation and Help Desk Documentation:** This discussed the necessity of ensuring any project-related documents pertinent to these two areas were updated appropriately. These functions are critical within the operation of the environment and have a need to remain up-to-date.

- **Workbook Documentation:** The workbook is the tangible document resulting from this manual and is required to be filed at the end of a project. The discussion identified what steps are necessary to complete this document.

- **CSO and INFO Management:** Lastly, once the project is truly complete (all the documentation is done), the change and project can be marked closed or completed. Each of these change management tools have their own status indicators and should be updated accordingly.

The final segment of the section identified the work necessary to address those projects which are really repetitive tasks. A number of questions were posed in order to help in determining whether or not this work is repetitive in nature. If found to be repetitive, you were then instructed on the steps necessary to turn this into a repetitive task and file accordingly.

This whole section revolved around those steps which are critical to closing a project or task. Without having performed this work, one cannot confidently say that the work is complete. These steps are a necessity in achieving those goals and objectives identified at the beginning of this manual.

V. TECHNOLOGY PROJECT MANAGEMENT PROCESS SUMMARY

This is the last section in the Technology Project Management Process. By now you should be well saturated with the ways of handling a project or task. This manual has attempted to provide a sensible approach to administering the work which you continue to perform on a day to day basis.

Throughout this manual it would not be difficult to identify the fact that this was written by someone who either is or was a software technician. Many of the procedures, recommendations, and examples are written with a software technician slant. This may make it a little difficult to apply it across functional boundaries. However, the hope is that over time, additional suggestions will be received to assist in sanding down the rough edges and making these guidelines valid and applicable across functional boundaries.

Another thought would be the application of common sense when executing a project or task. While common sense was not specifically identified within this manual, it was never the intent to exclude it from the process. All too often we attempt to follow the letter of "the law" (in this case, the procedures defined within this manual) without using common sense in applying their purposes. However, the previous statement is not meant to be a loophole which provides carte blanche freedom to avoid the established procedures. Rather, it is setting you up to be accountable for what you do when carrying out your project. If something stated within these confines does not seem correct or appropriate, you are then responsible to call this to someone's attention. Do not take this manual as gospel, and yet do not take it lightly. Again, use it as a means to increase the quality of the work that you and others like you will perform.

Best of luck to you as you go forth into your next project with this information freshly stored in the dark hollows of your mind. May this manual play a small role in the upcoming successes you experience in implementing future tasks and projects for those all-important people, our customers.

CHAPTER

4

Project Support Office

Royal Bank Financial Group

4.1 COMPANY PROFILE

Royal Bank is Canada's premier global financial services group with leading market shares in personal and business banking, corporate and investment banking, and wealth management. As one of North America's largest financial institutions, Royal Bank and its key subsidiaries, Royal Trust, RBC Dominion Securities, RBC Insurance, and Royal Bank Action Direct, have 58,000 employees who serve 10 million clients through 1,600 branches and offices in 35 countries.

Royal Bank is Canada's largest issuer of Visa and debit cards (by number of cards), serving 5.6 million credit card holders and 6 million debit card customers. It is also the largest provider of financial and electronic business banking services to small and medium enterprises and commercial accounts, servicing approximately

380,000 customers. It is one of the largest distributors of creditor insurance products by premiums, serving 1.8 million customers.

Royal Bank of Canada's Systems and Technology (S&T) group is
second only to the federal government as Canada's largest user of
technology, with spending around one billion dollars annually. Royal
Bank has a staff of more than 2,000 information technology professionals who maintain a sophisticated network system of 600 applications for its operations and clients around the world.

4.2 REASONS TO IMPLEMENT

Quality initiatives in an organization are often triggered by customer
dissatisfaction or quality problems. In the case of Royal Bank of Canada, an electronic payments system problem led to a quality initiative
in the S&T division in 1986 and 1987. This division has 2000 employees. Fourteen business units of the bank are S&T's customers.

During investigation of the electronic payments system problem,
it was discovered that there was no consistent development process
and no formal training or standards by which projects had to be
managed. Management subsequently replaced the System Development Life Cycle (SDLC) with a new Project Life Cycle (PLC), instituted ongoing PLC training, and established stronger, cross-
functional teamwork in projects.

In the early days, S&T recognized the need to change, but lacked
an overall strategy. In 1986, a Quality Group was formed within
S&T with full support from senior management. The group believed
that S&T could control its quality by measuring different attributes
of a project such as defects and scheduled completion date. For example, emphasis was placed on function point (FP) counting, which
was becoming popular at the time. Many people were trained to
count function points and many projects were measured. But without an overall strategy and a management process to support it, FP
counting lost credibility with most practitioners and could not be
sustained.

In 1990, the S&T Quality Group identified product and service quality factors to be measured. Eight *product quality* factors were defined for S&T deliverables:

- **Availability**: The system is accessible to the customer, as agreed.

- **Conformance:** The system adheres to architectural, data sharing, and other pre-established bank standards.

- **Correctness:** The system meets business and operational requirements.

- **Efficiency:** The system uses resources optimally and runs harmoniously within its environment.

- **Flexibility:** The system is easy to customize for specific needs.

- **Maintainability:** The system is easy to repair, enhance, and test.

- **Security:** The system is developed to prevent unauthorized access and ensure information integrity.

- **Usability:** The system is easy to learn, easy to use, and relevant to the rest of the bank's business.

Four *service quality* attributes were identified for serving S&T customers:

- **Caring:** Demonstrate empathy, courtesy, and commitment to the customer.

- **Competence:** Employees have and apply the appropriate knowledge and skills.

- **Dependability:** Meet cost and schedule commitments.

- **Responsiveness:** Address all customer inquiries and requests promptly.

Measurement plans were developed and initiated for all of the product and service quality factors. News of the quality focus and measurement program was favorably received in other areas of the Bank. The Quality Group started to gather feedback from individual departments for quality attributes that were most important to them. Project teams were encouraged to track their own performance, then identify and implement improvements. Performance data was collected, summarized, and presented to the senior vice president and senior management team, who were keen to see that greater emphasis was being placed on quality.

Results were compiled into a composite Quality Index (1992-94), showing the performance trend for each S&T department and S&T overall. Quality Index results were presented and discussed at a quality review committee that met each Friday morning. Suggestions made during the meeting were logged and investigated for continuous improvement.

In summary, S&T's early improvement efforts became focused on raising quality awareness through quality index reporting. The S&T Quality Index showed very gradual improvement over time, but did not identify what had improved or by how much. Performance increases or decreases within departments and across departments tended to average out. The Quality Index was discontinued in 1994.

4.2.1 AWAKENING

In 1990, S&T started its relationship with The Quality Assurance Institute (QAI), headquartered in Orlando, Florida. S&T participated in quarterly QAI Forum meetings (1990-94) with a small group of other companies. These meetings helped the S&T Quality Group to develop an understanding of quality management principles and applications in industry. Participants were encouraged to apply what they had learned, then share their experiences with Forum participants.

QAI suggested that the Bank use the Malcolm Baldrige framework to assess where S&T could improve its management practices. A Quality Council consisting of representatives from cross-functional areas was formed.

In 1992, the Quality Council developed a self-assessment survey based on the Malcolm Baldrige Award process. The assessment showed that many key management practices needed to be developed, improved, and matured. At the same time, a Customer Satisfaction Survey was developed and conducted with S&T's business unit customers to evaluate the performance of S&T project managers and staff who developed their technology solutions. The unfavorable survey results clearly showed that business units were dissatisfied with the way S&T projects were being managed. The Malcolm Baldrige Survey and Customer Satisfaction Survey were performed again in 1993, but the results did not show measurable improvement.

Also in 1992, the Quality Group started learning about the Software Engineering Institute's (SEI's) Capability Maturity Model (CMM). A survey based on the SEI document "A Method for Assessing the Software Engineering Capability of Contractors (CMU/SEI-87-TR-23)" showed that S&T's software capability maturity was at about SEI Level 1.5, which indicated an ad hoc development process. The survey respondents were 38 S&T developers in the Technology Planning & Development group. A detailed analysis of these results was presented to the Quality Council; however, there was not enough support to perform a proper SEI assessment at that time.

In 1993-94, IBM's Toronto Eglinton Lab made its customers aware that they had dramatically reduced defects over a three-year period, hence improving time to market, reducing costs, and improving productivity. S&T executives visited the lab and learned that IBM had improved their entire development process and had used the SEI's CMM as a guide.

In June 1995, an SEI assessment of S&T's software development process was performed, facilitated by the Quality Assurance Institute (QAI). Respondents were a management team and a non-management team. Assessment objectives were: 1) Via consensus, evaluate S&T SEI performance to the SEI model; 2) Ascertain S&T's maturity level based on SEI model criteria; and 3) Identify initiatives needed to mature to the next level. QAI analyzed the results and placed S&T at SEI Level 1.4 (Initial), along with 75% of IT organizations. S&T discovered that it really did not have repeatable system development processes, as defined for SEI Level 2. The results were reported to S&T management in September 1995.

The Quality Group started studying the SEI's CMM and realized that many previous quality improvement efforts had failed for lack of disciplined development processes that were needed to sustain them. For example, the S&T Quality Index focused on quantitative process management, which is an SEI Level 4 process!

4.2.2   S&T'S JOURNEY TO SEI LEVEL 2 BEGINS

A process improvement program was launched. In November 1995, approval was obtained to begin maturing S&T's SEI Level 2 processes. S&T focused on requirements definition methodology as the first process to improve because it is the foundation process in the SEI framework. A cross-functional team developed a new Requirements Management process in January-February 1996, and rollout began in April. An immediate benefit was instatement of the S&T Business Systems Analyst (BSA) position, which had been eliminated in 1990 in favor of Joint Application Design (JAD) sessions, due to management not understanding what needed to be changed.

In early 1996, S&T also engaged Quantitative Software Management (QSM) to perform a benchmark study of 12 projects, which represented the typical mix of projects being performed in S&T at any time. The results of this assessment were determined quantitatively and matched the results of the qualitative assessment performed in June 1995, rating S&T once again at SEI Level 1.4. Using the results of this benchmark and QSM industry statistics, S&T estimated that improvement to SEI Level 2 would reduce project schedules by 15% and reduce project cost 38%, on average. Even greater benefits would accrue by attaining SEI Level 3. The study showed that the first three SEI Level 2 process areas were key to enabling S&T to achieve these benefits, namely: Requirements Management, Project Planning, and Project Tracking and Monitoring.

The new Requirements Management process was a success from the beginning and quickly gained grass-roots support. Support from some executives extended to putting a Key Result Expectation (KRE) to perform Requirements Management in their middle manager's performance contracts, which was also very encouraging. However, the middle management rollout team decided on a low-key approach that was inadequate to change behavior and ensure process implementation (i.e., ad hoc presentations to management teams and practitioners, simple usage measures, and minimal resources for rollout and process support).

Despite CIO support and the results of the SEI and QSM assessments, all executives and group managers were not committed to implementing the improved processes. It was clear that middle management would need help to implement and sustain cultural change across the organization.

In October 1996, the S&T methodology group proceeded to define the next two SEI Level 2 key process areas: Project Planning and Project Tracking and Monitoring. They were carried to this point by the momentum generated by positive acceptance of Requirements Management based on actual usage feedback. But, the S&T rollout team realized that if they could not institutionalize Requirements Management, then they would not be able to implement the major changes needed for Project Planning, and Tracking and Monitoring, which would impact all developers and all levels of S&T management.

By this time it was clear that S&T needed to develop a comprehensive process implementation strategy and plan.

4.3 CULTURE CHANGE

S&T's Vice President for Business Planning & Technology Management, recently transferred to S&T after seventeen years of field operations and business background in the Bank, was responsible for bringing an "end-user and customer voice" to the executive table. She wanted simple information about S&T's core systems development function, such as how many projects were being completed on time and within budget. The metrics and management information teams had found that this data was not readily available, and were working with the methodology group to develop ways of capturing the data. They had also carried out the systems development productivity benchmark, described above, which reinforced the findings of the SEI CMM assessment.

In the meantime, the business units had one consistent message: "S&T is slow in delivering projects". Not having reliable data regarding project status, S&T management did not have the information to understand and address the true situation.

The S&T Project Office (called the Project Support Office until March 1998) evolved from earlier strategic measurement and SEI process improvement initiatives to address the need to implement and sustain cultural change. Jointly, the metrics and management information teams, and methodology group had been working to develop procedures for capturing project status information.

The team realized that project results are driven by a disciplined development process and that a project-process management tool suite would help with process implementation while providing much needed information to management about systems development projects. The team also realized that the Project Office was an essential vehicle for properly implementing and maintaining the new, improved processes and for developing professional project management competencies and practices. They developed a proposal to establish the Project Office, which included proposed acquisition of and justification for a process-project management tool suite.

The proposed plans for the Project Office were evaluated, enhanced, and presented to S&T executives for their understanding and approval. At this meeting, the Vice President for Business Planning & Technology Management elaborated on the fact that all indicators were saying something was wrong with the way projects were being developed and managed. At the same time, she discussed the time and energy it was taking S&T to re-vamp its systems development and project management processes. More emphasis was needed on providing creative solutions to the business units, continuing training for the integrated technology staff, providing automated tools, and supporting the idea that "we will help you to execute better projects". As each problem and potential solution was presented in the meeting, it became clear to the attendees that changing their culture and re-engineering the present way of doing business was not only inevitable, but a priority! S&T executives agreed to proceed with detailed plans to implement the Project Office.

The following objectives contributed core requirements for establishing the original Project Office:

◆ **Strategic Approach:** Position SEI process improvement in the S&T strategic plan, under the "Cost and Productivity" strategic driver. Target year-over-year S&T productivity increases based on actual project performance using a recognized metric, such as the QSM Productivity Index, which is benchmarked to SEI maturity level.

◆ **S&T / Business Partner Alignment:** Align S&T and sponsoring unit formal project review "gates". Establish S&T "gates" in alignment with Right Projects Right (RPR), the generic product development process adopted by S&T's key business unit customers. Ensure that critical project success factors are met at each gate.

◆ **Process Management:** Develop project plans based on defined, organization-wide management and software development processes. Provide repository-based automated tools to implement consistent project planning and time reporting based on actual project plans. Processes and tools must add value, as determined by the people doing the work.

◆ **Ongoing Implementation Support:** Build the foundation to establish a project management "Center of Excellence". Provide ongoing consulting and support to project managers for S&T project management standards, procedures, and tools. Continuously improve project processes based on actual usage feedback.

In late 1996, an evaluation of vendor project management planning and scheduling tools was carried out with the assistance of Price Waterhouse consultants to determine which tools fit the needs of S&T. The final choice was the ABT Tool Suite, complemented by the ABT Rapid Implementation process. These products were subsequently customized by the Royal Bank and used to install a standard project management tool suite in S&T.

A Project Office manager was selected who had strong project management experience, plus excellent negotiation, people, and communication skills. In addition, a project management consultant with Project Office expertise was hired from Electronic Data Systems (EDS) to plan and advise on the development of the Project Office. Regular status meetings were held to keep the managers and staff of S&T and business units in focus.

It is important to note here that without the full support of the CIO, establishment of the Project Office would not have been successful. It is easy to hide behind "culture" by something will not work because of company culture! But, it is management's responsibility to come up with new ideas, implement them, and emphasize that each manager will be evaluated based on the results they achieve. This simple idea in itself is enough to change the culture of any company fast! When individuals know their performance is based on successfully implementing new ideas and bringing positive results, they will force themselves to embrace the new "culture".

Having a team with strong business experience plus strong technical experience in S&T proved to be very powerful and focused team efforts on the satisfaction of S&T's customers, the Royal Bank Financial Group (RBFG) business units.

4.4 PROJECT OFFICE

The Project Office's charter was to focus on the development of professional project management as a strategic core competency within S&T. Key objectives were to help project managers become more successful and to institutionalize robust, consistent project management practices throughout the Bank. The mandate included:

◆ Provide consulting and coaching support to project teams in applying standard processes and tools.

◆ Develop, implement, and maintain systems development and project management processes.

◆ Roll out a project management tool suite within S&T.

◆ Identify and share best practices.

◆ Develop project metrics and project information for S&T management.

The Project Office seeks to achieve these objectives by providing just-in-time, hands-on training, consulting, and coaching to project managers and their teams.

4.4.1 STAFF

The initial Project Office team combined the people who had been working on systems development process improvement, metrics, and management information systems. The new Project Office manager soon joined the team, then hired several project manager consultants (PMCs) from among experienced S&T project managers.

In addition to project management experience, PMCs are fully trained in standard project processes and the project management tool suite, and are taking accreditation courses for Project Management Institute (PMI) certification. Skills such as communication, negotiation, and teamwork are essential for these individuals. The Project Office also has staff responsible for process improvement, coordination of project management education, project metrics, quality assurance, and management reporting. PMCs act as consultants to line project managers and may support a number of concurrent projects, the number depending on project complexity and the project manager's experience.

4.4.2 PROJECT OFFICE PRACTICES AND PROCEDURES

The Project Office has documented many repeatable processes in the form of project management processes, pre-built project plans, form templates, and guidelines to enable more consistent processes across projects. A planning guide for project managers was developed containing critical procedures and step-by-step instructions for the following key project management processes:

◆ Requirements Management is the foundation process for system development that enables S&T to maintain understanding and agreement on technical and non-technical requirements from the beginning to the end of a project. The driver for this process is the Business Project Definition, prepared by the sponsoring unit. Requirements Management is used by S&T in collaboration with sponsoring unit partners to define the strategic and core functionality that is essential to satisfy the business objectives.

◆ The three main steps are: High-level Requirements, which end at PLC Gate 2; Document of Understanding, Detailed Requirements, which end at PLC Gate 3; and Commitment to Deliver and Requirements Change Management. The latter step may return the project to Gate 2 or Gate 3 if unplanned changes to requirements make it necessary to re-establish understanding and agreement among project participants.

◆ The S&T senior management Project Review Meeting (PRM) process focuses on the Requirements Management gates to manage system development issues and increase project success by ensuring that pre-established process criteria have been met.

◆ Project Planning, Tracking, and Monitoring (PPTM) supports the key activities of Royal Bank's PLC and provides guidance on the tools and processes available within S&T to assist with project estimation, planning, and scheduling. The outcome of Project Planning is a consistent, coherent document that can be used to guide both project execution and project control. Project Tracking & Monitoring outlines the standard S&T processes designed to enhance and assist with tracking and monitoring the progress of a project and provides guidance on utilizing the project management tool suite repository for tracking and monitoring.

◆ The Communications Plan documents all communications events that should occur during a project and provides improved internal and external communications between project managers, team members, and other personnel within the RBFG. A Communications Matrix is used to capture, consolidate, provide communications information, and designate both the audience and the personnel responsible for each communications item. A Points-of-Contact List is used to capture, consolidate, and provide names and telephone numbers of those people important to the success of the project. A chart provides a quick reference as to the responsibilities of each team member and external support for all the key deliverables in the project. Project Status Reports provide group management with the changes to each project under their sponsorship so that they are aware of changes, slippage, scope creep, and any other problems occurring in each project.

◆ The Resource Management Plan provides the project manager with tools to set up the infrastructure for a project. The plan includes identifying functional areas and skill sets, strengths and weaknesses in the experience of the team members, functional and organizational charts, roles and responsibilities of each position, resource acquisition guidelines and procedures, and reward and recognition of team members for their work and effort on the project.

◆ The Process Management Plan ensures that the standards and procedures outlined in the PLC are consistently followed. The project manager plans the process-related activities the project is going to follow up-front, making adjustments to process templates depending on the size and magnitude of the project. The Process Management Plan outlines these activities. The plan is used at a later date to verify that the project followed specified activities outlined in the plan.

◆ The Risk Management Plan ensures that high-priority risks are aggressively managed and that all risks are cost-effectively managed throughout the project. The plan also provides management at all levels with the information to make informed decisions on issues critical to project success. Risk Management provides a proactive, team-based approach to continuously assess the project for the presence of risks, identify the most important risks, and implement actions to deal with them.

◆ The Financial & Contract Management Plan provides the project manager with infrastructure to assist in estimating, forecasting, and trending. The infrastructure contains automated tools, templates, and checklists that are effectively used to monitor the costs of a project. In projects where there are specific contractual obligations, the project manager is required to track contractual obligations and ensure they are fulfilled. The plan indicates how these requirements will be met and monitored.

- The Configuration Management Plan indicates the baseline
  configuration items of a project, their version number, and any
  documentation associated with the version. Any changes to baseline
  configuration items are tracked. It also outlines the commonly used
  procedures for tracking, version numbering, change control, and
  how the configuration libraries will be maintained. The process to
  assess change impact and control changes to schedules and
  deliverables are also supported by this plan.

- The Metrics Plan identifies the specific metrics that will be
  collected throughout the project. Typically, metrics are related to
  project functionality, schedule, quality, cost, and resources. The
  plan indicates how metrics will be collected, where they will be
  stored, the type of reports that will be generated, and the action
  items that will be taken based on the data. The plan also
  indicates how variance between estimated and actual results will
  be addressed to minimize any adverse impact on the project.

- Continuous Improvement provides feedback to the Project
  Office based on project team member experiences of what
  worked for them ("Winners") and what did not work for them
  ("Barriers"), e.g., automated tools, processes, communication, or
  senior management support. The feedback is documented and
  shared with senior management so that project management
  activities can be continuously improved. With assistance from
  the management team, items are prioritized and a process is
  designed to address each "Barrier". The "Winners" are also
  documented and made part of the Project Office library so that
  project managers can review what worked for other projects.

- The Training Plan contains personnel training records and
  outlines training required by a team, recommended training
  including self study courses, training available through outside
  vendors, and training available through the Royal Bank's online
  training curriculum. The plan provides guidance on related
  training procedures, templates, and standards.

- The Document Control Plan consolidates all administrative
  document control information. This plan ensures that all
  project-related documents, such as project plans, specifications,

test plans, data dictionaries, etc. are completed, reviewed, and then archived in a central system. The plan provides guidance on how to make revisions to existing documents, who needs to approve the revisions, and how new documents are to be distributed. It also provides for obsolete document disposal.

4.4.3 PROJECT OFFICE PILOT PROJECTS

A recent S&T snapshot showed 1,110 approved projects, comprised of development (618), enhancement (178), and maintenance (314) projects.

Nine pilot projects were selected to test the Project Office project management tool suite and PMC concept. Each project had a project manager and a PMC. It was made clear up-front that the PMC was not an additional resource to the project team, but was a consultant to the team. The PMC gave guidance and coaching in planning projects, using the tool suite, and carried out standard Project Office processes.

At the end of all nine pilot projects, surveys were conducted. The success of Project Office involvement was measured by surveying the pilot project's managers to determine whether they felt the Project's PMCs had assisted them in establishing the overall quality and productivity of the project. The results showed that the pilot program had been very successful.

4.5 CHALLENGES

The first challenge was lack of requirements management methodology and expertise. This was addressed by developing the Requirements Management Process, described above, and by reinstating the BSA role.

Next, S&T executives and the Project Office team realized that group and project management alone could not implement and sustain new work processes given all their normal project pressures. Therefore it became important to provide automated tools and support from

Project Office consultants to mentor the project managers on the job until they could perform the required activities on their own.

The lack of a rigorous process implementation program was another challenge. This was tackled by developing a detailed Project Office process, then integrating it with the implementation process for the project management tool suite. The result was a comprehensive plan and process that showed implementation staff what needed to be done, when, and how to do it.

The never-ending challenge is the constant project pressures that make it difficult to adopt new procedures, even for keen project managers. This is being addressed by the PMCs working closely with project managers to customize large-, medium-, or small-model project plans, and by using the Planning Guide for Project Managers to replace ad hoc work processes with improved procedures based on SEI and PMI guidelines. The model plans and guidelines are very detailed and give step-by-step direction on how to manage key project processes.

4.6 CUSTOMER SATISFACTION

4.6.1 BUSINESS PARTNER SATISFACTION SURVEY

S&T conducts an annual Business Partner Satisfaction Survey. The survey is structured into six categories that address S&T's strategic goals.

- **Business Focus & Alignment:** S&T group or relation manager who manages S&T development activities for a business unit.

- **Project Team Effectiveness:** Workmanship and caliber of the project teams that have done work for the unit.

- **Availability of Infrastructure & Common Systems:** Availability and effectiveness of the common technology infrastructure in RBFG, e.g., hardware such as PCs, servers, telecommunication services, data warehouses; systems software such as Windows, Notes etc.; and common business systems such as e-mail, calendaring, and client relationship management.

◆ **Proactive Application of Technology:** RBFG's position versus others in the financial market.

◆ **Overall S&T Business Relationship & Technology Solution Value:** Overall S&T effectiveness and solutions delivered by S&T.

◆ **General Comments:** Other important areas or specific concerns that are not addressed in the five categories listed above.

The management team reviews the survey feedback and assigns actions for addressing the issues and resolving them to individual project managers. In 1997, 68 surveys were sent out to the managers of 14 business units and 75% were completed and returned. S&T now has full-time relationship managers to oversee the relationship with business units and to provide information technology input to the units' management teams.

4.6.2   PROJECT PRIORITIES AND COMPLETION REVIEW

In addition to the above survey, there is a two-part survey called the Project Priorities and Completion Review. In the first part, the business unit ranks four key project attributes (functionality, schedule, quality, and cost) by relative priority and importance during the Requirements Management phase. The S&T project team uses this information as a guide if trade-offs are necessary during development.

At the end of each project, the following data is gathered from the business unit:

◆ Did S&T meet the business unit's agreed requirements?

◆ Was the project completed on time?

◆ Was the project completed within budget?

◆ Is the system reliable; does it provide acceptable response; is it easy to use?

The project ratings, weighted by the priorities set at the beginning, produce an overall project score.

4.6.3   METRICS

S&T currently maintains a Systems Development Productivity Index, developed by QSM Associates, Inc. This index tracks system size (source lines of code), elapsed time (months), effort (person months), peak staff, and defects for twenty recent projects in a database. The goal is to have every project in the database to provide timely information on trends and development efforts. This will assist S&T management in planning future projects.

Using the project management tool suite, which is rolled out to all S&T projects, the S&T Project Office will soon have a comprehensive base of project data to develop useful metrics for project planning or provide management reporting on any aspect of systems development.

4.7 CONCLUSIONS

Consistent, repeatable processes can be very powerful, but only if they can be effectively implemented and sustained through continuous reinforcement and continuous improvement, such as the Project Office enables. From the pilot projects onward, the Project Office continues to refine its processes based on project manager and project team feedback.

S&T management knows that the Project Office is definitely moving S&T forward in the right direction. They have learned that just being busy and getting results does not necessarily mean that the right work is being done or that the results being obtained are what is needed. S&T has learned to evaluate all results and ensure that what they are providing to their customers is what the customers really want.

The success of the Project Office is also due to the fact that the CIO uses all the project metrics and quality-related information he receives from different project teams and Project Office consultants. This data is shared with the rest of the business community in monthly status and operational meetings. As mentioned in the "Culture Change" section of this chapter, without full support of the CIO and the vice president responsible for the Project Office, the initiatives to improve the quality and reliability of projects would not have been successful.

The "teamwork" aspect was summarized from the top many years ago in the following ten key points:

- **Team Building:** Accepting responsibility for developing good working relationships among team members to achieve corporate values.

- **Participation:** Encouraging other team members to become involved in decisions that affect the team.

- **Cooperation:** Developing an atmosphere of cooperation and willingness to communicate about all aspects of the project's work.

- **Consensus:** Agreeing collectively on decisions to achieve solution ownership.

- **Responsibility:** Taking personal responsibility for team success without regard to individual effort.

- **Helping Others:** Sharing knowledge and experience to help solve problems and get work done.

- **Critical Feedback:** Accepting that opposing ideas are absolutely vital. Using group participation to provide a constructive forum to evaluate critical feedback.

- **Identity:** Identifying and visibly supporting team goals and objectives.

- **Commitment:** Ensuring that you deliver on your commitment to the team effort.

- **Sharing Success:** Taking advantage of every opportunity to credit the team for project success. Putting team achievement ahead of personal recognition.

The Project Office initiative is generating positive feedback from S&T's business unit customers. While no formal measurements have been put in place, it is estimated that the initiative has contributed to improving S&T's relationships by approximately 10%. Going forward, the Project Office will enable S&T to evolve from being cast in a supporting role toward becoming a proactive business partner and establishing a concrete plan to measure it's relationship with the business units.

C H A P T E R
5

Inspections
As An Agent Of Change

Primark Investment
Management Services Limited

5.1 COMPANY PROFILE

Primark Investment Management Services Limited is a part of Primark Corporation, a global information services provider which supplies the international investment management community with financial data, software, and investment accounting support services. The flagship back-office product, Icon, is a real-time, multi-lingual, multi-platform, client server investment accounting, fund valuation, unit pricing, and management and client reporting package. By its nature, the product is deeply embedded in its customers' business processes and is mission-critical to them.

It is worth noting that among its salient characteristics as a computer system, Icon addresses a complex application area driven as much by legislation, regulation, and market practice as by its own product strategy. Business requirements are often unclear and even unknown to any level of detail until close to the necessary implementation date.

Icon is usually installed on our customers' computers, and supported and fed with securities market data from our London headquarters. A number of generations of the product are supported because customers can only upgrade to the most recent when the demands of their own businesses permit it. This, of course, imposes a considerable support and maintenance burden on us; at the time of writing, we were supporting eight product generations on five hardware and operating system platforms.

5.2 REASONS TO IMPLEMENT

In 1994 when we started the journey described here, we were having obvious difficulties reconciling the seemingly irreconcilable: The gap between the needs of our customers and our ability to deliver solutions was often far too big. Consequently our product was perceived by its then small customer base as unreliable and our development process as unpredictable: They rarely knew what to expect in the next release or when to expect it. And when they finally received it, it was often broken!

The functionality offered by the product was, and had been since its inception, comprehensive and extremely flexible; but, most of its other characteristics were less endearing to its customers. The product was thus seen as being of poor quality, which was clearly a barrier to further sales.

5.2.1 A SNAPSHOT OF THE PRESENT

The quality of the software—its fitness for purpose, reliability, robustness, and predictability—is of paramount importance. If customers cannot rely on the performance and behavior of such a critical system, they must look elsewhere for a solution. And they do not want for choice; in the United Kingdom, our market is over-supplied and the competition is consequently fierce.

We have determined that as product differentiators, we shall offer not only the best functionality, but also exceptional service to our customers. Service, in this context, embraces such things as product reliability, performance, predictability, and our responsiveness to shortfalls in any of these. We have thus chosen our basic strategies to help us provide the service that really blows our customers' socks off. These strategies include document inspection and continuous process improvement to help us improve reliability, predictability, and those other key qualities; which, combined with total honesty and openness in the way that we deal with our customers (and ourselves), we believe will set us apart from all our competitors.

5.2.2   A VISION OF THE FUTURE

Petrozzo and Stepper in *Successful Reengineering* [Petrozzo94] define business process reengineering as "the concurrent redesign of processes, organizations, and their supporting information systems to achieve radical improvement in time, cost, quality, and customers' regard for the company's products and services." That's a very good definition of what we're doing; the difference in our case perhaps being that it is not a one-off exercise, for we are continuing to develop and improve the infrastructure, tools, and techniques, and, above all, to change our culture so that we are ready and able to redesign our processes, organization, and systems continuously.

In this way, we are using the powerful leverage effect of document inspection as an agent of change, and we now know that we can realize our vision and reach our goal of owning a product that is recognized as the best of its kind on every measurable scale.

5.3 MEASURES OF SOFTWARE QUALITY

There have been, and continue to be, many attempts to define software quality. Some have concentrated on measuring the delivered software itself, while others, such as ISO9000/BS5750, have focused exclusively on the development process presumably on the premise that if the process is of good quality, the software it produces will be of good quality as well.

Perhaps the most interesting example of the latter is the Capability Maturity Model (CMM) developed by the Software Engineering Institute (SEI) of Carnegie Mellon University [Paulk93]. The CMM came about from the pioneering work undertaken by, among others, Watts Humphrey while at IBM. It defines a set of criteria against which an organization can be measured to determine the quality of its development process and the software it produces. Therefore, software development organization is measured by the CMM according to the characteristics exhibited by its processes.

Figure 5-1 illustrates the five levels of capability defined by the CMM, as well as the criteria that apply to each.

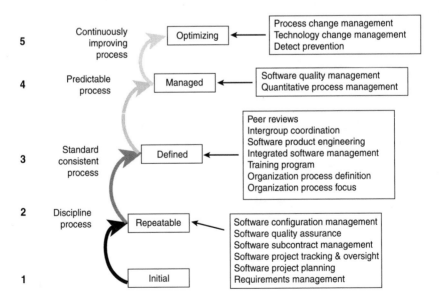

Figure 5-1: SEI's CMM

Although the CMM defines "software quality management" as a characteristic of a Level 4 organization, it does not prescribe the qualities that are to be measured and managed. It does say, however, that Level 4 and 5 characteristics are based on the concepts of statistical process control as described by J.M. Juran in *Juran on Planning for Quality* [Juran88].

The Juran Trilogy Diagram, illustrated in Figure 5-2, depicts quality management as three basic processes: quality planning, quality control, and quality improvement.

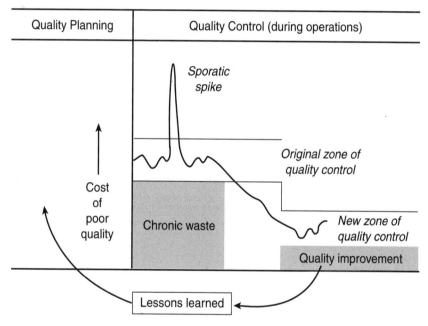

Figure 5-2: Juran Trilogy Diagram

The sporadic spike in Figure 5-2 represents what Juran calls firefighting activities—a term with which all those involved in software development activities are familiar. The Trilogy Diagram shows how the chronic waste caused by not managing quality can be reduced by introducing quality improvement and by feeding back lessons learned into the quality planning process.

Michael Fagan, who was also at IBM in the early 1970's, developed a method of formally inspecting program code against documented criteria as a means of improving software quality by removing defects before test [Fagan76]. This work was extended by Tom Gilb, as described in *Software Inspection* [Gilb93], into a method for formally inspecting any type of document. Gilb placed additional emphasis upon inspecting documents upstream of code in the development process on the basis that the earlier any defects are found, the cheaper they are to fix. What Gilb also did beyond Fagan was to build into his method a mechanism by which the process that created a document could also be examined to determine whether any systemic defects were being caused by the process itself. This introduced the element of process improvement into the method and resulted in a single technique that could be used for defect detection (a CMM Level 3 criterion) and defect prevention by process improvement (a CMM Level 5 criterion).

In addition to his work with inspection, Gilb was involved for many years in the field of software metrics and it is from this field that the notion of "quantified system attributes" came, described in his book *Principles of Software Engineering Management* [Gilb88]. This notion provides a means of defining attributes or objectives for a system which are measurable and hence quantifiable. Attributes can be chosen that refer to any aspect of a software system that will, if improved, contribute to an improvement in the overall "quality" of the software as perceived by its users. Thus, these attributes provide a very direct way of measuring improvement in software quality.

5.3.1   WHAT DO WE WANT TO MEASURE?

Quality can be measured along many dimensions. Some of the more interesting questions we might want to ask about a software system include: How many defects does it have? How easy is it to use? How easy is it to learn? How easy is it to install and upgrade? How well does it perform?

These qualities or attributes are important to a greater or lesser degree to all users of the software and it is therefore worthwhile to measure them to determine which ones require improving and to what extent. We can define as an attribute anything that can be measured numerically; *Principles of Software Engineering Management* [Gilb88] provides a "starter set" of such attributes.

5.3.2 WHAT ABOUT PRODUCTIVITY?

We've so far described the measures that we want to apply to the delivered software system, but what about productivity, which can be seen as a measure of development process quality?

We were sufficiently concerned about what we perceived to be a productivity problem that we presented Tom Gilb in November 1994 with our main objective (which had come to be known as our "time to market" objective):

"To improve time to market for new Icon developments and enhancements."

His response to this was a high-level definition of the quality of the software and our success at developing, installing, maintaining, and supporting it:

"To reduce the calendar time needed to deliver what customers really want. This is defined as:

◆ **Productivity:** Our ability to deliver customer needs in relation to cost of delivery, including training, installation, help service, and maintenance.

◆ **Reliability:** The degree to which the delivered functionality and quality of our total product and service meet the defined and real expectations and needs of our customers and prospects."

Clearly, by this definition, quality and productivity are two halves of an indivisible whole because the "time to market" objective includes delivering what the customer wants when he or she wants it. It also embraces all the necessary support activities and therefore addresses in a single definition many aspects of our business.

Four main strategies were proposed to help us meet this objective:

◆ Define quantified system attributes to set the quality standards for the software.

◆ Perform document inspection to detect and remove defects.

◆ Institute continuous process improvement to prevent defects from appearing by changing the development processes.

◆ Deliver evolutionary results to provide the required functionality incrementally in a timely and controlled fashion.

The powerful combination of these strategies is the essence of the Gilb "method": Quality measurement and improvement are embedded in the production processes (those that actually make your product). "Quality" thus requires no external agencies because it's in-process. You define the quality goals for your system, product, or service by means of quantified objectives, stating their current and target values and how they are to be measured. The method provides a number of strategies by which those goals might be reached.

The method is firmly rooted in a strong process orientation: It requires that the production processes be identified, and process ownership be recognized and assigned. Thereafter product and process quality, as measured by the values held by the quantified objectives, are raised continuously by means of techniques which include defect detection by document inspection and defect prevention by continuous process improvement.

It follows, therefore, that the first steps to take must include setting the quantified objectives and identifying the processes. This may (and we found that it did) require the redesign of existing processes and the recognition of hitherto undiscovered ones. It means that the supporting information systems need to measure, record, track, and report improvements in the objectives requiring redesign (as we also found), and it may also require organizational change (as we are continually finding).

5.3.3   QUANTIFIED SYSTEM ATTRIBUTES

As we have noted, quantified system attributes set the standards by which we wish to measure the software system, and an attribute can be anything that is directly measurable by some means. We look at attributes in two basic ways: those that are directly visible to the user of the delivered software system and those that are not. This gives us a first-level classification of attributes into externally—and internally—

focused ones, and we place each attribute that we want to define into one of these two classes.

A list of interesting externally-focused attributes, those that users of the system see, could include the following:

- **Reliability:** How frequently does it fail to produce correct results?
- **Facility:** How easy is it to use?
- **Installability:** How easy is it to install and upgrade?
- **Functionality:** Does it do everything that I want?
- **Performance:** Does it do it quickly enough?

We classify these as external attributes of our system: those which directly affect the customers of the delivered software.

A list of internally-focused attributes, those which the developers, maintainers, and supporters see, could include:

- **Serviceability:** How easy is it to fix things when they break?
- **Testability:** How easy is it to test and prove that a change works?
- **Diagnosability:** How easy is it to diagnose errors and find their causes?

We classify these as internal attributes, which are those that directly affect the vendors of the product and indirectly affect its customers. These are also related to the productivity aspect of our "time to market" objective.

We believe that it is imperative to publish the attributes, both within and outside our own organization. Doing this has a number of aims:

- To impress customers and prospects with the numbers themselves (always assuming that they are good!), and our willingness to share them publicly.
- To demonstrate to customers and prospects that we have a mission to improve continuously.
- To stimulate us to reach and maintain ever higher standards (and thus to improve continuously!).
- To put pressure on our competitors.

Attributes can therefore be used as very powerful marketing weapons, especially if competitors are less open about such things (as is indeed the case with our competitors). They can make a very confident and positive statement about us as a vendor, and they are also powerful agents of change for our own processes.

5.4 WHAT DO WE MEAN BY PROCESS?

Of the proposed strategies, document inspection and continuous process improvement are predicated on the existence of processes. So what are processes and how do we define them?

In *Reengineering the Corporation,* Hammer and Champy provide an excellent definition of a process: "a collection of activities that takes one or more kinds of input and creates an output that is of value to the customer" [Hammer93, p.35]. So, simply put, a process is anything we do to inputs to create outputs which are of value to our product or service. We extend the definition of customer in that we describe a process as creating an output that is also of value to another, downstream process. This may be a process within our organization or in a customer's organization.

We describe all of our processes in this way. We also define a taxonomy which contains two classes of process:

◆ A production process is one whose results are used directly by the product or service we are supplying to customers.

◆ A meta process is one which is concerned with the ulterior or underlying principles of the production processes.

Furthermore, by our definition, a meta process is also one whose results are used to monitor, measure, and improve the production processes, and hence one or more attributes of the product or service we are supplying. Thus, all processes such as defect detection, defect prevention, process ownership, and process change management are to be found in the meta process class.

To aid standardization of our definition, we adopt the notion of a "generic" process, which doesn't describe any process in particular, but rather shapes all of them. Figure 5-3 illustrates this generic process structure.

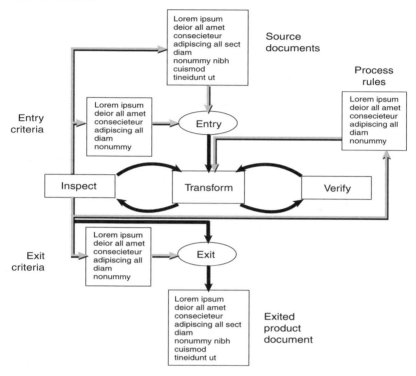

Figure 5-3: Generic Process Structure

The generic process includes the following components:

◆ One or more source documents, which are the inputs to the process.

◆ A set of entry criteria against which the source documents are checked by a sub-process (marked Entry) for compliance before the process is initiated.

◆ A set of process rules, or the procedure by which a process should be operated.

◆ An exited product document, which is the output from the process.

♦ A transformation (shown as Transform), which converts the source document(s) according to the process rules into the exited product document.

♦ One or more correctness verifications (shown as Verify), which establish that a product document's technical content is correct.

♦ One or more document inspections (shown as Inspect), which establish that a product document meets the agreed quality standards.

♦ A set of exit criteria against which a product document is checked by a sub-process (marked Exit) before the process is terminated.

The Transform, Verify and Inspect sub-processes are iterated until a product document is completed and exited from its final inspection. The Verify sub-process, analogous to what is known elsewhere as a review or walkthrough, can range from an informal exchange of views and information to a formal meeting with a variety of domain experts present. We have recently bounded the Verify sub-process by means of rules or procedures: It can either be invoked separately or by means of a formal verification role in a document inspection. The Inspect sub-process itself is always a formal event whose rules are clearly defined; the initial reference we used being *Software Inspection* [Gilb93].

Each process has a written procedure to be followed and a template form for its product document. The exit criteria that a product document must meet before the process is complete are those defined for its inspection through its inspection artifacts. Inspection itself is an instance of the meta process class, and is defined in precisely this way.

5.4.1 HOW WE INSPECT DOCUMENTS TO REMOVE DEFECTS

The primary objective of document inspection, when you first start out, is the detection and removal of defects from documents before they are used as sources in downstream processes; for this reason, it is also known as the defect detection process. As the process matures, it also becomes a means of preventing the injection of defects by helping the team discover where the development process is causing systemic defects and subsequently improving it. For a full treatment of the inspection process, refer to *Software Inspection* [Gilb93].

In an inspection, a document is checked rigorously against written rules, any breach thereof being classified as a defect. Defects fall into two categories: major defects being those likely to cause further errors and incur costs downstream, and minor defects being those unlikely to do so. The aim of any inspection is to reduce the number of predicted major defects remaining in the document to an agreed, and calculable, level as defined in the exit criteria for inspections. When a document reaches that point, it is suitable to be used as a source in a downstream process and, most importantly, it has a known quality status. Until a document has been inspected, its quality status is, of course, unknown and its defects undiscovered. It is therefore highly dangerous to use it as a source for further work downstream.

An inspection is carried out by an inspection team created for the purpose. All the members of the team are voluntary—including the author or editor of the product document being inspected. The inspection process is founded on the very sound psychological principle that people who are doing something they really want to do will naturally be motivated to do it to the utmost of their ability. An inspection is like a miniature project focused on a single goal—to help the author or editor of a document achieve the exit quality status in his or her document so it can go on downstream. Being so tightly focused and having a team consisting entirely of volunteers gives an inspection project the highest probability of success. Its objectives are clear and unambiguous, and every member of the team is there for one reason only: to help make the author a hero by producing the best document of its kind!

Within an inspection team, there are a number of special roles:

- **Leader:** The "project team leader" of the inspection.

- **Checker:** One who checks the product document and source documents against the rules and checklists. Checkers may also assume more specialized roles, for example, a procedural role or a verification role.

◆ **Scribe:** One who transcribes the issues raised during the Logging Meeting for subsequent use by the editor while cleaning up the document.

◆ **Author/Editor:** The editor of the product document, who may or may not be its original author.

The inspection process itself, illustrated in Figure 5-4 has a well-defined procedure:

◆ Ensure that the entry criteria are met.

◆ Check the product document against written rules.

◆ Log the issues raised by the checking.

◆ Edit the product document where defective.

◆ Raise document change requests for defects in source documents.

◆ Exit the product document when the exit criteria are met.

In this and other such models, the parenthesized codes in the boxes describing the sub-processes are the process identifiers; these will be seen again in Table 5-1, which enumerates the product documents and their intended readerships.

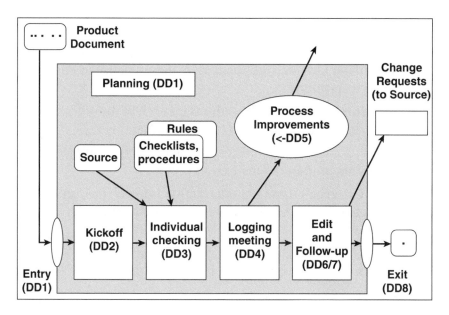

Figure 5-4: Defect Detection (Inspection) Process

A key feature of inspections is the automatic feedback loop to process improvement. This means that every inspection carries with it the potential to invoke a change to the process. Process improvement suggestions are ideas for changes to the process that produced the document being inspected. They are intended to reduce systemic defect generation, and can be raised by anyone participating in an inspection. Process brainstormings are held after some or all inspections to generate more improvement ideas from all inspection participants.

The results from both process improvement suggestions and process brainstormings are fed out of inspections to the process owner, who then decides whether to incorporate them into the process. This is depicted in Figure 5-3 by the arrow from the Inspect sub-process to Process Rules. The implication here, of course, is that every process which has product documents that are to be inspected must have a process owner to implement the improvements.

The document inspection process, like all others, is defined by a number of artifacts:

- ◆ **Rules:** Specify the criteria against which a product document is to be inspected. They include such attributes as form and content.

- ◆ **Checklists:** Provide additional help and guidance to checkers during inspections.

- ◆ **Procedures:** Define the procedures for each of the different roles to be performed by the inspection team members.

- ◆ **Forms:** Contain the templates for the inspection artifacts, the documents used in the inspection process.

- ◆ **Entry Criteria:** Define the criteria that must be met (unless specifically waived) before a product document can be inspected.

- ◆ **Exit Criteria:** Specify the criteria that must be met before a product document can exit an inspection.

Table 5-1 shows the product documents and their intended readership for each sub-process of inspection.

Table 5-1: Defect Detection Processes and Product Documents

	Process	**Product Document**	**Intended Readership**
DD1	Planning & Entry Check		
DD2.1	Kickoff—Leader	Master Plan	Checkers
DD2.2	Kickoff—Checker		
DD3.1	Checking—Leader		
DD3.2	Checking—Checker		
DD4.1	Logging—Leader	Data Summary	Inspection Leader
DD4.2	Logging—Checker		
DD4.3	Logging—Scribe	Author Advice Log	Editor
DD4.4	Logging—Author		
DD5.1	Process Brainstorming—Leader	Process Brainstorming Log	Process Owner
DD5.2	Process Brainstorming—Checker		
DD6.1	Editing—Leader		
DD6.2	Editing—Editor	Document Change Request	Source Document Editor
DD7	Follow-up		
DD8	Exit Check		
DD9	Product Release		

Table 5-1 also illustrates how we document every process we define. We record the following: each process' unique process identifier; its name or description; and its product document(s) and their intended readership.

The sub-processes of an inspection, as illustrated in Figure 5-4, include:

- **Planning & Entry:** The inspection leader establishes that a product document meets the entry criteria and then forms the inspection team.

- **Kickoff:** The inspection team meets, and the leader allocates any specialist roles and completes the Inspection Master Plan.

- **Checking:** The inspection team checks the product document against the source documents, rules and checklists.

- **Logging:** The team logs the issues raised by checking on the Author Advice Log and the leader completes the Inspection Data Summary.

- **Edit and Follow-up:** The editor, who may or may not be the document's original author, but is its current owner, cleans up the product document and raises any necessary document change requests for source documents and process improvement suggestions.

- **Exit:** The leader checks that all the logged issues have been addressed by the editor, calculates the predicted remaining defects in the product document, and exits it if it now meets the exit criteria.

- **Process Brainstorming:** The inspection team brainstorms to discover if any systemic defects are being caused by process deficiencies.

As you can see from this description, each inspection results in not only a cleaned-up product document, but also in a vital stream of process improvement ideas and suggestions. Inspection as a process also captures many of the values that we want to promote in our culture. We have a saying that every inspection is Voluntary, Open, Team-oriented, Egalitarian, and Supportive; everyone on an inspection team has VOTES.

5.4.2 HOW TO PREVENT DEFECTS FROM OCCURRING

The feedback loop from inspection is at the heart of Gilb's method and forms a key part of the process improvement framework. Thus it is the fundamental principle established for enabling the customers, practitioners, and owners of processes to change them as they determine from their real-world experience of process usage. It is continuous, occurring as part of every inspection that takes place, and requires no periodic review process because it's built into the way everything is done as a matter of course.

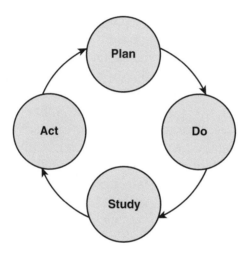

Figure 5-5: Shewhart/Deming Cycle

This feedback is based on the principle of the control cycle, long used in manufacturing industries for quality control and improvement. Figure 5-5 illustrates the Shewhart/Deming Cycle, which defines a simple framework for continuous process improvement. This was first described as a control cycle by Dr. Walter Shewhart, and later developed by W. Edwards Deming in his seminal work on quality, *Out of the Crisis* [Deming86].

The cycle defines four stages:

◆ Plan to do something.

◆ Do it.

◆ Study the results.

◆ Act to improve the process for the next time.

This cycle can also be clearly seen in the Juran Trilogy Diagram in Figure 5-2 as the Lessons Learned loop from Quality Improvement to Quality Planning.

In our context, the Plan and Do phases are those of the production process itself, while the Study phase is represented by process improvement suggestions from inspections and process brainstormings. The Act phase is the resultant process change effected by the process owners. Thus it can be seen that process ownership is a key element: Without process owners, processes cannot be improved.

Continuous process improvement, as we shall see shortly, is at the very heart of the method and is the element that gives it such leverage. Because document inspection and process improvement feed each other and are built right into the production processes themselves, we are automatically in a cycle of change and improvement, fueling further change and improvement.

5.4.3 SYNTHESIS

It is from all of these strands that we have woven our strategy for software quality improvement. Bringing together process ownership, document inspection, and the overarching continuous process improvement yields the "big picture" shown in Figure 5-6. We have seen how defining production processes and their product documents allow us to embed document inspections into those processes, and how the feedback mechanisms inherent in inspection together with process ownership provide the defect prevention framework of continuous process improvement.

Defining quantified system attributes for our software and processes is also a vital part of this picture, and in some senses is the well-spring from which everything else flows. Remember that the attributes describe the targets or goals that we wish to aspire to; everything else in Figure 5-6 can be viewed as a set of strategies to enable us to attain those goals.

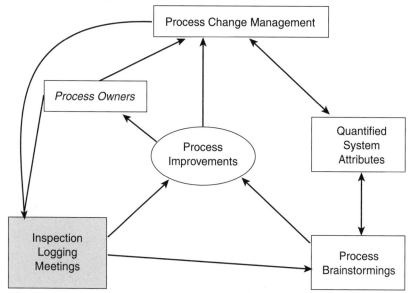

Figure 5-6: Continuous Process Improvement Framework

In Figure 5-1 we depicted the SEI's CMM as an interesting and industry-recognized model of software development capability. Everything that we have described since then has been with the intention of taking us towards CMM Level 5. We're now going to look at what we have done since December 1994, when we set out on our long journey to CMM Level 5.

5.5 HOW DID WE GET STARTED?

Our start-up comprised a number of parallel activities:

◆ Identifying and defining the quantified system attributes for the system that we deliver to customers.

- Identifying and defining our business processes, their inputs and outputs, and their relationships with each other.

- Learning about and practicing document inspection

- Setting up a support infrastructure for recording and logging all defect control activities, namely defect detection and defect prevention.

- Initiating the necessary change in mindset and attitude toward work and fellow workers. (This is often referred to elsewhere as culture change.)

5.5.1 DEFINING QUANTIFIED SYSTEM ATTRIBUTES

Principles of Software Engineering Management [Gilb88] defines "attributes" as being of the software system shipped to its users. We extend that term to include other measures that we believe are important not just to the delivered software, but also to the processes by which we develop and support it. Examples of such attributes include Completeness and Correctness, which measure how well we've understood a user's requirements and translated those into system functionality (Completeness), and how right our solution is (Correctness).

Each attribute is chosen to measure a single aspect of the system or a process and is classified as either externally-focused (external attribute) or internally-focused (internal attribute). Figure 5-7 shows the external attributes we have defined. In Figure 5-8, the darker boxes are "molecular" attributes which are broken down into the "atomic" ones shown in the lighter boxes. It is the "atomic" attributes for which the definitions following Figure 5-7 are made.

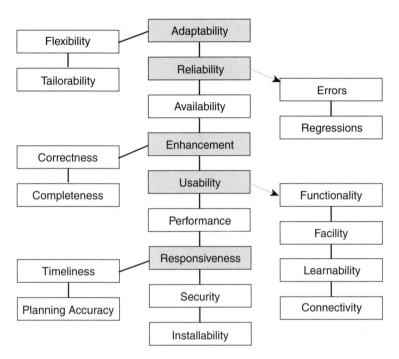

Figure 5-7: External System Attributes

♦ **Availability:** The percentage of scheduled time the software is available for customers to use.

♦ **Completeness:** The degree to which the development process delivers complete new functionality to customers.

♦ **Connectivity:** The degree to which the software can be connected to and integrated with other systems, services, and technologies that customers require for running their businesses efficiently.

♦ **Correctness:** The degree to which the development process delivers correct new functionality to customers.

♦ **Facility:** The ease with which a trained user can operate the system.

- **Flexibility:** The degree to which existing functionality can be adapted to customers' needs by on-site configuration, without requiring software changes.

- **Functionality:** The degree to which the software provides the functionality requested by customers and agreed by us.

- **Installability:** The degree of disruption required to a user's normal business for the installation or version upgrade of the software.

- **Learnability:** The speed at which a feature of the system new to the user can be learned and then operated with proficiency.

- **Performance:** The degree to which the software facilities which are part of a customer's critical business processes enable those processes to meet their business deadlines successfully.

- **Planning Accuracy:** The degree to which the planning process accurately plans and forecasts changes to the system.

- **Reliability:** The degree to which the software runs error-free for customers.

- **Security:** The degree to which the software detects and rejects intruders.

- **Tailorability:** The degree to which house style requirements for such items as report templates can be met by on-site configuration, without requiring software changes.

- **Timeliness:** The degree to which the problem management process meets its required fix times.

Figure 5-8 shows the internal attributes that we have defined. Again, definitions for the attributes follow the figure.

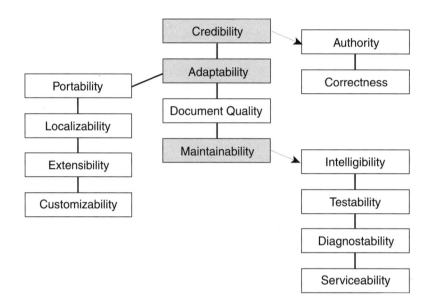

Figure 5-8: Internal System Attributes

◆ **Auditability:** The degree to which the system maintains an audit trail of its activities.

◆ **Correctness:** The degree to which the system behaves correctly in response to user actions.

◆ **Customizability:** The ease with which customer-specific functionality can be added to the system.

◆ **Diagnosability:** The ease with which a problem can be identified and its cause isolated.

◆ **Document Quality:** The permitted defect rate of all software engineering documents.

◆ **Extensibility:** The ease with which new functionality can be added to the system.

◆ **Intelligibility:** The ease with which the system, or parts thereof, can be understood to a sufficient degree to apply changes to it.

◆ **Localizability:** The ease with which the system can be configured for each target locale.

◆ **Portability:** The degree to which the system can be proven to operate with identical results in all target hardware and software environments.

◆ **Serviceability:** The ease with which changes can be applied to the software.

◆ **Testability:** The degree to which the system, or parts thereof, can be rigorously tested.

Notice the presence of Document Quality in the list above. We've defined it as an internal attribute so we can record an improvement in the exit criteria over time, just like all the other attributes. (The exit criterion at the time of writing is three predicted major defects per logical page; we intend to take that to 0.3 major defects per logical page over the next four years.)

Attributes, like any objectives, must be SMART: Specific, Measurable, Achievable, Results-based, and Time-bound. The format of an attribute accounts for all of these desirable characteristics; each attribute is defined in the following terms:

◆ **Gist:** Describes informally the essence of the attribute (in the attribute lists above, it is the Gist of each that is shown).

◆ **Scale:** Specifies the scale upon which it is measured.

◆ **Meter:** Describes how it is to be measured.

◆ **Past:** States the value that the attribute held in the recent past.

◆ **Record:** States any known industry or world best for the attribute (the ceiling to which we can aspire).

◆ **Must:** States the value to which we believe we must take the attribute in the short term to achieve an acceptable level.

◆ **Plan:** Describes a timed plan for longer term improvement of the attribute.

Of the numeric values shown for an attribute (Past, Record, Must, and Plan), Record perhaps requires some further explanation. The purpose of showing the "world record" for an attribute is to act as a reality check on our own aspirations to improve it—such records are typically set by organizations with considerable resources and are usually very costly to achieve. So the Record is there to stop us from "chasing rainbows" when we know there's no point in trying to beat, for example, IBM or AT&T.

To illustrate an attribute, this is how we have defined Reliability:

◆ **Gist:** The degree to which the software delivers error-free running for customers.

◆ **Scale:** Two numbers: reported errors per customer per year which require and those which do not require local fix releases.

◆ **Meter:** Sum error Software Change Requests (SCRs) raised in previous year by customers, grouped by Problem Severity Level(PSL): PSL 1-3 and PSL 4-6.

$$\text{Critical Reliability} = \frac{\sum(\text{error SCRs of PSL (1-3) in year})}{\sum(\text{customers})}$$

$$\text{Non-critical Reliability} = \frac{\sum(\text{error SCRs of PSL (4-6) in year})}{\sum(\text{customers})}$$

◆ **Past:** 51.4 : 54.4 [May94 - Apr95] ← Analysis of historical CR figures.

◆ **Record:** 0. Space shuttle ← IBM Systems Journal Sep94.

◆ **Must:** 24 : 60 [End 1995].

◆ **Plan:**18 : 45 [End 1996] 12 : 30 [End 1997] 6 : 15 [End 1998] 3 : 10 [End 1999].

The PSLs in this example are those defined in the "Problem Resolution Service" section of our standard Support Services Description, wherein Levels 1 through 3 refer to problems experienced with processes that are critical to the customer's business and Levels 4 through 6 refer to those problems with processes that aren't. The measures will be meaningful to customers in terms of the reliability of the system facilities that support their critical business processes. This is a good example of the customer orientation of an attribute and how we have approached the definition for all of them.

Pursuant to our goal of publishing openly all the key performance measures and indicators for the system, we engaged our product user group to help us formulate the external attributes. We now measure them by means of our change management system and publish them automatically every month in a mailing and on our website.

5.5.2 DEFINING PROCESSES

We started by identifying the processes that are used to develop the software. This was a relatively easy starting point since the processes are, or should be, well-understood. For each process thus identified, we enumerated all of its sources of input and its outputs, or product documents. To each product document we ascribed a readership. The inputs helped us define the procedure to be used to transform the sources into product documents. The outputs helped us define the rules for the product document, particularly the specific rules of content. As part of this exercise, we also defined the nomenclature to be used for document tags and the library (directory) structure into which all such documents are placed for subsequent access. This information is published in a navigational compendium, which is itself, of course, available publicly. The whole collection represents our document repository.

We saw earlier that each process must have an owner or owning group whose responsibilities include maintaining the process definition artifacts for subsequent use by process operators. We have found it easiest to define one person who performs the process and one who is a customer of the process—a recipient of the product document. Our process owners are also published in our compendium. We developed the first cut of the inspection artifacts using *Software Inspection* [Gilb93] as a source; these are now owned by the process owners who amend them and publish new versions in the document repository as part of the continuous process improvement program.

5.5.3 THE META PROCESSES

We earlier identified the meta processes to be those outside the production processes—primarily the defect detection and defect prevention processes. These are well-defined by Gilb in *Software Inspection* [Gilb93] and we have used, without embellishment, the definitions found there. There are other identified meta processes which we are still defining; for example, process ownership processes and process definition processes. Beyond those, there are certainly yet more processes, unidentified and even undreamed of.

The process owners of the meta processes are, by default, the Process Change Management Team (PCMT). The PCMT also has a broader responsibility to oversee all process change as illustrated in Figure 5-6.

5.5.4   TRAINING

Training for document inspection falls into two categories: that required for inspection leaders, and that for other inspection participants. The more important of the two is the former—well-trained leaders can perform very satisfactory on-the-job training for the other participants. It is also vital that every inspection be led by an accredited leader if time is not to be wasted and real benefits are to be realized.

We were very fortunate in that we received Tom Gilb's own Inspection Leader course; he packed a five-day course into three days by extending the hours and at the end we had eight accredited inspection leaders. We also had an inspection overview briefing for most of the other people in development. This briefing gave them an insight into what the process was all about and most importantly, explained the terminology that would be used. This clearly helped everyone feel positive about the process from the very beginning.

Training inspection checkers, scribes and editors is a continuous process; every inspection is a learning experience for everyone concerned, and we have found that new starters take readily to the process, even as authors, once their initial fears are overcome. In this respect, the positive and supportive attitude of their fellow inspectors has proved to be of immense benefit. Training in inspection is never finished: We are continuously learning more about how to run better inspections, how to do smarter checking, and how to improve the efficiency and effectiveness of defect discovery and removal.

5.5.5 SETTING UP THE SUPPORT SYSTEMS

We realized that it was important to begin recording the results of inspections right from the start, so we set up our QA database at the outset. It is simple but effective for our current needs. As our process matures, we shall enhance the database to cater to changes in our requirements; as we shall see later, it is already providing us with invaluable information about our progress. To provide for the introduction of document inspection into our development process, we enhanced our change management system so that we can record the quality status for software changes whose code is to be inspected.

We set up a document repository on our file server for all documents, whether part of the production processes or the meta processes, and we continue to work on navigation aids to help people find what they want. (Our first foray into the production of our navigational compendium resulted in a document so complex that it required its own navigational aid!)

To enable unambiguous identification of statements in documents, especially important in inspections and in citing them as sources in downstream documents, Gilb recommends that atomic statements be tagged. To assist with the tagging of documents and to help authors meet generic rules, we developed a Microsoft Word document template which provides a number of such facilities. The use of this template has the additional benefit of giving authors a framework within which to write their documents and ensures that all documents so produced have a standardized look and feel.

5.6 LESSONS LEARNED

The main achievements we set out to attain were:

♦ Improvements in software quality as a result of detecting and removing defects.

♦ Improvements in document quality as a result of having better product document definitions and templates.

♦ Improvements in the production processes themselves.

We have made very substantial gains in all of these areas, which we will now examine. There have, in addition, been many other smaller wins too, some of which we will describe on the way.

5.6.1 IMPROVEMENTS IN SOFTWARE QUALITY

We now have incontrovertible evidence that software quality is improving, and has been since the beginning of 1995 at a spectacular rate. History, as always, is the final judge as the results of inspected development projects filter into installed products and are used by customers. The scientific method would have us conduct a control experiment. We are, however, unable to do this and so the savings in downstream costs are simply predicted. As a measure of the effectiveness of the process, we're tracking the defects removed as a result of inspections against the error rate reported in usage of the system by both our own test and support staff, as well as by customers.

We have been collecting the statistics from all document inspections since the very beginning, in December 1994. It is worth noting that all the time spent by all participants in every sub-process of inspections is logged and accumulated; thus we track very accurately the true cost of the process.

From the number of major defects found in an inspection, we predict the hours saved downstream by their not being translated into errors discovered in test and field usage. This prediction is based on a conservative industry norm recommended by Tom Gilb of eight hours saved downstream for every major defect found in inspection; Trevor Reeve of Thorn-EMI has actually measured nine hours saved [Gilb93, p.20], and IBM has reported over a long period a ratio of one hour spent in inspection having saved 20 hours in testing and 82 hours should a defect get into field use.

The inspection metrics are, like everything else, made very public to help us feel good about our achievements and to spur us on to even greater things in the future!

Figure 5-9 illustrates some of the results achieved from all the inspections we have conducted to date. We show the number of major and minor defects, together with the process improvement suggestions and change requests for upstream documents ("Document

CRs") that are logged in inspections. Notice that the volume of major defects far outstrips that for minor defects, and recall that major defects are those which are likely to cause cost downstream. We exhort inspection teams to focus on finding major defects; the graph in Figure 5-9 illustrates how successful they are in their pursuit.

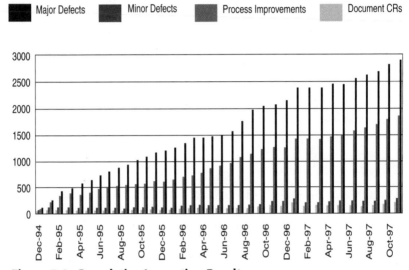

Figure 5-9: Cumulative Inspection Results

Figure 5-10 shows the cumulative amount of time spent in inspections since we started, together with the predicted time saved; the latter is based on the estimate of eight hours downstream saved by every major defect fund upstream. We intend to use the development capacity thus generated for other, more productive activities.

If you view this graph as an illustration of benefit (Hours Saved) to cost (Hours Spent), you get a real insight into the power of the inspection process.

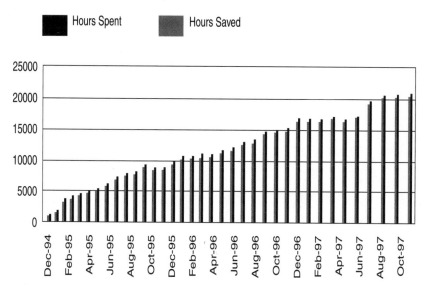

Figure 5-10: Cumulative Time Spent In and Saved By Inspections

We're also measuring effectiveness by plotting the Defect Density (number of major defects per logical page found) of each checker against the Inspection Rate (number of logical pages per hour checked). As you can see from Figure 5-11, the slower the checker, the more major defects found. The graph clearly shows two features: our optimum checking rate is between 0.5 and 1 logical pages per hour; and most of the time, most checkers are in fact checking at that rate. It also shows equally clearly that if the checker tries to go too fast, effectiveness falls off very rapidly.

Remember that the goal of every checker is to help the document author become a hero. Checking too fast is obviously not going to contribute to that goal, so we like to think of adopting an optimum checking rate as the best way of helping our author.

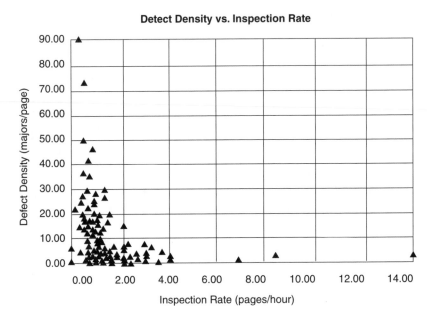

Figure 5-11: Optimum Checking Rate

Figure 5-12 is another graph of real checking results. This graph shows that document size affects the number of major defects found.

Our optimum document size appears to be somewhat less than three logical pages. So when we have a big document, we split it into many smaller documents for individual checking by such techniques as sampling (inspecting only a representative part of a document containing similarly structured sections) and chunking (breaking a document into chunks and having each chunk inspected by a different checker).

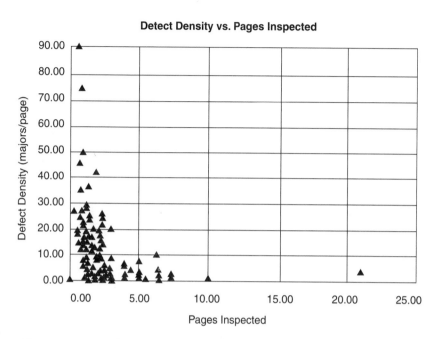

Figure 5-12: Optimum Document Size

For inspection to be a worthwhile process, it must remain efficient as well as effective. The graph in Figure 5-13 shows two measures of process efficiency: the number of major defects found per hour spent and the total number of defects found per hour spent. These help us learn how to maintain our efficiency and continue to justify the cost of doing inspections at all; for if we're not finding enough defects per hour spent in inspection, we might be better off spending the time finding them by some other means.

As you can see, the results vary quite substantially from one month to the next, and there appears to be no clear trend. But there does appear to be something worth investigating here. Perhaps our inspection process requires further refinement or tuning in some way; perhaps we need more training. We at least can see what's happening and decide what to do about it—we may even make inspection efficiency an internal attribute at some point!

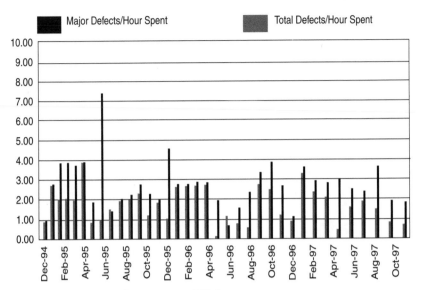

Figure 5-13: Inspection Process Efficiency

We have long recorded metrics on changes requested to software through our change management system—one of the things we measure is the arrival rate of error reports from all quarters (customers as well as our own in-house testing and usage of the system).

Now that we are also measuring defects found by inspections, we can compare the two sets of figures as in the graph in Figure 5-14, which shows, on a monthly basis, the arrival rate of error change requests (CRs) into our change management system (shown as "Total Count" since it includes those found both externally by customers and internally by ourselves) and the number of Major Defects found in inspections since they started.

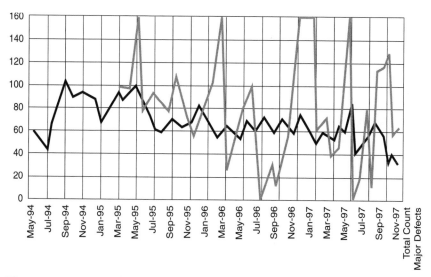

Figure 5-14: Inspection Process Effectiveness

There will, of course, be a time lag between the major defect removal rate and the reduction in error arrival rate from the field since it takes time for the improved software to get into field usage. We are going to track these two key indicators from now on and expect to see reliability improve (the software error totals to fall) as the number of major defects removed continues to rise.

As we saw earlier, we have an external quantified system attribute called Reliability. This measures the number of high- and low-severity errors per customer per year and is therefore a good indicator to a customer (or prospective customer) of what he or she might expect from our software. Figure 5-15 is the graph of that attribute, which we publish monthly for ourselves and our customers.

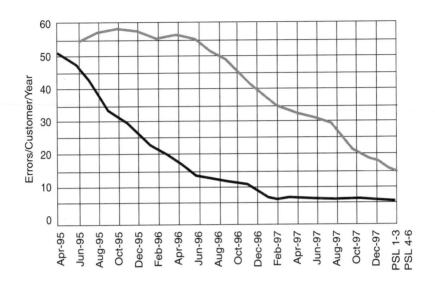

Figure 5-15: Reliability Attribute

Recall that we started doing inspections in December 1994. The results of those inspections would have started to reach the field in May and June 1995. You might imagine the impact this graph has had on us, on customers, and on prospects—and undoubtedly on competitors too!

5.6.2   IMPROVEMENTS IN DOCUMENT QUALITY

We are experiencing an amazing improvement in the quantity and quality of documents produced—people are now striving to produce better documentation because they want to. The inculcation of everyone with improved software engineering practice has led to a much clearer understanding and acceptance by most of the importance of sound documentation in support of the development and maintenance of the system. We are, of course, motivated very strongly by our having taken the radical step of defining our quantified system attributes, and making them available publicly to our customers!

We are always trying to find better and smarter ways of documenting the system and our processes, with most of the improvement suggestions originating, as expected, from inspections.

5.6.3   IMPROVEMENTS IN PROCESSES

Defining our processes has helped us understand them and the product documents; as a result, people no longer have doubt about what kind of document to write in any situation. Because process definition and ownership is now a responsibility visibly shared by everyone, most people feel that generally we have the "right" processes and, more importantly, that together we have the ability to change them whenever we see fit. Process definition has obviously helped us focus on the processes we want to have and the types of documents we want to generate in the development and support of our products. As with many other things, the trick is in striking the right balance between speed and safety: Just like driving a car, the faster you go and the more corners you cut, the more risk you run but the quicker you arrive (assuming you survive!).

There is nothing prescriptive, proscriptive, or mandatory at all about "the way we do things around here." We have guidelines published as rules, procedures, checklists, and entry and exit criteria and we publish best practice documents for people to aspire to. Everyone has the power to initiate any kind of change. We produce no documents simply to obtain sign-off, because we don't have any sign-offs: Every document we produce has a purpose in the process and a target readership or audience who need it as a source downstream. Everyone now understands the penalty of not doing it right: We deliver software of unknown quality. So, we are all strongly motivated to get the defect rate down, and we now have the tools to do that.

The process ownership/continuous process improvement framework gives us immense power to change things very quickly if we see the need, and we have made a surprisingly large number of changes since we started. We've redesigned the furthest upstream parts of the development process: requirements gathering, specification, verification, and what we call functional (external) design. We've redesigned the middle parts of the process: system (internal) design, coding, and unit testing. We introduced new code version management, change reporting, and tracking systems as well. And now we're redesigning the downstream parts: system test, regression test, packaging, shipping, and installation at customer sites. Aside from these major exercises, we've also implemented hundreds of small, incremental improvements to all of our activities.

In the space of three years, we've changed every part of our development process (some parts more than once), and we have had no management edicts, no committees, no external quality departments, and no cumbersome standards manuals. We've let the people operating the processes change them as they see fit and used the results to tell us which changes work and which don't.

As we shall see later, we have only just begun to understand the implications of having all this power at our disposal. We have not yet looked beyond the development processes to the wider issues of the Icon business as a whole. We are certain that when we do, we shall discover that further process improvements can be wrought to the lasting benefit of the product.

Our problem management and error correction processes have also benefited directly from what we've learned. In the first three years, our error correction process efficiency improved from 39 developers spending an annual 80% of their recorded time (31.2 work-years per year) correcting errors to 29 developers spending 35% of their time (10.15 work-years per year) doing the same. So, we have achieved a 67.5% reduction in software rework costs. In the same period, our defect detection and removal process effectiveness has also improved such that 80% of all errors were found by eight customers, whereas now only 60% of all errors are found by 25 customers between them. We have no evidence to suggest that our customers are any less effective in finding errors, so we assume that we are now more effective.

5.7 CULTURE CHANGE

One of the major difficulties we encountered was finding a way of giving people enough time to conduct inspections. We started by concentrating on selecting critical and high-risk developments and inspecting some or all of their product documents. As we became more familiar with the process, we expanded that strategy to embrace all new product enhancement projects and planned to inspect all, or at least the most critical (the ones furthest upstream) product documents generated. To help embed the process further, some people are starting to incorporate inspections into their annual objectives.

Allocating time to other activities such as process ownership tasks and artifact definition (rules, procedures, etc.) has also proved difficult, although we believe that one of the main reasons for this is that they were initially so unfamiliar to us. Although we had never had a strongly hierarchical "command and control" culture, the changes imposed on the way we think were sufficiently large as to make it difficult for us to appreciate the amount of effort we really had to put into these activities if we were to get the best out of them.

We believe now that our failure to address process ownership adequately is due to its not being part of anyone's objectives, so people have found it easy to ignore. The same goes for process change management, where our PCMT, comprising an author and two others, has done little of note to date, although to do something would elevate us, at least on that score, to CMM Level 5!

5.7.1 CHANGES IN THE WAY WE THINK

One of the benefits of the new mindset is that most people are now very keen on sharing their work with others. We encourage people to submit documents, either their own or those of others, to be included in our catalogue of best practice documents which is available for all to see. The purpose of this is to give good guidance to authors, new and old alike, without requiring cumbersome standards manuals to be followed. It also enables us to change the content and layout of documents, and even invent entirely new document types very rapidly by simply publishing a new best practice example and exhorting people to emulate it.

People now mostly understand that control rests with them, and almost everyone has responded well to the challenge this presents. Of course, with this empowerment goes real responsibility, and most are rising to it, exploring ways of doing things better, trying new techniques in documents, looking for ways of improving checking on inspections, inventing experimental rules to check by, and instituting a host of other incremental improvements.

Not everyone has grasped the nettle to the same extent, however. Because this is such an immense change in the way that work is carried out, it has proved to be a shock for many, and some are still having difficulty in coming to terms with the ramifications. One of the things we are still learning is how to convey the message of the method in such a way that we get people to "buy in." At the same time, we recognize that for some, the change required is too great and the environment too uncomfortable—we have indeed already experienced a limited amount of "fall out" as a result of the need for such radical change.

5.7.2   CHANGES IN THE WAY WE TREAT OUR CUSTOMERS

We're now engaging our customers much more in the development process. The verification process that we've already illustrated is a way we've invented of involving customers in at least part of the inspection process without the need for technical training. We've found, unsurprisingly, that when this process is applied, it has always resulted in a better product document at the Requirements Specification stage. Defects at that stage are, of course, far cheaper to correct than at any later stage of the development process. We've also found that customers who have been thus engaged do themselves gain a sense of real ownership over the development projects; more and more we find ourselves in real partnership with them.

5.7.3 "PROJECTIZING" OUR WORK

One of the greatest lessons we've learned from our experiences with inspection is that teams are the most effective organizing principle in focusing the attention and directing the efforts of a group of people to achieve a commonly shared goal: In the case of an Inspection, the goal is to help an author produce a document with a known quality status. We naturally became interested in pervading this concept to all of our activities, which, until 1995, had been largely organized along functional lines.

As a result of our vastly improved development process, we're now able to predict the future delivery of new and changed functionality with greater accuracy—and as a result of that, our customers now trust us much more than they did previously. We're also providing a better information service to them, based on openness and honesty. We now publish monthly future predictions in Release Bulletins, schedules, plans, and metrics in the form of the external attributes, including that all-important Reliability attribute.

5.8 STRATEGIC PLANS

One of the most tangible effects of our new-found culture is that decisions are no longer seen as the exclusive preserve of "management"—everybody is now actively involved in change. We continuously generate new ideas about how to build on the start we have made and maintain the momentum—these we shall describe next.

5.8.1 IMMEDIATE STEPS

We are concerned that document inspection is still too much of a "big deal" for us and is not yet sufficiently embedded into our way of life. To overcome this, we are continuously seeking (and sometimes even finding!) new strategies, including the following recent and current examples:

◆ Automate the capture of all data from inspections.

◆ Put the whole inspection process on-line electronically to eliminate paper entirely.

◆ Make inspections part of everyone's core objectives.

◆ Set inspection objectives for every project that we run.

◆ Invent better ways of sampling big documents so that we can do more, smaller inspections.

◆ Encourage people to inspect a document even while it's being developed.

We've also recently revitalized the PCMT and made it more fluid and dynamic and less management-oriented in an effort to concentrate on many of the process ownership issues that have lain fallow.

5.8.2   SPREADING THE WORD

So far, we have addressed the product development and shipment processes in isolation. They exist, however, in the context of the Icon business as a whole. Consequently we're going to develop a holistic process map for the Icon business (see Figure 5-16).

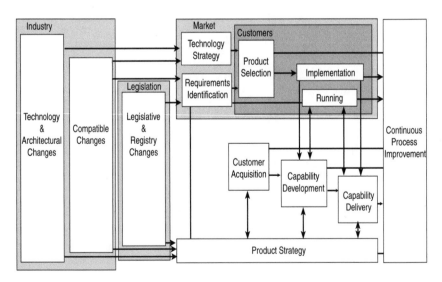

Figure 5-16: High-level Process Map

Within each of the process groups in the map are the atomic processes that we use to run our business—including software development and shipment, and all the support and service activities that we are going to be addressing next. This map helps us to look at the whole business from a process viewpoint and thereby ignore functional boundaries when designing new and better processes.

Our goal is to apply continuous process improvement to every part of the business. You can see that reflected in the process map as Continuous Process Improvement interacts with every other business process group we've identified.

Inspection as an activity encourages a very open, ego-less culture. We have formalized this in a set of policies and rules for processes and documents, with an emphasis on projectizing our work. Projectizing, a term coined by Tom Peters in *Liberation Management* [Peters92], means turning all of your activities into projects with defined targets, goals, or objectives, and running each with a defined project team.

5.8.3 CURRENT POLICY

Here is our current policy for projects and project teams:

A Policy for Development Project Teams
Version [0.3]; **Date** 22 March 1996; **Editor** DH; **Tag** POLICY.DT; **Rules** RULES.G;
Pages 0.5; **Readers** Unrestricted; **Status** Unexited > 60 defects/page; Unverified

DT1	PROJECTS	All work shall be carried out within projects, either for customers as defined in {CUSTOMERS} or for internal goals as defined in {GOALS}.
DT2	TEAM	A project team shall be created for each project and disbanded when the project objectives have been met.
DT3	LEADER	A team shall have a leader, who shall be selected by a method chosen by the team members.
DT4	OBJECTIVES	A project shall have written objectives, as defined in **"SPECIFIC RULES: Project Objectives"** {RULES.PO}, agreed between its customers and the project team.
DT5	START	The first task of the project team shall be to author the Project Objectives Document as defined in {OBJECTIVES}.
DT6	CUSTOMERS	The two classes of customer herein defined are external (commercial product customers) and internal (other parts of the vendor organization) who, as downstream processes, are de facto customers.
DT7	GOALS	Internal goals for all teams include, but are not limited to, education, customer business exposure, and project team leadership; external goals are defined in **"SPECIFIC RULES: Project Objectives"** {RULES.PO}.
DT8	AIM	The ultimate aim, when this policy is pervaded across all technical and commercial processes, is an organization of self-managing Case Teams.

The final tag, DT8 AIM, refers to Case Teams. Case Teams are self-managed work teams which are characterized by being small, fast, empowered, and highly focused on their project; what Tom Peters calls "Customerized" [Peters92]. We are already making significant strides in that direction with an increasing number of customer-focused development projects, every one of which has, of course, document inspection embedded in its process.

The policy above also refers to a Project Objectives Document, and this is the current rule set for that document:

> **Version** [0.6]; **Date** 12 July 1996; **Editor** NR; **Tag** RULES.PO; **Rules** RULES.G;
> **Pages** 0.5; **Readers** Unrestricted; **Status** Unexited > 60 defects/page; Unverified

PO1	READER	Readership is unrestricted.
PO2	PRODUCT	Project deliverable products shall be defined.
PO3	TARGET	Tracking methods and progress reporting including estimate revision, communication with customers, and milestones shall be defined.
PO4	STRATEGY	Variations from product strategy, both business and technical, shall be documented with an impact and risk analysis.
PO5	ATTRIBUTES	Relevant system attributes {←ATTRIBUTES} shall be listed and estimates of improvements on them shall be enumerated.
PO6	PEOPLE	Targets for developing the people on the project team by adopting new team roles and learning and applying new skills and expertise shall be set.
PO7	EXPERIMENT	Conducting at least one organizational, project management, or technical experiment in pursuit of the continuous improvement goal.

As you can see, there is considerable emphasis on developing more than simply application functionality: meeting our targets for quantified system attributes and developing the people on the project team attract as much attention. The last rule, tagged PO7 EXPERIMENT, enjoins project teams to try at least one new thing on every project and to share the results with others; in this way, we believe we can enjoy a constant influx of new insights and discoveries through the activities of the project teams.

5.9 CHALLENGES

It is a constant battle against the forces of evil—deadlines, schedules, promises made to customers, and the very weakness of our own flesh. We continue to seek ways of doing everything better. Document inspection is clearly not a complete answer; there are other mechanisms that we must look for to bring domain knowledge, skills, expertise, energy, and commitment to bear on every aspect of our business.

We are now continually asking ourselves questions:

◆ Do we have too many document types? Should we dispense with some of them?

◆ Do we have too few document types? Does this make documents too big?

◆ Are we doing inspections optimally?

◆ Are there smarter ways of doing checking? Can we automate any of it?

◆ Are there smarter ways of choosing inspection teams to make it more efficient?

5.9.1   OUR TOUGHEST CHALLENGE YET

The toughest challenge of all is the goal we've just set for ourselves. The methods we've adopted have been so successful for us and we now have such high confidence in our processes and our people that at the end of 1997 we proposed to our customers that we offer them a software reliability guarantee.

5.10 CONCLUSIONS

Recall that we described earlier our classification of software errors into high- and low-severity errors. The high-severity errors, Problem Severity Level (PSL) 1-3 errors, are those which impact a customer's critical business processes, and the low-severity, PSL 4-6 errors, are those which do not. The software guarantee that we have suggested to our customers is that:

"For every high-severity (PSL 1-3) error raised which we subsequently action we will credit an amount against future charges."

We are seriously offering our customers money back when they have errors in our product which impact their critical business processes. We believe this to be a first in our industry: We know of no other vendor organization that dares to suggest such a thing; and it is the strongest possible confirmation that we believe we have chosen the right path to software quality. Indeed, the principles are so sound and the results so spectacular that it remains a wonder to me that there are still software development organizations that don't practice inspection!

Thus ends the chapter for this book. We have many more chapters yet to write; where our journey will take us, we know not, but what we do know is that at every turn, we shall be continuously striving to reach our goal of owning a product that is recognized as the best of its kind on every measurable scale.

C H A P T E R

6

Software Reliability Engineering

Digital Technology International

6.1 COMPANY PROFILE

Digital Technology International (DT) is a company specializing in the development and marketing of newspaper software in the international marketplace. DT provides an integrated solution for large and small newspapers, based on advanced database technology. DT software allows a newspaper to automate the entire work flow associated with collecting news stories and advertising, and using the information to publish the newspaper.

DT also provides an "off-the-shelf" software package that gives anyone in the multi-media and publishing industries the ability to interface with popular publishing packages, attach them to an appropriate database, and use them to make information available to appropriate customers.

DT has been in the software business for over 12 years in Orem, Utah. The core software is made up of around 4 million lines of code, written mainly in C, C++, 4D, and Apple Script. A relatively high percentage of the current code in use is "legacy code," i.e., existing code that has been modified and/or extended to keep up with customer demands rather than code representing entirely new applications. New projects tend to be small products (e.g., 200,000 to 300,000 lines of code) designed to be "interoperable" with existing applications, and "scripted" interface-type software designed to "customize" DT systems to individual customer environments. The number of employees worldwide is around 100.

6.2 BASIC CONCEPTS AND GOALS OF SOFTWARE RELIABILITY ENGINEERING

Software Reliability Engineering (SRE) is defined to be the quantitative study of the operational behavior of software-based systems with respect to user requirements concerning reliability [IEEE95]. Various measurements relating to SRE are [Lyu95]:

◆ **Mean time to failure (MTTF):** The expected time that the next failure will be observed.

◆ **Mean time to repair (MTTR):** The expected time until a system will be repaired after a failure is observed.

◆ **Availability:** MTTF/[MTTF + MTTR].

Some basic definitions are:

◆ **Service:** Expected service (or "behavior") of a software system is a time-dependent sequence of outputs that agrees with the initial specification from which the software implementation has been derived, or which agrees with what system users have perceived the correct values to be.

◆ **Failure:** A failure occurs when the user perceives that a program has ceased to deliver the expected service. This may involve several levels of severity or failure.

◆ **Fault:** A fault is uncovered when either a failure of the program occurs or an internal error (e.g., an incorrect state) is detected within the program. The cause of a failure or internal error is a fault.

◆ **Defect:** When the distinction between a fault and a failure is not critical, "defect" can be used as a generic term to refer to either a fault (cause) or a failure (effect).

◆ **Error:** The term "error" has two different meanings:

1. A discrepancy between a computed, observed, or measured value or condition and the true, specified, or theoretically correct value or condition.

2. A human action that results in software containing a fault. Examples may include omission or misinterpretation of user requirements in the software specification and incorrect translation or omission of a requirement in the design specification. This is handled in DT's current methodology by designing in a *failure mode* solution (see [Jarvis97] and [Snow97]).

Within this framework, the goal is to generate an estimate of MTTF which is beyond the operational time of the system, or to maximize the estimate of the "availability" of the system during operational time. It is important to note in the context of SRE that the goal of the estimation is to determine if the MTTF is beyond the operational time of the system. It is NOT to help you "extend" the estimate to be beyond the operational time by a given amount. In ISO-9000 terms, this is neither a "corrective" nor a "preventive" action, nor is there any associated strategy to help you design or modify the system to reflect "reliability standards," i.e., it is "testing-" and "estimation-" oriented rather than "design-" oriented. This made a big difference as we looked at SRE to help us solve a critical problem!

The basic steps to implementing an SRE program may be defined as follows:

◆ Define an operational profile based on customer modeling.

◆ Generate test cases automatically based on "frequency of use" reflected in the operational profile.

◆ Deliver software in increments to System Test with quality factor assessments (reliability being one factor). At DT, quality measures (attributes) are defined in the Product Positioning filter, as defined in the Product Delivery Process [Jarvis97]. These include such "behaviors" as usability, trainability, installability, interoperability, migrateability, performance, etc. These are similarly defined in [Lyu95] and many other testing references on the market.

◆ Employ clean room development techniques (see [Humphrey95]), together with feature testing based on the operational profile. Note that there are other effective software development methodologies besides "clean room" (see [Jarvis97] for a list).

◆ Test to reliability objectives.

These basic concepts are based on the "best current practice of SRE" described in [Lyu95] for AT&T's International DEFINITY® PBX quality program (see also [Abrahamson92]).

Once you decide to an operational profile to estimate various parameters, you need to create models of the system as well. [Lyu95] and [Musa87] present various mathematical models which can be applied to operational profile(s) to create estimates of MTTF and other relevant measures. These are usually based on maximum likelihood estimates of the parameters of the competing probability distributions and other types of mathematical models. How we were able to avoid dependence on such modeling assumptions will be presented below.

6.3 REASONS TO IMPLEMENT

We discovered that it is impossible to implement SRE without considering the entire set of quality issues and putting in place a complete Product Delivery Process. This process must be both marketing-driven and feedback-oriented.

In DT's Systematic (Product) Delivery Process, the concept of a "filter" is used as the fundamental feedback mechanism. It is defined such that it contains the following components:

- **Completeness:** All the components of the deliverable, including those for the Product Positioning Filter, Preliminary Marketing Plan, Preliminary Sales Plan, Software Specification, software architecture, Project Plan, and the code itself, must be completely documented. Trip Reports and other documents can also be used as filters. If a "filter" is to be modified, based on feedback, a new version is created. This can be done on a weekly basis, if necessary.

- **Quality:** Each component of the deliverable has an associated measure of quality. This is also evaluated as part of the filter, and modified through feedback, as necessary.

- **Accuracy:** For appropriate components, an accuracy characteristic is also attached. It should be noted that accuracy evolves into precision.

"Filters" usually take the form of standards, checklists, forms, outlines, or prototypes. They work similar to the filter for a pot of coffee except that as the coffee passes through the filter, not only does the filter remove the grounds (defects), it also adds quality to the taste. If a defect gets through, root cause enables us to trace the failure back through each applicable filter, correcting those which were not transparent to the defect and thus should have caught it. (See [Jarvis97] and [Snow97].)

We also found SRE to be meaningless unless software quality standards in terms of quality attributes (defined later in this chapter), software coding standards, and software architectural standards, accompanied by effective information modeling and data modeling strategies, were available as well.

For DT, the goal of a Deming-oriented Product Delivery Process is based on the concept of identifying all meaningful measures of quality and "designing them in," while designing out any defects. In

Deming terms, it is better to design defects out and quality in than it is to "inspect" quality in or "test" quality in. With SRE, the original intent is to study what is wrong with an existing system, rather than designing it correctly in the first place. This latter approach is the concept discussed in [Jarvis97].

About four years ago, it became obvious that the quality of DT's software was gradually decreasing and the operational time of the software system for certain users was also decreasing. In addition, the typical maintenance problem of "push-and-pop" (i.e., every defect fixed introduced one or more additional defects; defects "fixed" at one point did not remain "fixed" later on) was also negatively impacting the code. New products, built in the same manner as the legacy code, quickly degenerated into the same pattern. This problem led to increased customer dissatisfaction and required more and more programmers to go on site to support both technical support personnel and software trainers. This led to the observation that unless something was done quickly, with respect to the legacy code as well as with respect to the new code being created, the company's bottom line could be severely impacted.

Just as with the airline industry, where a system being unavailable may cost around $20,000 per minute (see [Jarvis97], [Crandall93], and [Crandall94]), in the newspaper industry, a missed publishing deadline could cost advertisers thousands of dollars in a single day. The ripple effect of being even one hour late might be that the distributors would not get the newspapers to the paper's delivery personnel on time, i.e., young people who deliver the papers between (say) 5:00 AM and 7:00 AM, before school. Should this happen, the papers could not be delivered until after (say) 3:00 PM, making that day's advertising totally ineffective. Even if the distributors were to deliver the papers themselves, if the delivery time was after someone had left for work, the cost to the advertisers would cause excessive damage to their business. Thus the potential damage to the advertisers could be far worse than someone not seeing the news in a timely fashion. Ultimately, this cost could further damage a newspaper through lost advertising, lost subscribers, and lawsuits.

This scenario illustrates our "publishing-critical" defects, which need to be corrected within minutes if a newspaper wants to meet its publishing deadline.

Because DT's software is based on a MAC platform, rather than a PC platform, very few automated tools exist to aid in testing. This means that we do not have the luxury of running large numbers of test cases to "certify" that the availability of a piece of software is within proper parameters. This suggests that whatever solution is appropriate, it will not be found in the traditional approach to software design and testing, even using SRE.

As we attempted to solve the problems we were encountering, we noted that a large percentage of our newspapers were putting their papers out without any problems. Those who called our customer support desk with "publishing-critical bugs" had put their paper out on time the day before. This led us to ask, "What are you doing differently today than you did yesterday?"

Initially, we looked at this in terms of the operational profile, and we attempted to list the functionality to see what the relative frequencies were. This proved practically impossible to do, given the time-critical nature of the bugs. This led us to do two things differently from SRE.

First, we defined a user profile to be the exact sequence of operations through a "work flow" as a user created "deliverables." Therefore, work flow is a sequence of operations leading to a sequence of "deliverables." This might be "writing a newspaper story," "sending it to a database," "retrieving it by a copy editor," "editing the story," "putting it back in the database," "planning a page," "retrieving the story (along with other stories and photos, pictures, and advertising) to place on the page," etc.

A deliverable is the result of any action, function, or set of functions performed during a work flow, using the basic functionality of the software system. This might be viewed as a static set or distinct set or sequence of functions. This allows the operational profile to be viewed as a finite set of distinct, deterministic user profiles. "Deterministic" in this context means that a specific set of functions, which either occur in a specific sequence (if there are dependencies among the functions) or merely as a set, and are performed at the same time (if they are independent), will produce exactly the same software system response each time it is executed. In this context, the "response" is the creation of a pre-specified product or deliverable.

The probability distribution of the operational profile is based on taking the aggregate of all the user profiles, recognizing that the basic function frequency of usage and user profile frequency of usage added together create the operational profile probability distribution. This means that within a given user profile, a given function either always or never occurs. This makes it possible to "certify" that if a newspaper produces their paper a certain way, it will "always work." Further, since failures (formal definition above) can now be defined to be "deterministic," i.e., always occurring within a user profile, we no longer need to test for random failures or non-reproducible failures; we can duplicate a failure by narrowing down the failure to a small set of user profiles (based on a description of the failure) and then fix it directly, rather than waiting until we can reproduce it.

Second, as we began to create mathematical models of our software systems, we noted that the actual number of user profiles could become countably infinite, i.e., if you have (say) 100 functions with (say) 100 lines of executable code in each one, and they are all mutually independent of each other, then you have only 100 possible states (e.g., 10^2) the software system can take on. This means that no matter how many functions are used to create a given deliverable or in what order they are taken, the software system takes on only 100 states. If, to test the system, one provides adequate test cases for 100% path coverage, and this requires (say) 10,000 test cases per function, you must use 1 million (e.g., 10^6) test cases to achieve that coverage. Note that this is merely a generalized example to give you a feel for the testing process.

It can be seen, therefore, that traditional SRE (see [Lyu95], [Musa87], and [Musa97]), when there are large numbers of dependencies in the user interfaces, may not be the best approach to take. In addition, it shows that traditional testing is also not effective and why.

6.4 SOLUTIONS TO THE PROBLEM

Once we saw the problem with DT's software, it became obvious why much of the automated testing performed at other companies was not effective regardless of the white box or black box coverage. This led us to approach the solution to our problem in two ways.

First, we formalized and put in place a Product Delivery Process. This process lent itself nicely to ISO-9001 quality process standards, ISO-12207 life cycles standards which are currently still under development, and ISO-9126 internal and external standards also still under development. It turned out to be marketing-driven and it represented a true Deming process. This also led to a new paradigm based on the concepts of:

♦ Total quality and Total Quality Management.

♦ Continuous process improvement.

♦ Six sigma and zero defects.

♦ Cycle time reduction.

♦ Software quality definitions.

♦ Software code quality definitions.

♦ Software architecture quality definitions.

♦ Direct testing versus indirect testing definitions and strategies.

♦ Elimination of regression testing.

♦ Feedback processes based on general systems theory, with mini-processes, intermediate and final deliverables based on quality definitions and measures, and the use of self-modifying filters in place of traditional metrics.

♦ Customer satisfaction teams.

♦ Input-driven software development methodologies.

♦ Customer-oriented quality measurements.

♦ User profile modeling and development, with impact on software architecture and usability. Dependencies in user profiles were designed in explicitly and evaluated in terms of impact on "usability" and "trainability." Dependencies were evaluated in terms of "failure modes" (with appropriate error messages and constraints) and "certification" (where violation of a failure condition might under some conditions be valid, i.e., a user would be warned of potential failure conditions and then shown recovery strategies when overrides were necessary).

There are other related concepts documented in [Jarvis97] and [Snow97; see also [Musa97].

This paradigm led to DT's recent qualification for ISO-9001 registration and is impacting its goal of SEI's CMM Level 5 achievement, anticipated in 1998, as a direct consequence.

Second, we re-defined software code and architectural quality to minimize dependencies and to reduce the number of states the software could take on. This allowed us to "certify" the code by inspecting or auditing it, i.e., direct testing, rather than by assuming all functionality needed to be processed before being certain it worked, i.e., indirect testing. When you recognize that you need to be testing the states rather than the code, you can readily see the problems with traditional testing. In addition to "state coverage" inadequacies, there is also the problem with the indirect testing model itself: test case = input data + expected output (i.e., test oracle) + actual output. If you have (literally) millions of test cases to run, what exactly is your "test oracle"? Usually, you can "visualize" the states as easily as you can identify them and write a test case for each one.

If you can assure that there is no dependency between two pieces of code, no matter how close or far apart they occur at execution time or physically within the code source listings, changing one can have absolutely no impact on the other! This eliminates the "push-and-pop" syndrome and the need for regression testing. When you realize that with state-oriented testing, your coverage may actually be less than 0.0000000001% (by whatever measure you use!), it can be seen that it is not worth the effort. In addition, a test case which actually "covers" the broken code (caused by a maintenance fix), may not actually be guaranteed to "uncover" the "newly-caused" defect.

6.4.1   IMPACT OF THE SOLUTIONS ON THE LEGACY CODE

When we recognized the inadequacy of attempting to maintain the stability of our legacy code using a "find-bug-fix-bug," or, more accurately, "uncover defect-fix defect" mode approach, we realized that it was actually more effective to certify the code by identifying and tracing dependencies manually (visually) through the code and then having the activity re-certified by additional programmers (auditors).

6.5 CULTURE CHANGE

When the seriousness of the code stability problem was truly recognized, everyone realized that the future of the company was being negatively impacted and was in need of quality improvements. There was never a problem of knowing or accepting the fact that a radical change was needed. Our major problem was to get the customers to become satisfied, without undue risks. This was almost immediately accomplished by identifying "user profiles" that were stable at various newspaper (customer) sites. We then radically cut the number of changes being made, while "enforcing" the profiles that we could prove "worked."

During this time, we modeled the software to determine the seriousness of the dependencies it contained. As patterns of dependencies were discovered, we attempted to document them and ascertain their impact. At first, the question of how to eliminate the dependencies and their impact was difficult to solve. But as we gained more experience, patiently tracking each dependency through the remaining code allowed us to solve each problem and eliminate the introduction of subsequent defects.

In terms of impact on corporate culture, major problems related to:

◆   Getting the users, trainers, and others reporting the defects to report them in terms of "what they were doing" rather than "what the error was," i.e., user profiles.

- Getting the help desk personnel to think of capturing error-reporting information in terms of user profiles rather than functions.

- Getting the programmers to think in terms of:

  - Spending adequate time tracing the dependency through the code until they could "certify" that it did not cause a defect anywhere. The rule was: "When you finish fixing an error, you must have reviewed your work to the point that you can 'certify' its correctness. You then have it reviewed by a peer; that peer must also 'certify' its correctness. If he/she cannot or does not feel 'comfortable' doing so then a senior programmer must also 'certify' it. If that programmer cannot, then the fix should be 're-programmed' until everyone involved can 'certify' it." This direct testing approach has proven much more effective than traditional regression testing. The proof of this is not a metric studied over a long period of time; rather, it is due to direct observation based on the "corrective-action/preventive-action/root-cause" approach of our new paradigm and the ISO-9000 enforcement process (with its associated periodic third-party auditing).

  - Recognizing that they could not skip this phase (due to time constraints or simply feeling uncomfortable with the approach) and catch existing/remaining problems later on through traditional regression testing. Programmers tended to feel that if the code did not "break" during regression testing, then it worked, i.e., contained no defects, rather than feeling that if the code did not break, it merely meant that "none of their test cases could uncover an error IF IT EXISTED." Eliminating this comfort zone was difficult to do and required strong enforcement of signatures and auditing by the quality team, as well as coaching. It was difficult to get everyone to understand that it is more effective to demonstrate that something works through direct testing than to assume it works through indirect testing, i.e., because some particular test case was successful. But, it is so easy to demonstrate that this approach works, that mainly it is a question of training programmers and auditors to be effective. In our paradigm, if a defect does get through, it means that there was a state of the system that went unrecognized. Root cause allows us to adjust our certification and auditing process to reflect the class of states containing the unrecognized state.

♦ Getting the entire company and its customer base to think in terms of user profiles.

♦ Modifying our software architecture development process to reflect:

❑ Identification of work flows and user interfaces rather than functions.

❑ Creation of software from an "input-driven" approach rather than a "function-definition" approach.

❑ Creation of software architecture definitions and standards based on independent "mini user profiles" rather than functions (or objects).

♦ Continuing to study and develop this new approach to software development and maintenance.

Probably the most effective step in overcoming resistance due to problems in our corporate culture was the pressure of satisfying third-party auditors who would be on-site on a particular date, i.e., the ISO 9000 auditing team. The corporate culture was modified to reflect the following:

"Just one person failing to follow the process could keep us from qualifying."

"Assuring a quality process is more important than simply satisfying the ISO 9000 auditors."

"Following our quality process is not something you do in addition to performing your assignment, it is how you perform your assignment!"

This approach allowed us to eliminate the cynicism that sometimes exists when quality programs are used merely to achieve ISO 9000 registration rather than actually achieve and maintain a corporate quality process.

6.5.1 DESCRIPTION OF OTHER ISSUES THAT REQUIRED ATTENTION

The major issues that required and are still requiring attention are related to the continual need to identify and refine user profiles and to implement them into the work flow of our new customers. The new paradigm defined in [Jarvis97] and [Snow97] is theoretically sound, but it requires a major change in the way a company operates. This requires the implementation of a living quality process rather than a static one. At DT, this has meant that we are constantly modifying the filters (often on a weekly basis), monitoring the quality process, and using ad hoc teams to keep the process active and current.

We still have not completely matured this process either in terms of the process itself or in terms of personnel. We see this as an ongoing improvement process that continually moves towards a moving goal. The maturation is towards a stable, living process rather than towards a static, reachable goal.

6.5.2 SUPPORT AND BUY-IN FROM MANAGEMENT AND STAFF

Because of the recognized need and desire to improve quality and eliminate existing problems at DT, upper-level management and the employees did not need to be convinced that there was a problem. Neither did they need to be convinced that the solution we proposed was the correct one. This was mainly due to the fact that the feedback filters associated with the process implemented under the new paradigm worked so quickly and were so easily demonstrable that everyone was able to perceive their value and buy in.

The biggest problems were related to three situations. Note that this relates to more than just the concept of SRE; it relates to the entire concept of quality and its introduction as a part of software engineering and user profiles, i.e., it relates to the entire paradigm it was necessary to install at DT to achieve our goals.

- ◆ Upper-level management needed to be disciplined enough to use the new process and paradigm. This was related not to their acceptance of the process, rather it was related to their understanding the process and remembering to use it. As with all employees, it required and still requires a maturation in its use. DT feels that to maintain a high-quality process, wherein highly reliable software in terms of SRE, as defined in terms of our user profiles, continues to be produced and delivered to our customers, we are required to add to our corporate quality goals the necessity to mature in our quality process. We have our upcoming goal to achieve SEI CMM Level 5 at our next ISO 9000 third-party audit.

- ◆ Management and employees at all levels of DT needed to change the way they conducted meetings and solved problems. This meant that everyone needed to understand that all problems and failures were related to process defects, not just problems occurring at DT that needed to be solved. This involved:
  - ❏ Recognizing failure.
  - ❏ Defining it in terms of a process.
  - ❏ Identifying the filters that allowed it through the process.
  - ❏ Repairing the filters and process causing the failures in the deliverable or product being created, whether it related to software or other deliverables such as specifications, training materials, sales materials, etc.
  - ❏ Walking back through the process after a solution was proposed to make sure everyone understood the new process.
  - ❏ Documenting and disseminating changes to the process to everyone involved, i.e., at DT, we place them in a public file with a version, date, and manager's signature.

- ◆ Continuous research into software development strategies needed to be done, including:

❏ More appropriate information models. Our experience at DT has been that the use of object-oriented paradigms has not been as effective as other strategies such as structured analysis and structured design, information engineering, and other similar techniques listed in [Jarvis97].

❏ More appropriate data and database models tied to work flows, user profiles, and business rules. We want to pioneer the use of entity/attribute/relationship models for customer processes, as well as to use them to build data models. This should help us create better work flows and associated user profiles.

6.6 PROJECT PLAN/TIME-LINE

At the time the author of this chapter joined DT, it was obvious there were serious problems that needed to be addressed immediately. It should be noted that these problems were not unique to DT; they exist in every software company in the industry, regardless of how effective their emphasis on quality. DT was blessed with a very enlightened management team whose desire was to produce a quality product and to create and maintain satisfied customers. The problem was rather how to accomplish it with a customer base using a complex product based on legacy code going back 8 to 12 years. The fact that this problem relative to the entire software industry has not yet been solved even though it has been recognized for 20+ years can be seen in the fact that Brooks' 20-year Anniversary Edition of the *Mythical Man-Month* merely has four additional chapters. Nothing else has changed essentially in the 20 years since the first edition. (See [Brooks95], [Jarvis97], and [Snow97].)

As was described earlier in this chapter, the solution required the development of a completely new paradigm. Because of management commitment, we were able to define and install the Deming-oriented Product Delivery Process at DT within two weeks! (See [Jarvis97] and [Snow97].) At DT, this has become known as the Systematic Delivery Process. It differs from the Product Delivery Process described in [Jarvis97] in its additional emphasis on a "newspaper-oriented Product Release Process." Because of its specialized nature, it was not addressed in [Jarvis97] or in the more recent [Snow97].

In terms of a time-line, it has taken us around four years of experimentation, mainly with the technology, to create the quality process under which we currently registered for ISO 9001. Once we felt our delivery process was stable enough to allow us to qualify, it took us around six weeks to be ready for the first visit of the third-party auditors.

At that point, our main weaknesses were found in our Quality Manual and in our high-level auditing practices; at the lower levels, the auditing was extremely effective. Other weaknesses we uncovered during the audit were localized weaknesses in employee understanding of the quality process and weaknesses in both new and old employee training. The auditors also uncovered a few inconsistencies in our documentation and sign-off policies—one of the difficult concepts for employees and management to understand related to the concept of "accountability." Almost everyone was oriented to hierarchical accountability through management. In the new paradigm defining the Product Delivery Process, accountability is linear and relates to handing off products in a network-type process. Accountability is defined as:

- "Whenever a sub-process is started, the person (position) who initiates it terminates it."

- "Hand-off from one sub-process to another is always 1 to 1."

- "The person who 'ends' one subprocess is 'accountable' for the 'quality' of the product to the person who 'initiates' the follow-on process. One place this was extremely effective was in the 'scheduling accountability' between Installation Schedules as defined on Sales Contracts and product availability schedules as defined in the Product Delivery Process' Product Development Plan."

6.7 IMPLEMENTION

The formal beginning of the implementation process came when DT hired a new Vice-President of Software Development. This individual was given the mandate by both the CEO and the president to identify the existing problems and solve them as soon as possible.

Using existing processes already in place and the existing organization, the VP constructed a preliminary view of the process. Because there would be a need for change, a Configuration Control Board (CCB) was organized and a document created for managing the impact of change. All changes were implemented within the framework of this CCB. This was what allowed us to implement everything in a meaningful manner.

When we started building process definitions, each department was asked to create its own processes and checklists which later became "filters." It took around three months to get these finished. In the Operations part of the company, they tended to stabilize and become effective faster than in the Development part of the company. This was because more technological change was needed in Development. In Operations, it mainly involved a "formalization" of what was already being done.

The biggest problems involved:

◆ Operations:

- ❑ Placing the checklists inside the processes.
- ❑ Turning the checklists into filters.
- ❑ Achieving management sign-off.
- ❑ Tracing accountability to other parts of the organization and to the rest of the company.

◆ Development:

- ❑ Creating the checklists.
- ❑ Maturing in the use of the checklists.
- ❑ Turning the checklists into filters.
- ❑ Developing and mastering the underlying technology.

❑ Tracing accountability to other parts of the organization and to the rest of the company.

◆ Marketing:

❑ Actually defining and implementing a process. Problems here were due to the lack of a large (enough) marketing organization to perform its newly needed functions. This is just barely starting to happen as a part of our continuous process improvement process.

The person to spearhead the implementation of quality movement was the vice president, but all of upper-level management, middle-level management and senior programmers immediately signed on.

We found that, other than for general meetings with the entire company, training was usually on a department-by-department basis. The implementation worked best through coaching, especially in the technical areas. But it also proved useful when the VP, or one of the quality team, sat in on critical meetings and provided an evaluation afterwards. Problems both in terms of training and process modification differed both with respect to point-in-time and part-of-the-organization. We found the entire process with its associated need for training to be dynamic and people who were trained did not always remain trained.

Initially, it was the VP who insured that the implementation guidelines were followed by all participants, reporting problems to both the CEO and the president. As we got closer to ISO 9000 registration, we created a more formal, complete company-wide quality committee. Emphasis also shifted, with organizational maturity, to auditing more than coaching.

It should be noted that under the concept of "continuous process improvement," we will never have the process completely implemented in terms of its becoming static. Rather, it will continue to adapt and mature as DT faces new challenges and marketplaces.

On the other hand, since we were starting from scratch in defining a completely new paradigm, it took us around four years to completely learn what we were doing and get it implemented. From the time we felt we were ready for a third-party audit, i.e. the ISO 9000 registration, it took around six weeks to prepare and an additional month to clean up outstanding issues.

6.8 RESULTS

Since we have an on-going, continuous process improvement process, our next goal relates to maturing in our process and maintaining a high level of maturation. To us, this implies setting the goal of achieving SEI CMM Level 5 at the time of our next ISO 9001 third-party audit.

One of the most valuable parts of the ISO 9000 third-party audit was getting our personnel to understand the concept of "root cause." This was always a part of our feedback process, but it was more generally accepted after the registration.

Since the Product Positioning Document was one of the first ones to identify and make use of user profiles, it suffered from the fact that we needed to identify a technology and strategy for creating them and then to implement it. Actually defining and implementing a process in Sales was also difficult due to the fact that the majority of our sales personnel were outside the area and it was difficult to either define how their processes should change or to figure out how to effectively use them.

As was mentioned in an earlier section, it was impossible to find defects and fix them in the existing environment. For this reason, it was obvious that we needed to look at our operational profile, as defined in [Musa87] and [Musa97]. We quickly saw that there was not enough time, nor was it realistic to determine a usage distribution for the functions. This led us to the related concept of user profiles. The need to impose standards and move to direct testing was seen and immediately implemented at the same time.

As a result of all the quality initiatives we have taken, our legacy software and our new software are more stable, and our customer satisfaction is extremely high. Customer problems are more easily identified and more quickly and effectively dealt with. Occasionally,

DT faces a new customer who has personnel problems and management problems which translate into an unsatisfied customer. Things that would not normally be considered faults or errors are angrily reported to our help desk by employees attempting to sabotage the installation/use of our product(s). Since these problems are basically political in nature, we use a Customer Satisfaction Team to help solve the problem(s). Often, special customized changes must be made to the code; at other times, we must send technical people to the site who can enforce valid DT/customer policies, since the company's management cannot or will not. By having an entire team focus on the site, we can often turn such potentially dangerous situations around either from a political, technical, or "reality check" point-of-view. This type of customer can quickly get out of control and eat up all our profits while degrading our code and creating bad press for DT with other customers and with the industry. To DT, these problems are failures that must be solved as much as problems with the code or the software. We have found that many customer problems are not related to code quality as much as to process quality, i.e., how we deal with them in solving their "real" rather than "perceived" problems.

By obtaining tighter control of our entire delivery process, almost all of our products are being completed on time and within schedule. We have further been able to show that when a product is late, it is because we have violated one or more of our project guidelines or checkpoints, with its accompanying quality filter. We find we must do a lot of training and coaching, but very little selling.

By finding a non-traditional way to deal with SRE and recognizing the need to manage software reliability as a part of a complete quality process and not just as a solution in and of itself, we were able to find a fast, timely solution to our quality problems and have it validated through third-party audits, i.e., the ISO 9000 registration.

We are delighted to report that the ultimate result obtained by DT is a 25% reduction in defects.

6.9 LESSONS LEARNED

As a result of our quality initiative at DT, we have learned the following:

◆ The traditional approach to quality is extremely ineffective.

◆ Traditional solutions to software problems are also ineffective.

◆ Traditional life cycle approaches are ineffective. Software development life cycles must be implemented in the context of a complete Deming-oriented Product Delivery Process. This process must be marketing-driven and input-oriented.

◆ Quality must be based on user-perceived quality issues such as "trainability," "usability," "installability," "interoperability," "migrateability," and other similar attributes. With good software design, "error rates," "failure rates," and other similar concepts should indicate process failures rather than coding errors. This seems to be the future of software quality initiatives.

◆ Metrics and measurements are less effective than filters for providing feedback to a software development process. They take too long to implement and the results of quality initiatives are evaluated too far out in the future to be of effective use.

We found that had we taken the traditional approach to SRE, with its emphasis on gathering statistics and performing modeling and estimation, we would never have found a timely enough solution to our quality problems. Emphasis on quality pays for itself many times over, but if what you are doing is not working, "trying to do it faster with more people will make it 'not work' even faster." Running from one new technology to another rarely helps, either. Sometimes the simplest, most inelegant, common sense solution is the best!

Using third-party audits to help enforce deadlines on quality and to certify that you are doing what you set out to do using ISO 9000 and other quality initiatives pays for itself and makes quality achievement realistic and accessible.

Building corporate quality goals around a realistic three-stage quality program pays off. While DT has not reached its final goal, we feel that our program will pay off within the next six months.

6.10 CONCLUSIONS

The concepts and results of our new product delivery paradigm are extremely powerful. If we had been using our product delivery paradigm from the outset instead of needing to develop it from scratch, we feel we could have reached the point where we are today within six months to a year. We believe our efforts over the past four years have paid for themselves over and over.

C H A P T E R
7

Release Planning

Cisco Systems

7.1   COMPANY PROFILE

Cisco Systems, Inc. (NASDAQ: CSCO) is the worldwide leader in
networking for the Internet. Cisco products include routers, LAN
and ATM switches, dial-up access servers, and network management
software. These products, integrated by the Cisco IOS™ software,
link geographically dispersed LANs, WANs, and IBM networks.
Cisco Systems is headquartered in San Jose, California.

Cisco's networking solutions connect people and computer networks, allowing people to access or transfer information without regard to differences in time, place, or type of computer system. Cisco
provides end-to-end networking solutions that the public uses to
build unified information infrastructures of their own, or to connect
to someone else's network. An end-to-end networking solution is
one that provides a common architecture that delivers consistent

network services to all users. The broader the range of network services, the more capabilities a network can provide to users connected to it.

Cisco offers the industry's broadest range of hardware products that are to form information networks or give people access to those networks; Cisco IOS software, which provides network services and enables networked applications; expertise in network design and implementation; and technical support and professional services to maintain and optimize network operations. Cisco is unique in its ability to provide all these elements, either by itself or together with partners.

Cisco serves customers in three target markets:

♦ **Enterprises**: Large organizations with complex networking needs, usually spanning multiple locations and types of computer systems. Enterprise customers include corporations, government agencies, utilities, and educational institutions.

♦ **Service providers**: Companies that provide information services, including telecommunication carriers, Internet Service Providers, cable companies, and wireless communication providers.

♦ **Small/Medium business**: Companies with a need for data networks of their own, as well as connection to the Internet and/ or to business partners.

The Multi-service Switching Business Unit (MSSBU) of Cisco Systems is the pioneer of cell switching technology and a leading supplier of high-performance multi-service switching systems in both the frame relay and ATM markets.

7.2 REASONS TO IMPLEMENT

What is known as MSSBU today was formerly a company called StrataCom. In 1993, StrataCom received ISO 9001 registration. Since then, we implemented, maintained, and controlled a development system that ensured adherence to all product specifications and standards and was based upon the requirements of ISO 9001. To adhere to our policy that all new products be designed, developed, tested, and manufactured to the highest level of excellence in engineering, workmanship, reliability, and performance, we introduced the New Product Introduction (NPI) in 1993.

The NPI was divided into a seven-phase process, using checkpoints to synchronize our efforts regarding products:

- **Product Marketing:** Management makes a first cut estimate of resources, features, and cost.

- **Proposal:** The project proposal plan to the executive staff is presented prior to proceeding with implementation to verify that the marketing requirements are understood and agreed upon.

- **Definition:** To complete the Functional Specifications and interface definitions for the product, including hardware, software, and firmware sections.

- **Development:** The purpose of this phase is to design, document, and test the product and its manufacturing process.

- **Limited Availability:** To test the product in limited settings so that it can be released as the "standard" shippable version.

- **General Availability:** For shipment of standard product.

- **End of Life:** To perform the necessary tasks to remove a product from the price list.

On July 10, 1996, Cisco Systems completed its purchase of Strata-Com, now known as MSSBU. To meet the challenges of this new relationship, MSSBU started evaluating the old NPI against Cisco System's development methodology called the Great Engineering Methodology (GEM). A team of cross-functional employees was selected to spearhead the rewrite of NPI. The rewrite of the development process was named the Multiservice Switching Great Engineering Methodology (MSSGEM).

For MSSBU, the release of products was becoming a critical factor for customer satisfaction and quality. During old NPI days, seven to eight product releases with several features would be taken to market in a year. The development engineers were constantly working on several releases at the same time, thus getting exhausted. To minimize employee frustration and customer complaints, the newly selected Vice President of Engineering decided to address the issue of release management.

A new release process was developed and made part of MSSGEM. This process, which is illustrated in Figure 7-1, has four checkpoints. Each checkpoint acts as a "gate" through which each deliverable is developed and approved for accuracy, consistency, and quality. Since the success of a release depends on cross-functional activities, a lot of emphasis is given to the approval process as this ensures that individuals from different organizations are involved. Listed below are the checkpoints:

◆   Project Definition Checkpoints.

◆   Release Commit Checkpoint.

◆   Time To Market First Customer Ship Checkpoint (FCS-TTM).

◆   Time To Volume First Customer Ship Checkpoint (FCS-TTV).

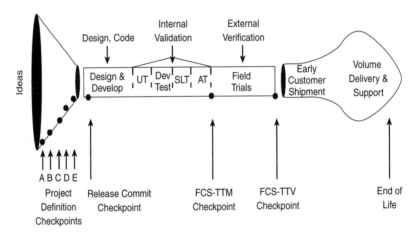

Figure 7-1: Release Planning Overview

7.3   RELEASE PROCESS

The release methodology described in this chapter has worked for us, and the intent of this chapter is not to discuss the entire MSSBU development process, but to cover in detail the process for defining and planning a release. In addition, it covers the steps to execute the delivery of a release, the release level checkpoints, release participants, and documentation. Where we feel that readers would benefit from additional details on a particular phase of development, we have described these details.

A MSSBU release is a collection of projects (features) delivered on various platforms. Each release consists of the following:

1. A set of projects (customer features).

2. A set of documentation such as Project Specifications, Design Specifications, and Functional Specifications that describes the operation, installation, and configuration of these features.

3. Release Notes that specify the release content, limitations work-arounds and issues related to the release.

4. A set of baselines consisting of software for our products. A "baseline" is a particular kind of software that contains specific features and functionality.

5. A set of upgrade and downgrade procedures for moving from one baseline to another in a manner that is least service-affecting.

6. New hardware, if applicable, in terms of new platforms or new boards for existing platforms.

7.3.1   RELEASE TEAM AND KEY LEADERS

The formation of a release team consisting of appropriate individuals with the required skill sets is vital to the success of the release. The release team consists of:

1. Release Manager, Engineering and Marketing.

2. Project Managers.

3. Marketing Product Managers.

4. Engineering Project Sponsors who can be either directors or senior managers.

5. Project members as appropriate.

6. Manufacturing representative for NPI.

7. Cisco Customer Advocacy (CA) representative for NPI.

All of the above resources, implicitly, report to the Release Manager to facilitate the planning and execution of the release. The Release Manager is responsible for release-level planning, running release meetings, and overall inter-dependencies and issues at the release level.

7.3.2   RELEASE MEETINGS

Each release has weekly release meetings. These are held by the Release Manager and attended by Project Managers, Director-Sponsors, the CA, Manufacturing, Documentation, Compliance, etc. as the Release Manager deems necessary. The purpose of the meeting is to ensure that on a weekly basis the progress of a release is tracked, release-level issues are raised and addressed, and release-level inter-dependencies are noted and addressed.

7.3.3   RELEASE-LEVEL DOCUMENTATION

Each release must have a Release Plan. A template for the Release Plan is developed to eliminate revamping of the process and to ensure there is a common document from release to release. The purpose of this document is to track the release. The document is used at the release team meetings to discuss issues and dependencies. For easy access, the Release Plan template resides on the Web. Typical contents of the template are:

◆ Release overview.

◆ Release contents (project list and brief description).

◆ Development Test Plan.

◆ Key project dates.

◆ Project interdependencies.

◆ SLT (System Level Test) entrance criterion and milestones.

◆ Key milestones for new hardware.

◆ Upgrade plans.

◆ External (to MSSBU) release-level dependencies.

◆ Performance: Reliability, Availability, and Serviceability (RAS) measurement plan.

◆ Release policies.

◆ Key manufacturing dates.

◆ Key customer advocacy dates.

◆ Key technical publications dates.

◆ Field trial support plan.

The Release Manager maintains the Release Plan based on input from and work assigned to Project Managers, Manufacturing, and the CA.

7.3.4 PROCESS FOR DEFINING AND PLANNING THE MSSBU RELEASE

Prior to understanding the release planning process, our project planning process must be reviewed briefly. Each project holds its own Project Definition/Forecast Checkpoint. This checkpoint is chaired by the director or senior manager who is the Project Sponsor and executed by the Project Manager. In this checkpoint, the Project Specification is reviewed to ensure it meets customer and market requirements. Also in this checkpoint, the Project Development Plan is reviewed to ensure the project has been planned properly. The checkpoint also ensures that the project meets market requirements and that it can be staffed to be included in a forecasted release. At this checkpoint, the following activities must be completed prior to moving to the next phase of release:

◆ Candidate projects approved.

◆ Project Sponsor and Project Manager identified.

- High-level System specification approved.
- Project Development Plan completed.
- Project Specifications completed.
- Initial Manufacturing Plan developed.
- Pricing target established.

All releases are on pre-scheduled release "trains." This means each future release has a targeted date for Time To Market–First Customer Ship (FCS-TTM). FCS-TTM addresses field trials. After this milestone is achieved, the product is ready to be tested at selected customer sites. Thus, as stated above, the project team, based on careful and detailed planning, forecasts which release train they would be ready for in the future.

It is important to note that after the Project Definition Checkpoint, a project is not committed to a release yet. This is due to release-level priorities; once release-level planning starts, the project may or may not fit into the total resources available to deliver the release. Stated another way, after the Project Definition Checkpoint, the project is only forecasted for a particular upcoming release. It is not committed to that release until the release-level Release Commit Checkpoint is held.

7.3.5   RELEASE PRIORITIES

Release priority refers to the "ordered priority" of each project targeted for release. Each project is evaluated as to the size of its market opportunities, customer commitments, and the value it brings to the business unit relative to core competencies such as reliability, availability, and serviceability.

In summary, the measures used to rank a project are:

1. Market potential, revenue potential, and competitive challenges.

2. Customer commitments.

3. Improving core competencies.

The project is ranked as Priority One, Two, or Three as follows

◆ **Priority One:** The project addresses a large revenue potential, market opportunity, competitive challenge, customer commitment, or valued increase in our core competencies. The project must be done as part of this release. Resources must be assigned to it to finish it in time for the FCS-TTM target or the date for the FCS-TTM must be pushed out to make the project fit. Priority One projects can "hold the release train," meaning the release will be delayed until the project is completed and ready.

◆ **Priority Two:** The project addresses a good revenue potential or increase in our core competencies. The project will be staffed as best as possible. Every attempt will be made to accommodate the project and make it fit into the release schedule, but if it does not, the project will be pushed out to the next release.

◆ **Priority Three:** The project addresses a particular niche or set of customers, or makes a small improvement to our core competencies. The release-level resources will be assigned first to Priority One projects, then to Priority Two projects, and then to Priority Three projects. Thus, Priority Three projects will generally only be included in the release if they are small and require resources that happen to be available.

The MSSBU marketing team decides the priorities, and projects with initial priorities are stored in a database that the marketing team maintains. The priorities may be changed periodically based on competitive changes, market changes, commitments made, and technology changes.

It is important to point out that project priorities are not categorized by:

◆ Different hardware platforms.

◆ Baseline.

◆ Technology segment.

Each project is prioritized against all other projects for a targeted release. For each release, there is only one priority list. Furthermore, to facilitate the tough task of assigning resources from such central organizations as System Level Test (SLT) to each project, each project is ranked top to bottom in the Priority One and Two lists.

The maintenance, accuracy, and validation of this priority list is up to our marketing team. For example, if customer commitment is not ranked as a Priority One project, it represents a serious problem for future customer satisfaction and credibility issues.[1] Also, the marketing team is responsible to ensure that projects that are ranked high bring significant value to the business.

It is Engineering's ultimate responsibility to ensure that projects are staffed according to the priority list generated by Marketing.

7.3.6   RELEASE PLANNING MEETINGS

Release planning starts up to twelve months prior to the targeted FCS-TTM. The first step is that a release priority list is generated by Marketing for the release. Note that the release planning meeting does not start until this list has been generated. Engineering directors and senior managers begin the planning process by having a series of informal planning meetings whereby project resources are assessed. Available resources are allocated such that the highest priority projects are staffed properly.

The first pass of the planning process is complete when the results of the above are presented by each director/senior manager listing Priority One projects that are either un-staffed, under-staffed, or need more time to finish, thus delaying the release. This presentation is made to the joint team of the VP of Marketing and VP of Engineering. The executive staff makes additional suggestions, assigns resources, or takes other means to remedy the situation.

---

1.   We do not make customer commitments outside of the project and release planning process. However, in our business environment, sometimes key customer commitments have to be made at the executive level to meet certain business and customer needs. These commitments are then folded into the project and release planning process to ensure they are properly planned and delivered.

The <u>second pass</u> of the planning process is a formal meeting that may last one or more days, where all projects are presented to the VP of Engineering and VP of Marketing, or the Marketing Director. Each project has an allocated time slot and follows a previously designated format for the review. In this meeting, representatives from CA and Manufacturing may be present to understand and comment on upcoming products. However, this is primarily a meeting for the marketing and engineering teams to assess which projects fit into the release, which do not, and which require additional resources. At the end of this pass, development test resources are assigned.

Each project is presented by the Project Manager. Each Project Manager represents all aspects of the project such as software, hardware, and firmware. The Director/Senior Manager-Sponsor for the project is also present. In this meeting, the Project Manager merely "requests" resources from an area and discusses his/her plans for staffing the development test cycle.

At the end of this meeting, an approximate view of the projects that fit into the release is formed. Next, the <u>third pass</u> provides any "make-up" sessions for the projects that did not show a sufficient level of planning. Sometimes, time permitting, the second and third passes are combined.

The <u>fourth pass</u> involves assigning development test resources such as people, nodes, and cards. The results of the fourth pass are presented to the VP of Engineering and VP of Marketing. At the end of this pass, a nearly complete view of the release content is formed.

The <u>fifth pass</u> is the final pass before the Release Commit Checkpoint. Its purpose is to assign the SLT resources.

Finally, the Release Commit Checkpoint is held. It is only after this checkpoint is held and successfully approved by the cross-functional team of Engineering, CA, Manufacturing, etc. that the release contents can be committed to customers, with rare exceptions such as those stated in Footnote 1.

7.3.7   RELEASE CHECKPOINTS

Release checkpoints represent a formal mechanism by which the release passes through specified quality and planning gates en route to delivery to first a limited set of customers and then to all customers.

No new release is ever executed without these checkpoints. All release-level checkpoints are a cross-functional effort. The functions represented are:

◆   Engineering.

◆   Marketing.

◆   CA.

◆   Manufacturing (the portion responsible for MSSBU products).

◆   Documentation.

7.3.8   RELEASE COMMIT CHECKPOINT

This checkpoint is the culmination of all of the planning done by the release team, Project Managers, the SLT team, the development test team, Marketing, Manufacturing, CA, etc. The purpose of this checkpoint is to validate to the VP of Engineering and VP of Marketing (or Director of Product Management) that the contents of the release are satisfactory, and the projects are properly planned and staffed in all areas such as Hardware, Firmware, Software, Test, Marketing, Manufacturing, CA, Documentation, etc. In addition, this checkpoint is the final opportunity for anyone in the business unit (BU) or in the functions surrounding the BU (Manufacturing, CA) to raise any concerns or issues. Such concerns and issues should have been previously raised to the Release Manager and previously addressed. But, this checkpoint is the final opportunity to do so.

The outcome of this meeting is that if the stated criteria (see below) are met, the Release Commit Checkpoint is a success, the release content is committed, and the release moves into the next phase (en route to FCS-TTM). If the stated criteria are not met, the checkpoint is re-held until the checkpoint is a success. The Release Commit Checkpoint is typically held 7-10 months prior to the release FCS-TTM.

7.3.9 RELEASE COMMIT CHECKPOINT PROCEDURES AND REQUIRED ITEMS

Attendance of the following is mandatory:

- MSSBU VP, Engineering.
- MSSBU VP, Marketing (or MSSBU Director, Product Management).
- Release Manager (executes the meeting).
- MSSBU Director, Engineering Operations/Release Management.
- Project sponsors.
- Product Managers (may be represented by Director, Product Management).
- Manager, Test.
- Quality Manager.
- Manager, Documentation.
- Manager, Compliance.
- Director, CA (or appropriate senior-level representative).
- Director, Manufacturing (or appropriate senior-level representative).

The required format is:

Release Manager and team members review the Release Plan:

a) Release Manager presents release timetables.

b) Release Manager presents release contents.

c) Release Manager presents projects that were rejected (not included).

d) Release Manager presents release-level dependencies on other BUs.

e) Release Manager presents release policies (e.g., inspections, RAS, test automation, etc.).

f) Development Test Manager presents the allocation of development test resources (such as testers, automation test beds, equipment, labs, boards, etc.).

g) Director-Sponsors present their plan for supporting a limited number of early field trials (Beta customers). This list is co-developed with the marketing team on each project. While the need to do early field trials (EFTs) is dictated by market conditions and varies by project, it is entirely the Director-Sponsor's call to support or not to support EFTs, and how many.

The following activities must also take place at the checkpoint:

◆ Documentation Manager presents the Documentation Plan.

◆ Compliance Manager presents plans for compliance testing.

◆ Product Marketing Managers present the list of trial customers for the upcoming FCS-TTM phase of this release. The list is reviewed to ensure proper feature coverage is given (that is, new features are properly tested by trial customers). In this checkpoint, this is a preliminary list only as the full list of trial customers will not be known until the FCS-TTM checkpoint.

◆ CA New Product Trial Manager presents plan to support FCS-TTM customers. Again this is a preliminary assessment which is co-developed with the marketing team.

◆ CA, Marketing, and Engineering state that the release team has identified the field trials (FT) team members. This is very important because each field trial request must be approved by this team.

◆ Manufacturing representative presents plans for supporting the new pieces of hardware through the engineering development cycle and field trial cycle.

7.3.10 EXCEPTIONS

Any new release must pass the Release Commit Checkpoint. If a Release Commit Checkpoint is held, and all of the required items are not properly planned for and presented, or the required attendees are not present, the Release Commit Checkpoint must be re-scheduled and re-executed until all requirements are met.

It is possible that certain projects may not fit the release time-frame and as such are not included in the release, but due to business reasons, some projects are reconsidered or new projects are intended to be added back into the release after the original Release Commit Checkpoint is completed. If this is the case, the Release Commit Checkpoint, as pertaining to these specific projects, must be re-executed and re-approved.

It is possible that certain key projects that originally did not fit the release time-frame or certain key new projects should be strongly considered for a "post-regular" release for business. Such projects should have had their own Project Definition/Forecast Checkpoints and should have met the specified requirements (e.g., Project Specification, Project Development Plan, Project Management, Director-Sponsor, etc.).

Table 7-1: Release Commit Checkpoint Process

OVERALL OWNER FOR THE RELEASE COMMIT CHECKPOINT: RELEASE MANAGER

Activity	Deliverable	Approval	Template	Activity Owner
1. Release planning: All release contents identified and confirmed	Release Plan	Release Mgr. VP Engineering VP Marketing Dir. Eng. Ops. Dir. CA & Mfg.	Release Plan	Release Manager
2. Document Plan completed	Document Plan	Dir. CA & Marketing.		Mgr. Doc.
3. Field trial planning process started	Field Trial Request Form	VP Marketing.	Field Trial Request Form	Marketing Product Mgr.
4. Manufacturing Plan finalized	Manufacturing Plan	VP Engineering Compliance Mgr.	Manufacturing Plan	Mfg. Program Mgr.
5. Prior exceptions reconciled	Exceptions noted in Checkpoint Forms	Exceptions reviewed and the checkpoint approved by: VP Engineering VP Marketing Dir. CA Dir. Eng. Ops. Dir. Mfg. Mgr. Doc.	Release Checkpoint Form with exceptions	Project Manager
6. Checkpoint meeting	Approved Checkpoint Form	VP Engineering VP Marketing Dir. CA Dir. Eng. Ops. Dir. Manufacturing Mgr. Doc.	Release Checkpoint	Release Mgr.

236

7.3.11 FCS-TTM CHECKPOINT

The purpose of this checkpoint is to determine if a release has met all of the criteria required to be FCS-TTM. After a release passes the Release Commit Checkpoint, each project continues to work toward its own milestones and the release-level milestones set for it. The Release Manager holds weekly reviews to assess the issues and progress on each project.

Each project, at some point, finishes its implementation, unit-level testing, and product-level integration tests. The project then moves into its Development Test, where the project is tested functionally against a series of test cases and test plans. The Development Test is focused on all functional testing, upgrades in small network, compatibility, data transfer, traffic management, product-level stress, and product-level performance. The Development Test exit criteria must be met prior to moving to the SLT phase.

7.3.11.1 *Development Test Exit Criteria*

◆ All sets of features delivered in a release are functionally tested and verified. (Note: This means NO feature is released on an individual basis).

◆ All new functionality is tested and verified.

◆ All connection types supported by product are verified with traffic over all supported trunk types.

◆ All baseline support for the new features introduced in the product is verified.

◆ Open bug count is within established limits.

◆ All planned tests are completed with 100% pass, with no blocked test cases.

◆ All new product limits are verified. All existing limits are verified in the "Continuous Systems Regression" network.

◆ Demonstration of all supported upgrade paths are completed with no unresolved issues.

◆ Non-conformance to the release policy is negotiated, agreed to, and documented by Release Manager.

◆ Configuration save/restore is verified.

Note that up to this point, the project is asynchronous from the release timetable. A project's Development Test may finish earlier or after the Release Commit Checkpoint. Also, a project's Development Test may finish earlier than the SLT start date. The only requirement is that all project-level development, unit test, product integration, and Development Test must end two weeks prior to the start of SLT. These two weeks are used to validate the entrance criteria for SLT on all projects targeted for the release in a pre-SLT environment.

All of the projects that pass the SLT entrance criteria, bundled together in the form of various software baselines and new boards, transition to SLT. The release, consisting of many projects and baselines, is tested in the SLT environment. The SLT is focused on performance, upgrades, stress, regression, limits, failure, and recovery It is a requirement that no new functions can be added to software baselines after the start of SLT. All exceptions must be signed by the VP of Engineering.

7.3.11.2   SLT Entrance Criteria

◆ All Development Test exit criteria are met.

◆ Systems limits requiring verification are documented by Release Manager.

◆ List of all work-arounds and known problems are provided.

◆ All SLT test plans with 100% of test cases are written and formally inspected, with appropriate inspection reports duly completed.

◆ Any customer-specific requirements are specified, and documented by Release Manager.

◆ All prototype hardware is available in required quantity at the start of SLT.

◆ Required upgrade paths and network topologies are documented by Release Manager.

◆ Upgrade procedures for each required path are demonstrated, documented, and reviewed by Development.

◆ All tested firmware and hardware revisions are documented for SLT by Release Manager.

◆ Performance requirements and conditions for measurements are documented by Release Manager.

◆ Critical systems performance parameters are documented for the release.

◆ Any exception to the above criteria is documented by the Release Manager in the Release Plan and agreed to by the Project and Development Test Managers.

Prior to leaving the SLT phase, the exit criteria must be met.

7.3.11.3 SLT Exit Criteria

◆ 100% of required system limits verified; 100% of test cases pass.

◆ All required upgrades paths verified; 100% of test cases pass.

◆ All required performance criteria verified.

◆ 100% of service-level regression test cases completed; 100% pass.

◆ 100% of test cases for final code verification phase completed; 100% pass.

Once the SLT is complete, a two-week Acceptance Test is done to verify that all baselines and new hardware are ready to go to the next phase. The final step in Quality Assurance is a week-long Final Code Verification (FCV). Final Code Verification is done with no code changes to verify the stability of the system over a relatively long period of time. The QA testing is focused on customer usage and emphasizes interoperability, conformance, and usability.

When all of the above steps are completed, a release FCS-TTM checkpoint is organized and executed by the Release Manager. This ensures the release is ready to transition to field trials. It is important to point out the difference between early field trials (EFTs) and field trials (FTs), which are enumerated in Table 7-2.

Table 7-2: Difference between EFTs and FTs

Early Field Trials	Field Trials
Done before FCS-TTM milestone and after the end of Development Test	Done after the FCS-TTM milestone
Supported by Engineering only; exceptions are approved by Director-Sponsor	Generally supported by Technical Assistance Center only
Numbers are very limited	Numbers are limited
Totally at the discretion of the Director-Sponsor and based on business needs	Trial customers are approved by the release team and designated field trial team
Duration is predictable—1 to 2 weeks	Duration is not predictable; it is dependent on how fast customers test, how many bugs are found, and possibly other factors
Equipment is planned for and supplied by Engineering	Products are purchased by customers
There must be an Engineering-approved test plan; this test plan must be supplied by the account team or customer	Each field trial request must accompany a test plan for the request to be considered for approval
Engineering "pre-executes" the test plan in the appropriate lab and then "demonstrates" the test plan in front of the customer	Customer does the actual testing and generally there are no development engineers on-site

7.3.12 FCS-TTM CHECKPOINT PROCEDURES AND REQUIRED ITEMS

Before entering the FCS-TTM Checkpoint, the release must have completed the SLT and the exit criteria of SLT must be met.

7.3.13 FCS-TTM EXIT CRITERIA

An FCS-TTM Checkpoint must be attended by the following individuals:

♦ VP of Engineering

♦ VP of Marketing or Marketing Director

♦ Release Manager executes the meeting

♦ Director of Engineering Operations/Release Management

♦ Project Managers may be represented by Project Sponsors

♦ Product Managers may be represented by Director, Product Management

♦ Manager of Documentation

♦ Manager of Compliance

♦ Director of CA or appropriate senior-level representative,

♦ Director of Manufacturing or appropriate senior-level representative.

The format for the checkpoint outlines certain activities that must take place, such as:

♦ Release Manager and SLT Manager state the SLT results, including:

   ❏ Open bugs, open issues.

   ❏ Areas that were not tested and why.

♦ Engineering Design Verification Test, Manufacturing Design Verification Test, and other manufacturing-related test results are presented jointly by the Hardware Development Managers and Manufacturing Engineers.

- Manager of Compliance states any compliance issues.

- Manager of Documentation presents the state of documentation for all new features in the release.

- Release Manager confirms that all project-level and release-level documentation is stored properly on-line.

- Director of CA presents the plan to support the trial customers. This includes the status of the availability of new hardware in the Technical Assistance Centers worldwide. This presentation should also address any concerns (such as product defects) that CA has with allowing the release to move to FCS-TTM.

- Director of Manufacturing presents the Manufacturing Plan for shipping and supporting the trial customers. This also includes any issues that Manufacturing views may hinder FCS-TTM.

- Field trial team presents the field trial customer list. Test coverage areas are presented. Lack of test coverage is highlighted. Any unique trial customer issues and requirements are highlighted.

- Release team presents the release notes and outstanding issues.

All releases must pass the FCS-TTM checkpoint. No exceptions are allowed.

Table 7-3 shows the activities, deliverables, required approvals, templates, and activity owners related to this checkpoint.

Table 7-3: FCS-TTM Checkpoint Process

OVERALL CHECKPOINT OWNER: RELEASE MANAGER

Activity	Deliverable	Approval	MSSBU Template	Activity Owner
1. Release Notes finalized and published	Final Release Notes	Dir. Eng. Ops. Release Manager	Release Notes	Release Manager
2. SLT and exit criteria met	SLT Plan Checklist indicating SLT criteria met	SLT Mgr. Release Mgr. Dir. Eng. Ops.	SLT Plan, SLT Exit Criteria	SLT Mgr. Release Mgr.
3. Design Verification Testing (DVT) and Manufacturing Design Verification Test (MDVT) complete and reports sent to Manufacturing.	DVT/MDVT Plan DVT/MDVT Test Results	Mgr. of Compliance Dir. Eng. Ops. Dir. Manufacturing	DVT and MDVT Plan	Mgr: DVT and Homologation
4. Compliance review per project	Review Minutes, Review Report, or Review Results	Compliance Manager		DVT and Homologation Mgr.
5. Limited orderability available		Dir. Manufacturing		Mfg. Prog. Mgr.
6. FT Support Plan complete	Field Support Plan	Dir. Marketing Dir. CA		Mktg. Prod. Mgr.
7. CA, Technical Assistance Center and Logistics readiness evaluated for unlimited support		Dir. CA		MSS Mgr.
8. Field trial team established		Dir. Marketing Dir. CA		Mktg. Prod. and MSS Mgrs.
9. Transfer of information to CA complete	Presentation to SE and CA	Dir. of CA Project Mgr.		MSS Mgr.
10. Field/customer training	Training materials development and delivery	Dir. CA		Dir. CA
11. Technical publications complete	Technical Publication Plan	Dir. CA Mktg. Prod. Mgr.		Mgr. Doc

Table 7-3: FCS-TTM Checkpoint Process *(continued)*

	OVERALL CHECKPOINT OWNER: RELEASE MANAGER			
Activity	**Deliverable**	**Approval**	**MSSBU Template**	**Activity Owner**
12. CA and Technical Assistance Center ready for FT support		Dir. CA		Release Mgr.
13. Orderability review complete		Dir. Manufacturing		Mfg Prog. Mgr.
14. All plans and specs approved and archived in document control system	Changes to following plans or spec: SW, HW, FW, Design	Project Mgr. Sponsor Dir. Eng. Ops. Mg. Compliance SLT Dir. or Sr. Eng. Mgr.	See individual plan and spec in the Project Definition Checkpoint, Release and FCS-TTM Checkpoints	Release Mgr. with individual Project Manager
15. Yr. 2000 requirements addressed for all new and old code	Yr. 2000 requirements addressed in all code and SLT cases	Dir. CA and Eng. Ops. Release Mgr. Dir. or Sr. Eng. Mgr.	Project Development Plan	Release Manager
16. Hardware ready for FT shipments; orderability review held for FT		Dir. Manufacturing Mktg. Prod. Mgr.	Hardware Orderability Review List	Mfg. Prog. Mgr.
17. Prior exceptions reconciled	Exceptions noted in the Checkpoint Forms	VP Engineering VP Marketing Mgr. Doc. Dir. CA Dir. Eng. Ops. Dir. Manufacturing	FCS-TTM Checkpoint Form with exceptions	Project Manager
18. Checkpoint meeting	Approved Checkpoint Form	VP Engineering VP Marketing Mgr. Doc. Dir. CA Dir. Eng. Ops. Dir. Manufacturing	FCS-TTM Checkpoint	Release Mgr.

7.3.14 TIME TO VOLUME FIRST CUSTOMER SHIP (FCS-TTV) CHECKPOINT

The third and final checkpoint a MSSBU release must pass through is called the FCS-TTV Checkpoint. The purpose of this checkpoint is to ensure that the MSSBU release can be priced, ordered, shipped, supported through CA, and maintained by MSSBU for an unrestricted number of customers.

At the point the FCS-TTV checkpoint is executed successfully and all of the required items are satisfactorily met, the current sub-release of the release is declared TTV.

7.3.15 FIELD TRIAL PLANNING AND SUPPORT PROCESS

The field trial process allows customers to try new products prior to the FCS-TTV milestone, and provides Cisco with valuable technical information regarding customer-specific product and application usage.

Marketing Product Management sends communication to the field announcing the field trial dates and the process in place for the field to submit requests to participate. Requests from the field are submitted through the field trials Web site. Each field trial request must accompany a test plan for the request to be considered for approval.

The field trial team is composed of the CA, the Marketing Release/Product Manager, the Field Trial Planning Coordinator, and the Engineering Release Manager. The field trial meetings begin before the FCS-TTM milestone to evaluate and approve/disapprove customer trial requests. Criteria for approving trial applicants include:

◆ Ability to test features that will allow the product to be brought more quickly to FCS-TTV.

◆ Revenue opportunity.

◆ Customer commitment.

◆ Strategic deal.

◆ Competitive bake-off.

A list of approved customers is provided to Customer Service (Order Administration) and Manufacturing. Upon receipt of orders through the new product hold process, shipments are scheduled from Manufacturing, and CA resources are allocated to support trials whenever possible.

The field trial team meets on a weekly basis to:

◆ Approve/disapprove new trial requests submitted by the field.

◆ Address field trial planning issues, such as ordering process, manufacturing equipment availability, CA NPT resource allocation, etc.

◆ Discuss TAC and escalation engineering feedback on specific customer issues.

◆ Review SEs/AMs feedback and issues at the customer trial site.

◆ Plan and execute communication to field trial SEs/AMs, informing them of next planned maintenance release or requesting that customers upgrade to the latest maintenance release.

◆ Review and evaluate overall field trial issues.

The question of how many customers should test a release and declare it ready for deployment before the release is allowed to enter the TTV Checkpoint is a matter that varies from release to release. It also varies depending on the number of and complexity of features in the release.

Field trials are very crucial to the success of a product/release since it's impossible to test for all various customer application scenarios in the SLT phase. One requirement for considering this phase successful is to have a very limited number of customers deploy the field trial product in their live network.

The field trial team continues planning for, supporting field trial customers, and providing status to executive management during the phase between FCS-TTM and FCS-TTV.

7.3.16 FCS-TTV CHECKPOINT PROCEDURES AND REQUIRED ITEMS

Before entering an FCS-TTV Checkpoint, it is paramount that the release be subjected to various customer trials and test labs. This is because in spite of extensive automated and manual tests that are done on the components of and the whole release, it is not totally proven until tested in customer trials and labs.

An FCS-TTV Checkpoint must be attended by the following individuals:

♦ **Release Manager:** Holds the checkpoint.

♦ **Director of Engineering Operations:** Chairs the meeting and ensures all WANGEM processes are executed as documented.

♦ **VP of Engineering:** Approves the release for FCS-TTV based on presented material.

♦ **VP of Marketing:** Approves the release for FCS-TTV based on presented material.

♦ **Director of CA or representative:** Approves the readiness, quality worthiness, and volume supportability of the release.

♦ **Director of Manufacturing or representative:** Approves the readiness, quality worthiness, and volume manufacturability of the release.

♦ **Manager of Documentation:** Presents material that demonstrates release and product documentation is ready for volume distribution to customers.

♦ **Manager of Compliance:** Presents material that demonstrates all new products in the release are compliant with national and international standards and compliance requirements.

The underlying goal of the FCS-TTV "gate" is to ensure that the release is volume-orderable, supportable, and manufacturable. Volume refers to unrestricted availability of the release to all existing and future customers.

7.3.17 EXCEPTIONS

Every business must allow for exceptions so as to fit the changing needs of its customers and marketplace. Such exceptions must strictly be limited and must be approved by the VP of Engineering, VP of Marketing, VP of CA, and Director of Manufacturing.

It is the goal of the FCS-TTV "gate" to demonstrate that all features and product sets within the release are ready for volume shipment, volume support, and volume manufacturing. Occasionally, for business reasons, a release may be allowed to pass the FCS-TTV gate with known defects in certain aspects of the product set within the release. Again this must be approved by the individuals above. The purpose here is to allow certain key customers who use a subset of the features and products in the release to proceed with the deployment of those features and products. This is while the known defects in the other features and products are clearly documented and targeted for future maintenance releases.

Other exceptions, applicable to documentation, for example, may be allowed if the impact to customers and the CA organization's ability to support the product is deemed to be insignificant. Again, the individuals above must approve the exception. In regard to volume manufacturability and orderability, exceptions may be allowed to let the release pass the FCS-TTV gate with one or more sub-products not having passed Manufacturing's stated criteria. These too have to be approved by the individuals above.

All exceptions are reconciled later through the re-execution of the FCS-TTV Checkpoint with the express intent of removing those exceptions. Table 7-4 shows the activities, deliverables, required approvals, templates and the activity owners related to this checkpoint.

Table 7-4: FCS-TTV Checkpoint Process

		OVERALL OWNER FOR FCS-TTV CHECKPOINT: PROJECT MANAGER		
Activity	**Deliverable**	**Approval**	**MSSBU Template**	**Activity Owner**
1. Field trial satisfactory	Field Trial Summary Report	VP Engineering VP Manufacturing VP CA		CA Trials Manager
2. Updated Release Notes from field trial published	Updated Release Notes	Dir. Eng. Ops. Release Manager	Release Notes	Release Manager
3. Technical publications complete	Finalized technical publications	Mgr. Doc. Dir. Marketing Dir. CA		Mgr. Doc. Dir. Marketing Dir. CA
4. Distributed Defect Tracking System (DDTS) Release Notes complete	All defects on DDTS to have DDTS Release Notes	Release Manager	DDTS System	Release Manager
5. All SW, HW, Firmware, Design Plans/Specs approved and archived	Release Checkpoint and FCS-TTM Checkpoint; any new documents and updates to previous documents	Project Mgr. Sponsor Dir. Eng. Ops. Mgr. Compliance Mgr. SLT Dir. or Sr. Eng. Mgr.	See individual plan and spec in the Project Definition Checkpoint, Release Checkpoint, and FCS-TTM Checkpoint	Release Manager
6. Manufacturing ready to volume ship		Dir. Manufacturing		Manufacturing Prog. Mgr.

Table 7-4: FCS-TTV Checkpoint Process *(continued)*

		OVERALL OWNER FOR FCS-TTV CHECKPOINT: PROJECT MANAGER		
Activity	**Deliverable**	**Approval**	**MSSBU Template**	**Activity Owner**
7. Prior exceptions from FCS-TTM Checkpoint reconciled	Exceptions for FCS-TTV noted in the Checkpoint Forms	Exceptions reviewed and checkpoint approved by VP Engineering VP Marketing Mgr. Doc Dir. CA Dir. Eng. Ops. Dir. Manufacturing	FCS-TTV Checkpoint Form to note exceptions	Project Manager
8. Checkpoint meeting	Approved Checkpoint Form	VP Engineering VP Marketing Dir. Manufacturing Dir. CA Mgr. Doc. Dir. Eng. Ops. Mgr. Compliance	FCS-TTV Checkpoint	Release Manager

7.4 CULTURE CHANGE

Since the adherence of the new release process was supported by the VP of Engineering, everyone had to follow it. Our BU employees, however, are too familiar with the old process and are reminded frequently by the senior management to follow the new release methodology. In addition, any Project Manager who persists on using the "old way" cannot have his/her project go through a checkpoint. This has created a new awareness.

As part of the new release process, all project-related documents have standard templates that must be used. Project Managers must re-do the documentation that follows the old format.

A number of internal presentations were held to train the employees. We now have put all our project-related templates, processes, checklists, and inspection data on the Web for easy accessibility.

7.5 LESSONS LEARNED

The new release process has brought discipline to various project teams. The team members know that no exceptions will be allowed unless they are approved by a VP; therefore, every Project Manager has become extremely conservative in making deviations to the documented process.

Since the checkpoints require certain attendance without whom the checkpoint cannot be conducted, all of a sudden the gates of communication have opened up! Project Managers have learned by experience that if their Development Plans do not address risks and other project-related dependencies, they will be asked about these at the checkpoint meeting. Therefore, each Project Manager is very thorough in his/her Development Plans, as well as in other project-related deliverables.

We take inspections very seriously. The new release process ensures that the Project Manager has made a commitment up-front to inspect the new code. The time required to conduct the inspections is incorporated in the beginning of the project schedule. The Project

Managers receive bi-weekly reports on the number of lines inspected versus the commitment they made. The reports are taken very seriously and where the rate of inspections have dropped, the Project Managers rectify the situation by conducting remaining inspections.

7.6 CONCLUSIONS

You will note throughout the process that we have emphasized the job titles of individuals who need to either attend a checkpoint meeting or sign a deliverable. Without an approved signature or individual, a document or checkpoint meeting is considered incomplete. The job titles indicate the ultimate person responsible for a particular activity. Where a lot is at stake, senior management such as a VP of Engineering or Marketing or CA is required to authorize and approve. This structured process has raised awareness of quality in MSSBU, which has resulted in improved, unambiguous, detailed project-related documents.

In addition to this release process, we now have also developed a project process. We have experienced that our staff is willing and eager to implement the new release and project processes when the value-added is clear to them. Our engineering staff has discovered first-hand that following a well-documented and clear process saves time, improves quality, and avoids frustration at work.

CHAPTER
8

Release Metrics

TANDEM Telecom Network Solutions

8.1 COMPANY PROFILE

Tandem, a Compaq company headquartered in Cupertino, California, provides 24 X 7 fault-tolerant Intelligent Network (IN) servers that keep applications running around the clock. Tandem provides products and services that the telecommunications industry has depended on for more than 20 years.

Tandem Telecommunications Network Solutions (TTNS), located in Plano, Texas, provides Tandem's IN platforms for 30 of the world's leading carriers. Nearly 140 public telecommunications companies from the Americas to Europe and Asia-Pacific rely on Tandem technology to better serve their subscriber base. Most US cellular phone calls are in some way connected with a Tandem fault-tolerant Intelligent Network server (INS).

Tandem is the technology leader in IN systems and solutions. The solutions support a wide array of open network interfaces, global intelligent network/advanced intelligent network (IN/AIN) standards and applications, while providing a unique parallel processing architecture.

Tandem is the product leader, with more than 15 million wireless subscribers already calling Tandem platforms "home." When these subscribers roam, solutions like Tandem's Home Location Register (HLR) and Authentication Center (AC) functions, calling card validation, debit card services, customized number translation services (E800), and mobility management systems give subscribers intelligent networking features and virtually seamless service access anywhere.

The significance of being the market-leading platform provider is that TTNS's delivery schedule directly impacts the schedules of its customers. A scheduled release of capability by a telecommunications customer is often based on the timely receipt of the supporting software from TTNS. This potential domino effect of schedule slip, as well as the criticality of the quality and functionality, adds pressure and risk to the TTNS release management process.

8.2 INTRODUCTION

One of the most critical questions asked during a software development project is: When will it be ready? This question becomes more and more pressing as the scheduled delivery date draws near, and inevitably is the penultimate question that release management must answer.

Although trade-offs are made throughout the development cycle, it is during the final test phase that the impact is most measurable and the pressure most intense. All schedules are based on assumptions, and if those assumptions are disproved during testing, risk mitigation must occur. Unfortunately, the later issues are identified, the less time there is to react.

In this case study, a fast-growing telecommunications software company reveals how it developed a set of measurements that serve as an early warning system when release readiness is at-risk. These measurements, which are combined into a Confidence Rating, guide the core product team in evaluating release status and implementing risk reduction or mitigation strategies.

What is especially interesting about our approach is that, unlike the traditional software reliability "S" curve, the techniques we have developed provide a linear view that projects readiness based on desired quality, not on defect arrival rates. This linear approach means the release date can be projected earlier in the cycle; instead of waiting for the "S" to flatten, we can foresee a schedule slip from week to week and take corrective action early.

This is the story of how and why we developed our release metrics, as well as the lessons we learned about applying them.

8.3 REASONS FOR IMPLEMENTATION

TTNS management understands the benefit of project planning, including setting dates and milestone criteria. But, as with every software project, there are a series of trade-offs, customer demands, market pressures and resource constraints that occur throughout the life cycle and compromises are unavoidable. Realizing that these risks were a fact of life, the Manager of Development Services at TTNS set out to manage them.

Clearly every project plans an end date, but unfortunately this was the only release measurement communicated to management. Whether the date would be met was traditionally measured by monitoring test execution and comparing planned to actual and defect arrivals. This measurement was not only insufficient to detect the effect of other decisions and factors, it was available too late in the cycle to employ mitigating strategies.

For example, the software reliability curve predicts an "S-" shaped plot of defect arrivals; readiness can only be predicted when the curve begins to flatten at the top. Usually, this is too late to do anything about it.

The Manager of Development Services also realized that there were additional factors that affected release readiness that were not being communicated to management. These factors included business risks, the significance of mature processes, and the balance of time and budget versus quality. TTNS was maturing as an organization and needed a completeness indicator that was more meaningful and could be used to continuously improve their processes.

Although trade-offs occur throughout the development life cycle and measurements are useful at each phase, it is the final system test phase where the impact is most acute and the schedule most critical. Therefore, it was decided to begin the refinements of the release measurements during this phase.

System test at TTNS reported their status weekly to the program core team. A program core team is made up of Product Management, Development, Test, Technical Publications, Customer Support, Training, and Systems Engineering, and is led by a Program Manager.

Change management decisions are made by the core team based on analyses presented by the various functions; they are also affected by customer needs. Release dates may have to be coordinated with customers, who often have their personnel at the ready to incorporate and test the TTNS components into their own products.

The test team traditionally reported their weekly status to the core team in discrete items, such as test pass/fail and defect discovery rates. Unfortunately, these measures made the test process appear flawed. A test cycle planned for four weeks that ballooned to eight weeks surprised the team because they were not aware of the implications of the backlog of defects that were left from prior release cycles, those that had accumulated from customer-reported problems, or the significance of discrepancies that were waived during the cycle and reported in Release Notes.

It became apparent that the usual test process measurements were inadequate to convey the "big picture" to the core team and that they were unable to provide an early enough indication of the status of the system to allow the team to take corrective action. So, we set out to develop a tool that would concisely communicate to the team on a regular interval the readiness of a project and provide a basis for decisions and compromises. The tool needed to be objective and easily understood.

8.4 OBTAINING BUY-IN

For the tool to be understood by the core team and accepted as a useful measurement, it was important to obtain the contribution and buy-in of all affected parties. To accomplish this, a representative group was assembled from the core team areas and an outside consulting firm was engaged to lead the team through the process of developing the tool.

At the time, TTNS was maturing as an organization and had initiated process improvement teams aimed at progressing in the SEI's CMM. The managers, whose compensation was based in part on making both schedule and quality goals, were seeking a better way of managing projects and willingly invested the time to participate in the process.

The team began by discussing the importance of mature processes and the effects of prematurely promoting a project to the next phase. The life cycle phases were broad and included objectives, requirements, design, implementation, and validation. The team reviewed each phase of the life cycle, specifically focusing on the entry and exit criteria from one phase to the next, and identified the factors that made a project "ready" for promotion to the next phase.

Although each member of the team had knowledge of the life cycle and all were highly experienced, discussing the phases in terms of readiness encouraged new thinking. It raised the question of how to measure the inevitable trade-offs made throughout the life cycle in the larger context of their impact, and the difference between a project being "finished" in the sense of completing all the phases and being "ready" in the sense of being complete in its quality and functionality.

For example, the team member representing Customer Support recalled a recent project when the test execution rate was reported to the core team as being on-plan, and although discovered problems were discussed, their impact was not fully communicated. A part of the system of particular interest to the customer, which had been planned for validation early in the test phase, was blocked from being tested by some of the discovered problems.

Because the test team executed other tests to keep their resources productive, the blocked tests became off-plan while the run rate remained on-plan! The team realized that simple execution and pass/fail rates were inadequate to convey both the true state of the project and the business risks of time and budget versus quality.

In parallel to the core team discussions, a team composed of System Test and Development members met to discuss the objectives of the phases of testing. Test objectives of each phase of development were identified, including inspection, unit-test, integration, and system test. Other issues came to light. As the system test group described their automated test scripts, it became apparent that they were focused on unit-level tests that more accurately belonged in the development test phase. Allocating testing to the appropriate phase would alleviate some of the burden previously on System Test, which could be reinvested in refining the system test function.

Finally, all agreed that the idea of a "readiness" rating that measured exit criteria components could be derived for any phase. However, the requirement phase was being redesigned and inspections were only recently introduced. These phases did not have the institutionalized data collection methods available from the test group, and although data was presented to the core team from other areas, it was not yet well-understood.

The life cycle review session was cut short when members recognized that the phase of the life cycle with the most data available for decision-making at this time was the system test phase. The team decided the most immediate rewards could be achieved by focusing on the validation phase of the life cycle: development integration and system test.

8.5 ASSESSING MEASUREMENTS

The next step was to convene a session to assess the measures currently being captured and reported during the validation phase for their value in the decision-making process. Some metrics, while of value in planning, were not of benefit to the core team during project execution. For example, the number of media refreshes received during the validation phase and the number of staff hours expended were two metrics that were valuable to the test manager for future planning, but meant little to the team.

Other metrics were altered. Previously, the Test Manager reported only those problems opened by the Test organization. Following the principles of SRE, the Test Manager used staff effort between discoveries to estimate remaining effort. However, during the validation phase, the customer community using the prior release may also uncover new issues that exist in the project under test. Thus, the core team needed to be apprised of all open problems for the project—from all sources.

This realization caused the Test Manager to view the tool as not just a measure of the status of the test phase, but of the project itself. The overriding question was not whether the test phase was on or off its plan, but whether the project in its entirety met the overall criteria of quality and completeness.

Once the existing measures were evaluated and either kept, modified, or rejected, the team searched for new factors. For example, the Customer Support member wanted an early alert that testing for a subsystem was in trouble. Since test cycles are planned with priorities in mind, if high-priority tests are blocked, a flag should be raised. Similarly, it was decided that while a complete test cycle may not be executed on each and every refresh, there should be a set of core, or essential, tests that must be passed or the core team is alerted and the release is at risk.

Each of the measurements was defined, agreed-upon, then listed and ranked according to priority and importance. Next, the team assigned a score to each component such that the composite made 100%. The goal was to arrive at a grade or score, which came to be known as the Confidence Rating, which would summarize the release readiness of a project as it moved through the final validation phases.

8.6 DESCRIPTION OF THE RATING

The Confidence Rating comprised nine measurements whose total was targeted to be no less than 90% for release. The components of the Confidence Rating and their relative weights are described below. At the end, Table 8-1 illustrates how each measure is calculated and weighted and how the final rating is derived.

8.6.1 COMPONENT 1—INPUTS TO PHASE

The first component measures the availability of required inputs to the test cycle. System Test must often make a trade-off between completing some preliminary testing with incomplete inputs and then perform rework when those inputs become complete.

Six inputs were defined for the system test phase:

1. Completion of the test strategy, including the priority of tests and the planned execution sequence.
2. Availability of defined test procedures.
3. Known problem documentation.
4. A verified software build.
5. Preliminary Release Notes, including special installation instructions and application impacts.
6. The Installation Guide.

This component and its elements are used to alert the core team of any shortfalls in the inputs to the system test phase and their potential effects. Mitigation strategies are discussed.

8.6.2 COMPONENT 2—PASS RATE

Pass rate is the traditional measure of the number of tests currently in a pass state divided by the total number of tests to be run. Retests, which are failed tests that must be re-executed, are not included in this measure; a test executed twice to achieve the pass state is counted as one. This is a "unique" test count only.

8.6.3   COMPONENT 3—FAILURE RATE

Fail rate is the number of tests in a failed state divided by the number of unique tests run. Again, retests are not included in this measure. However, the sum of the fail rate and the pass rate does not necessarily add to 100%, because tests that have been attempted but are blocked or tests that were newly developed but discovered to not be valid for a new capability are counted in the aggregate denominator.

For example, say there are 20 tests planned, 15 are executed with 10 passing, 3 failed, and 2 are blocked due a documented failure. The pass rate is 67% (10 out of 15) and the failed rate is 20% (3 out of 15). The remaining 13% are in an uncertain status (2 blocked out of 15).

8.6.4   COMPONENT 4—DEVIATION FROM PLAN

The test plan contemplates the execution sequence of test suites organized by functional area. Problem areas that prevent or block test suites from being executed cause a slip in the test plan. At each status report period, the test suites that have been executed are compared to their planned completion date. Any test suite or part of a suite that is not on-plan deducts from the score. Each suite has equal weighting.

This measurement alerts the core team that, although the execution rate of tests may be on schedule, the sequence of functional areas is not. This would apprise Customer Support in those instances where high-priority functions are at risk because they are behind plan.

For example, if there are three suites and Suite A is not scheduled for completion, Suite B is scheduled for completion but is only 50% complete, and Suite C is scheduled for completion and is 100% complete, the score would be $1/3 + 1/2*1/3+1/3$, or 83%.

8.6.5   COMPONENT 5—EXECUTION COMPLETION

Execution completion is the number of tests completed from the inventory of tests to be run. In this measure, the inventory can increase or decrease based on core team decisions. If defects are discovered that need to be corrected in the software, the re-tests are determined immediately and added to the inventory.

For illustrative purposes, say there are 100 test cases in the inventory initially, and after the first week, 20 are executed, but only 10 of them pass. The core team determines that the defect(s) causing the 10 failures must be corrected and retested, so the 10 are added back into the inventory. Now, the percentage completion is not 20%, it's only 18% (20/100+10).

If addition of the correction indicates the entire suite must be redone, then all of them—even those that passed—are added back. Alternately, a time and budget decision by management may be made to eliminate an area of testing and restrict shipment of the release to customers not requiring the dropped functionality. The inventory is then decreased by the dropped test cases.

This measure reflects the impact of both the discovery of defects and the decisions by the core group on the test effort.

8.6.6   COMPONENT 6—CORE TEST SUCCESS

As described above, the test team identifies a set of essential or core tests that are required for any refresh of the media. These tests represent functions that, if not present and accurate, compromise the release to the point that it is not usable. Every time a media refresh is required during the test cycle, the core tests are always run on the released tape. Management is alerted if any of the core tests fail.

Unlike some of the measurement components, this one is all or nothing: Either all core tests are passed or no points are available.

8.6.7   COMPONENT 7—CRITICAL OPEN PROBLEM REPORTS

A critical problem is one that compromises the system's essential functionality. A critical open problem is like a core test failure in that it is an all or nothing component: None are acceptable. The problems included in this component are not only those discovered to be open by test, but also those found in the field or by other internal organizations such as Development.

8.6.8 COMPONENT 8—MAJOR OPEN PROBLEM REPORTS

Major open problems are those that impact functionality, but have suitable work-arounds. The team agreed that no more than ten major problems should be acceptable in a release; more than ten problems decrease the component measurement proportionately.

8.6.9 COMPONENT 9—MINOR OPEN PROBLEM REPORTS

Minor or cosmetic problems are those that are non-conforming, but not an impediment to using of the system. The team agreed that no more than 50 should be present; any more than this indicates that while the release is functionally acceptable, an annoying number of issues exist that require analysis and mitigation.

8.7 CALCULATING THE CONFIDENCE RATING

The above components are summed and the overall rating calculated as follows:

Table 8-1

Component	Calculation	Goal	Points for Making Goal
Inputs	# Completed/Total	100%	15
Passed	# Passed cases/Total test cases planned	>=90%	13.5
Failed	# Failed cases/Total test cases planned	<=10%	1.5
Deviation from Plan	# or portion of suites on plan/ # Suites planned	100%	15
Executed	# Tests executed/Total inventory	100%	15
Core Tests Passed	Successful completion of all core tests on current media	100%	15
Critical Problems	All or none calculation	0	15
Major Problems	100% for <=10, 10-20 is proportion of 100%, >20 is 0%	<=10	7
Minor Problems	100% for <=50, 0% for >50	<=50	3

8.7.1 GRAPHING THE CONFIDENCE RATING

The goal for any release was at least a 90% rating.

These component calculations are made on a weekly basis and then summed into the overall Confidence Rating. This rating is then plotted using a spreadsheet pivot table, which projects actual progress against the goal. The purpose of this table is to visually depict the effects of project decisions and test phase results on the schedule through a linear projection that can be compared to the goal (see Figure 8-1).

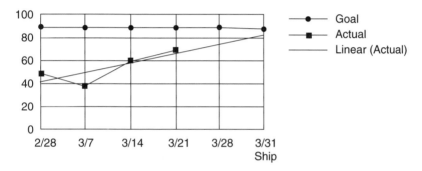

Figure 8-1: Overall Confidence Factor

For example, at Week 3 of the test cycle, the graph shows the confidence factor is 75%. A linear extrapolation indicates the ship date to be on-target. However, during the first week, the line would have been quite different—in fact, it would have projected downward. This shift in the line acted as an early warning to the core team, which examined the factors that were depressing the Confidence Rating and discussed the contributing factors and how to mitigate them. For example, additional resources might be added or functionality dropped from the release.

The Test Managers found that the entire core team participated in the effort to bring the chart to an upward trend and assess all the components.

8.7.2   GRAPHING THE TEST EFFORT

The fifth component, test execution, is also shown as a graph (see Figure 8-2). The number of tests executed from the inventory is reported at each interval, and another line shows the size of the inventory at report time. Again, a linear extrapolation is drawn through the execution ratio values to indicate prediction of a completion date.

Figure 8-2: System Test Cases Executed

This chart also shows that by Week 3, the execution rate appears off-target for the planned ship date. This was caused because a decision was made during Week 2 to add re-tests; this raised the "effort" bar. The core team was now alerted to the effect of this decision and acted to mitigate the resulting risk to the ship date with additional resources.

8.7.3   ANALYSIS

The two graphs delivered at the reporting intervals enabled new forms of analysis and discussions in the core team that were previously unsupported. As shown in Table 8-1, the individual component values of the Confidence Rating are assigned such that deficiencies in certain areas will result in failure to meet the overall confidence goal. For example, failure of any core test drops the confidence below 90%.

In some cases, the core team may choose to lower the confidence bar due to time and budget trade-offs. A platform or middleware development organization has some unique options in this area because projects ship to a lab where a partner or third party integrates an application. Holding the shipment and delaying the integration phase must be evaluated against the early grief the partner can experience with premature promotion of the project.

However, any project released at a Confidence Rating below 90% necessitates special handling. Special handling can include a developer or customer support person traveling with the release. Or, the project can be shipped on a limited basis while corrective activities are initiated and the official project release delayed. The core team makes these decisions based on the components of the rating and knowledge of the business case.

In addition to the Confidence Rating, the core team is also kept advised of the impact of re-tests. Change management of a project is the responsibility of the core team. While in the System Test organization, the impact of changes in scope of the project due to the correction of problems and associated retest is immediately visible. Retests increase the inventory of tests, thus increasing the "effort" bar in the System Test chart.

The raise in the "effort" bar communicates ever-increasing work. This is a very different message than reporting that System Test is behind plan, which tends to imply the need to work harder and faster. It also demonstrates the problem with promoting software too early. Are the problems requiring correction of a system level, or are they of an integration level? If the problem is acute, the decision can be made to demote the project to integration-level testing and begin the system test phase anew.

8.8 IMPLEMENTATION

These release management techniques and metrics were implemented first on a pilot project. This project consisted of a development effort of about 20 persons and a six-week cycle. Many of the core team members on this project had participated in the session where the Confidence Rating was derived.

A training session was held on the Confidence Rating at one of the weekly core team meetings. The Confidence Rating was presented weekly and reviewed by all. Charts were posted on the intra-company Web site. Typical occurrences were identified defects bringing down the rating and corrections increasing the "effort" bar. This relationship is now a well-known trade-off for core teams.

The selected pilot demonstrated a characteristic that surprised Customer Support in previous projects. A function of particular interest was off-plan early and required additional time beyond the planned test cycle. The function in the past had presented problems due to its complexity in project after project.

However, this time, the situation was visible early and the causes were discussed. The Manager of Customer Support supplied an experienced staff member to assist in raising the skill set of the tester. The problem is thus improving with each project due to these team actions.

Following the pilot, the Confidence Rating concept was presented to all other core teams and at management staff meetings. Program Managers enthusiastically accepted the new presentation for project status and now include the graphs in meeting minutes. Initial projects for each program were identified for initial use of the report.

Like any metric, the Confidence Rating requires focus and time to be maintained effectively. The Test organization brought in a co-op student with skills in information management to support the tool. This individual formats the Excel workbook that accumulates the data for reporting to the core team and performs a sanity check at each reporting interval.

The first couple of projects were carefully managed and the roll-out went well. However, then the blessing of a fast-growing organization necessitated implementation of the Confidence Rating by new test leads and managers. As more groups became involved, insufficient training in the Confidence Rating resulted in some inadequate communications to core teams. One common misunderstanding was that the test leads minimized the report as a formality. The analysis opportunities and resulting control over change in the core team were not well-understood.

With a year of fast growth and the outlook of another year of growth at the same pace, materials are being formalized for regular refresh training on the Confidence Rating. The goal of the training will be to present the defined standards of the components and the process for analyzing of the resulting graphs. The result will be the consistent and reliable reporting of results. Additionally, test leads will understand the control over change available with the Confidence Rating.

8.9 RELEASE MANAGEMENT IN ACTION

To get an idea of how the Confidence Rating and System Test charts work as an early warning system to support the core team's decision-making process, Figures 8-3 and 8-4 show the charts for one project and a behind-the-scenes look that occurred on the real-life project.

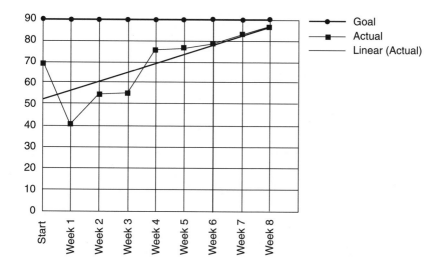

Figure 8-3: Real-life Confidence Rating Chart

The chart above depicts the week-to-week Confidence Rating assigned by the core team as compared to a linear projection to reach 90% by the desired date. Certain characteristic trends in the graphs have been noted following use of the Confidence Rating in multiple releases. One is the downward trend early in the test phase. The frequency of this occurrence in the early stage of system testing prompted the assessment that installation testing in the development phase was deficient. The System Test organization worked with Development Test to make it more rigorous and use more complex databases.

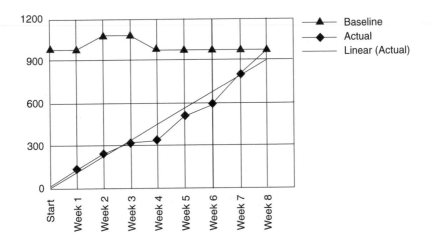

Figure 8-4: Real-life System Test Chart

The System Test effort chart above depicts the run rate of system tests as a percentage of tests passed to the inventory. It is important to note that retests are added back to the inventory, illustrating that a project is promoted too early, before proper unit or integration testing, there is a price to pay during System Test.

The information below explains the events and decisions that were driven and affected by the charts above:

Week 1: High severity discovery causes rating to drop.

Week 2: The high-severity problem is fixed and the necessary retests are planned. System Test effort bar is raised as a result.

Week 3: Test effort is off-plan due to discoveries. Both charts project failure to meet target.

Week 4: The core team decides to limit shipment and drop some customer-specific tests. The System Test effort bar drops as a result. The Confidence Rating improves following re-test of corrections received in Week 2.

Week 5: Critical discoveries with work-arounds are waived. Confidence Rating reflects a critical discovery count above the goal. Mitigation planning begins.

Week 6: The decision is made to add test resources to get back on-plan.

Week 7: Back on-plan.

Week 8: The core team reaches decisions about how to mitigate the critical problems with work-arounds.

As you can see, instead of waiting until the last week or two to take corrective measures, the metrics provided an early warning system so that issues could be discussed as they occurred and decisions could be made in time for action to be taken.

8.10 RESULTS

The release management metrics have been a success. For example, a major release was recently shipped on time; this was accomplished in part by making the decision to drop functionality that customers did not plan to use for another year. As a result, the customer-initiated application development was on time and without early problem grief because of focusing TTNS resources on validation of the critical system components. This trade-off between scope and schedule is natural and inescapable; what is special about our approach is that these trade-off decisions are made early enough to alert customers so that their expectations can be managed.

Other types of decisions that have been made include holding the release if it does not meet acceptable ratings levels, or arranging for a developer to accompany the release to the customer site to mitigate the known risks in certain functional areas.

Overall, this approach has served to shift the core team's focus from the schedule to the completeness of the project. By being constantly aware of whether a project is going to be quality-ready for release at the appointed time, the core team can take action to improve the quality long before the scheduled date arrives.

Aside from shipping quality projects on time, the major benefit of this process is the opportunity for the core team to evaluate the status of a project on a continuous basis, with objective measures understood and accepted by everyone, and to encourage decision-making early in the process.

It has also helped to remove the perception that everything is fine until it reaches System Test, where it somehow mysteriously falls apart. In the past, testers were sometimes viewed as not working hard enough to stay on-plan, when in fact they were working harder than ever because their workload was increasing due to discoveries, retests, and blocked tests.

Like all new processes, these require training, support, and reinforcement to remain effective. There are also ongoing discussions and ideas about refinements and improvements. The key is not whether any particular metric or tactic is perfect, but whether it supports the team involvement and decision-making that is essential to project quality and success.

8.11 LESSONS LEARNED

There were a number of lessons learned along the way. During the sessions where the development process was reviewed and the entry/exit criteria defined, members of the core team gained a new appreciation for the interlocking nature of the process, and how prematurely promoting a release from one phase to the next could have a disproportionate effect on later phases. Although this concept might be intellectually understood, it became clearer when illustrated with actual examples.

Likewise, enumerating the elements that make up a quality release shed new light on the consequences of past practices. Items such as deviations from the test plan, for example, were effectively "hidden" in the past because the number of tests being executed was consistent with the plan, although the areas being tested were not. By revealing this element, it drew attention to the real reasons behind it—areas of the system that were simply not ready for test because of outstanding issues.

It was a surprise to see new test leads view the metrics as a mere formality and not a hard-won, well-thought-out management tool. This is typical of new processes: While the original team that develops and implements changes has a clear mission and understanding of their goals, those who come along later may have a narrow if not inaccurate view. Thus, constant training and reinforcement are required for any new process to become institutionalized.

8.12 CONCLUSIONS

With schedule squeeze being the predominant challenge for almost all software releases, managing readiness is a constant battle. By redefining release management as an ongoing process that involves all members of the core team throughout the test phase, instead of a hastily negotiated decision at the very end, issues can be raised and managed before they become too critical or too late.

Creation Of a Software Development Process Handbook

Phoenix Technologies Limited

9.1 COMPANY PROFILE

Phoenix Technologies Ltd. is the leading innovator and supplier of enabling software and services fundamental to PCs, servers, peripherals, and information appliances. The company works closely with manufacturers to integrate key emerging standards such as USB, IEEE 1394, and AGP. Phoenix enables OEMs to optimize engineering resources by licensing advanced software with full integration services to help them increase product differentiation and reduce time to market. Phoenix is a publicly traded company (NASDAQ:PTEC). The company is headquartered in San Jose, California, and has offices worldwide.

9.2 WHY PHOENIX CREATED A PROCESS HANDBOOK

Today, the PC industry is intensely competitive, marked by falling prices, even shorter market windows, and rising customer expectations. To remain competitive, a number of our major customers have implemented continuous quality improvement systems. These systems typically include some form of supplier control as a component, and several companies have requested that Phoenix, as one of their key suppliers, put a continuous improvement system in place.

While Phoenix Technologies is a relatively small corporation (around $100 million in annual revenues), it is a global company, with eight engineering offices located in five countries on three continents. This strategy of geographic diversity allows us to serve a worldwide customer base. Some of our customers, however, who are also international corporations, have complained that when they are working on multiple projects with multiple engineering offices of Phoenix, they sometimes feel as if they are dealing with separate vendors. Our customers increasingly expect to see a more uniform set of documented engineering processes practiced by Phoenix offices worldwide.

To meet this demanding challenge, a Core Steering Team, guided by a process improvement consultant, set out to reach consensus among over 400 engineers on their worldwide best practices. The goal was to document agreed-upon best practices in a small, practical handbook so that processes could be consistently used and controlled to improve software development worldwide. Of course, Phoenix also recognized that quality and productivity are closely related, and efficient systems that increase product quality can result in improved profitability as well. Everyone agreed that the first step toward building an efficient quality system was to document the software development processes.

9.3 CULTURAL ISSUES

From the beginning, it was clear to us that cultural issues would be a major factor in unifying and improving our software development processes. Not only is Phoenix Technologies spread geographically all over the world, in several countries with several different cultures; several of our offices came to us through the acquisition of small software development companies, each of which came with a company culture and a set of different, mostly undocumented, processes. Additionally, the Phoenix workforce is highly diverse, especially in the American engineering offices, with several dozen different races and nationalities represented. National, ethnic, and company cultures all had to be considered. Since English is a second language for many of our employees, the handbook had to be simple and clear.

Our customer base also had to be considered. Phoenix has developed long-term working relationships with numerous key customers; these working relationships typically develop in a way that allows us to relate to and communicate effectively with each key customer using processes, procedures, and terminology which the customer understands. An effort to unify working processes would have to allow us to keep intact, while continuously improving these working relationships that were developed over a period of years.

9.3.1 THE CORE STEERING TEAM PARTNERS WITH CORPORATE SYSTEMS ENGINEERING

A Core Steering Team (CST) was responsible for documenting the Software Development Handbook. The team was comprised of three members from Quality Assurance, the Engineering Director, two members from Corporate Engineering Systems, and the process improvement consultant. They began to work on documenting the key processes. To be successful on a world-wide basis, the team had to have representation at the corporate level. The Vice President of Corporate Systems Engineering (CSE), who reported to the CEO, agreed to co-lead the effort. The consultant would work directly with him and head up the Process Improvement Team to implement consensus building, documentation, and auditing processes.

The CSE team enlisted the participation of key individuals worldwide to form a task force that became known as the summit leaders. Summit leaders were responsible for representing the views of their respective sites on the documentation progress and effort, as well as communicating the views of the CST back to their departments. It was critical to gain the support of these influential site leaders.

The CSE team also opened channels of communication with key customers through surveys and interviews to gather data on what customers were most and least satisfied with regarding Phoenix products and services. These customers were pushing to see evidence of process documentation and improvements in product quality. This created a sense of urgency. Some customers were even willing to share with us their ideas and experiences regarding software development processes and continuous improvement systems.

9.4 DRAFTING THE SOFTWARE DEVELOPMENT HANDBOOK

A major goal set by the CST was to document a baseline set of the diverse current processes that were being effectively used at one or more of the worldwide sites. These would be captured in the Software Development Handbook, which could be referenced by all employees. However, since current processes were not uniform between different company sites or divisions, it was decided that the handbook should represent a set of minimal current best practices, that when combined, would result in the required outputs for a given key process. Best practice candidates would be selected from among the processes that were being successfully used at one or more of the sites and divisions.

To make this a manageable project, the CST originally identified 23 key processes. The consultant used the ISO 9000-3 Software Development Guidelines and the SEI's CMM guidelines for improving software processes as baseline standards. She performed a gap analysis of what elements were missing and made recommendations. Raymond Kehoe and Alka Jarvis' work, *ISO 9000-3, A Tool for Software Product and Process Improvement*, was also used as a reference guide.

Champions for each of the 23 processes were selected. It was their job to form teams of experts who could bring together, and agree upon, the best practices for a given process at each site. Over six months, parallel activities were designed and conducted worldwide by the consultant and CSE team. These included a series of process improvement training sessions, internal process audits, and individual and small group conflict resolution sessions with management and employees. All this effort was focused on driving toward consensus and integrating and/or reducing the 23 key processes. Senior management, at this point, decided to separate the software development processes from the process improvement ones listed below. These processes would belong to CSE to be implemented fully at a later date as management tools.

◆ Internal auditing.

◆ Corrective and preventive action.

◆ Intellectual property protection.

◆ Lessons learned.

◆ Training.

◆ Document and data control.

◆ Product development reviews.

The remaining proposed software development processes were condensed to 15 and documented in a draft of the handbook. The draft was published and circulated company-wide for review and comments three months after the project began. After the first round of review and editing was completed, we shared the draft Software Development Handbook with our key customers as well and seized the opportunity to ask for their feedback. We received very positive, supportive feedback and suggestions. Later, through an intense, carefully orchestrated, consensus-building process, these 15 key processes would be dramatically reduced to the final 11 key software development processes at a worldwide Engineering Summit.

9.4.1 THE ENGINEERING SUMMIT

In a true demonstration of corporate commitment to process improvement, the CSE team arranged to bring together more than 50 key individuals from Phoenix offices worldwide to spend a full week reviewing, understanding, integrating, and refining the key processes and Software Development Handbook. The consultant designed and facilitated a complex consensus-reaching process. Small and large group sessions were designed to help groups resolve conflicts while continually driving toward a final consensus and plan for implementing the use of the handbook.

The first three days of the Engineering Summit were spent mostly in breakout sessions. The small groups of typically five to seven representatives met to work on each key process. The groups were assembled so as to include those who were most knowledgeable in each process area, and also to include representation from all of the different Phoenix sites. Hundreds of internal process audit findings, gathered from the working engineers prior to the summit, were introduced strategically into each group and resolved. It was critical to represent this information from the "grass roots".

During the final two days of the summit, representatives from each team presented the finished process documents to the group and the inputs and outputs from process to process were correlated and adjusted. These sessions were very dynamic and interactive. Many were conduced by the process champions or summit leaders and resulted in solid agreement after some pretty heated discussions. It was critical to deeply involve the key engineers and leaders in this process. They had to create it, validate it, and claim it as their own. Leaders for championing the new process began to emerge. The final integrating session was charged with excitement and promise; the excitement a group feels when a major and very difficult goal is about to be achieved.

The effect of the Engineering Summit was like a Tower of Babel in reverse: We came to the summit speaking different languages about the engineering process. By the end of the summit, we had a common language and a shared understanding of our engineering processes. Phoenix had reached consensus, as a whole for the first time, on the software development process that would be used worldwide. The 12 summit leaders, supported by the CEO, agreed to return home, with a revised handbook in hand, and follow up to insure that their people would use, control, and start to improve the newly fought for processes listed below:

◆   KP001 – Initial Requirements Analysis.

- KP002 – Business Planning.
- KP003 – Project Planning.
- KP004 – Contract Creation.
- KP005 – Project Management.
- KP006 – High-Level Design.
- KP007 – Low-Level Design.
- KP008 – Coding and Testing.
- KP009 – Product Validation.
- KP010 – Problem Tracking.
- KP011 – Product Release.

9.4.2 THE HANDBOOK

In its introduction, the Software Development Handbook states its goals and objectives: To define a consistent set of processes and practices for software development and to set a baseline for incremental process improvement. The introduction also contains a call to action for everyone involved in the software development process to study, use, control, and improve the processes in the handbook.

Thirty days after the summit, the CSE team carried out internal audits worldwide to insure that the 437 handbooks that had been distributed to all engineers within two weeks of the summit were actually being used by management and engineers. Over 67% were using the handbook at this time. Audit results were shared with management and corrective action plans were set up for those who needed encouragement. CSE then followed up on the effectiveness of the corrective action plans to increase the use of the handbook.

The pages that follow contain excerpts from the Phoenix Technologies Software Development Handbook. These include a responsibility matrix (Table 9-1), showing clearly which groups within Phoenix have primary or secondary responsibility for each step of the software development process, a portion of a flowchart showing how inputs and outputs flow from process to process (Figure 9-1), and some examples of specific process documents (numbered 1 through 6 on the following pages).

Table 9-1: Responsibility Matrix for Software Development Processes

Key Process #	Key Process	Eng. Mgmt.	Eng.	FAEs	Legal	Mktg.	Proj. Mgmt.	QA	Release	Sales
KP001	Initial Requirements	X	X	X		P	X	X		X
KP002	Business Planning	P	X	X	X	P	P	X		P
KP003	Project Planning	P	X			X	P	X		X
KP004	Contracts				P		X			P
KP005	Project Management	P	X				P	X		
KP006	High-level Design	P	P			X	X	X		
KP007	Low-level Design	P	P					X		
KP008	Code and Test	X	P					X		
KP009	Validation	X	X					P	X	
KP010	Problem Tracking	X	X	X			X	P		
KP011	Release	X	X			X	X	X	P	X

P indicates functional position with primary responsibility.
X indicates functional position with secondary responsibility.

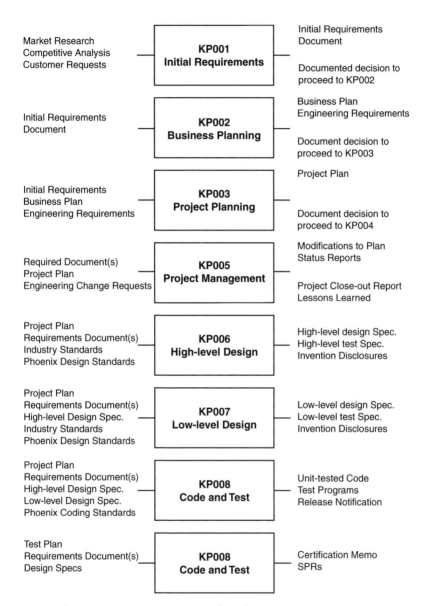

Figure 9-1: Inputs/Outputs Flowchart

1. PROJECT MANAGEMENT PROCESS DOCUMENT

Project Management Key Process	KP005	Revision Date: 14-May-97
Accountable Functions: Project Management, Engineering Management		Revision: 1.0
		Documented by:

1. Purpose

To ensure that all projects (development and deployment) are monitored against the Project Plan, progress is reported, and projects are re-planned as appropriate.

2. Scope

The Project Management Key Process applies to all projects, including both development and deployment projects.

3. Inputs / Dependencies

3.1 Initial Requirements Document

3.2 Project Specifications

3.3 Executed contract, if applicable

3.4 Project Plan

3.5 Engineering Change Requests (ECRs)

3.6 Release Notifications

3.7 Certification Memos

3.8 Test Reports

3.9 Escalation Reports

4. Project Management Steps

4.1 Initiate the project

    4.1.1 Distribute Project Plan and related documents

    4.1.2 Conduct kick-off meeting to review the plan with the project team

    4.1.3 Establish Project File

4.2 Manage project status

    4.2.1 Obtain project status from team

    4.2.2 Conduct project meetings

4.2.3 Monitor progress according to the Project Plan

4.2.4 Identify and resolve project issues

4.2.5 Produce and distribute Project Status Reports

4.3 Manage boundary conditions

4.3.1 Identify any out-of-bounds conditions which impact the Project Plan

4.3.2 Escalate out-of-bounds conditions as necessary

4.3.3 Prepare and present an Out-of-bounds Recovery Plan

4.3.4 Obtain approval of Recovery Plan

4.3.5 Update and redistribute the Project Plan

4.4 Manage milestones

4.4.1 Conduct milestone reviews

4.4.2 Determine if milestone criteria have been met

4.4.3 Manage the release of milestone deliverables, as appropriate

4.5 Manage requirements changes

4.5.1 Identify any changes to requirements and their impact on the plan

4.5.2 Prepare and present modified Project Plan

4.5.3 Obtain approval of the modified Project Plan

4.6 Close out the project

4.6.1 Conduct a project post-mortem

4.6.2 Prepare and distribute a Project Close-out Report, including lessons learned and root cause analysis of problems

5. Outputs / Deliverables

5.1 Updated Project Plan

5.2 Project Status Reports

5.3 Out-of-bounds presentations, if applicable

5.4 Project Close-out Report

5.5 Project File

6. Customers

6.1 Phoenix Technologies Ltd.

6.2 Customers of Phoenix

6.3 Development partners of Phoenix

7. Key Measures

   7.1 Estimated vs. actual time to complete

   7.2 Estimated vs. actual effort to complete

   7.3 Customer feedback

2. HIGH-LEVEL DESIGN PROCESS DOCUMENT

High-level Design Key Process	KP006	Revision Date: 14-May-97
Accountable Functions: Project Management, Engineering Management		Revision: 1.0
		Documented by:

1. **Purpose**

   To produce a complete functional specification for a design that will satisfy all project requirements, as specified by the Requirements Document(s), the Project Plan, and any other related documents.

2. **Scope**

   This applies to the development or maintenance of all software/firmware.

3. **Inputs / Dependencies**

   3.1 Project Plan

   3.2 Requirements Document(s)

   3.3 Statement of Work, if applicable

   3.4 Industry/technical standards documents, if applicable (Institute of Electrical and Electronic Engineers (IEEE); American National Standards Institute (ANSI), etc.)

   3.5 Other related Phoenix-generated specifications

   3.6 Third-party specifications, if applicable (e.g., Microsoft, Intel)

3.7 Customer-supplied documents, if work is at customer request

3.8 Phoenix design standards, both documented and undocumented

3.9 Undocumented industry standards (e.g., IBM AT compatibility)

4. **High-level Design Steps**

    4.1 Analyze all inputs

    4.2 Consider possible functional solutions

    4.3 Consider technical factors (design time, testability, design standards, design constraints, etc.)

    4.4 Confer with customers (internal and/or external) on possible revisions to requirements

    4.5 Select a concept for an optimum solution

    4.6 Create an outline for the specification(s)

    4.7 Add detail to the specification(s)

    4.8 Search for possible patentable ideas in the design

    4.9 Notify Project Manager if any problems were found that require changes to the Project Plan

    4.10 Conduct Design Review

    4.11 Revise specification(s) as required based on results of the Design Review

    4.12 Repeat 4.10 and 4.11 as necessary until exit criteria are satisfied (consensus is reached that the design meets requirements)

5. **Outputs / Deliverables**

    5.1 High-level Design Specification

    5.2 Possible revision of Requirements Document(s)

    5.3 Possible notification to Project Manager of required changes in the Project Plan

    5.4 High-level Test Plan

    5.5 Invention Disclosures

6. **Customer**

6.1 Engineering uses the outputs of this process to proceed to the low-level design process

6.2 Marketing uses the outputs of this process to understand and influence product functionality

6.3 Management uses the outputs of this process to make a decision to continue funding the project

6.4 Salespeople and Project Managers use these outputs to help manage customer expectations

7. Key Measures

7.1 Estimated vs. actual elapsed time to complete

7.2 Estimated vs. actual effort to complete

7.3 Number of errors and defects

3. LOW-LEVEL DESIGN PROCESS DOCUMENT

Low-level Design Key Process	KP007	Revision Date: 14-May-97
Accountable Function: Engineering		Revision: 1.0
		Documented by:

1. **Purpose**

    To produce a complete Low-level Design Specification that will accurately and efficiently implement the design as specified in the Requirements Document(s) and High-level Specification(s).

2. **Scope**

    This applies to the development or maintenance of all software/firmware.

3. **Inputs / Dependencies**

    3.1 Project Plan

    3.2 Requirements Document(s)

    3.3 High-level Design Specification(s)

3.4 Industry/technical standards documents, if applicable (Institute of Electrical and Electronic Engineers (IEEE); American National Standards Institute (ANSI), etc.)

3.5 Other related Phoenix-generated or third-party specifications

3.6 Customer-supplied documents, if work is at customer request

3.7 Phoenix design standards, both documented and undocumented

3.8 Undocumented industry standards (e.g., IBM AT compatibility)

4. **Low-level Design Steps**

    4.1 Analyze all inputs

    4.2 Consider possible implementations

    4.3 Consider technical factors (design time, testability, design standards, design constraints, etc.)

    4.4 Confer with customers (internal and/or external) on possible revisions to requirements or specifications

    4.5 Make design decisions based on technical and other factors

    4.6 Create an outline for the specification(s)

    4.7 Add detail to the specification(s)

    4.8 Generate Test Specification

    4.9 Search for possible patentable ideas in the design

    4.10 Notify Project Manager if any problems were found that require changes to the Project Plan

    4.11 Conduct Design Review

    4.12 Revise specification(s) as required based on results of the Design Review

    4.13 Repeat 4.10 and 4.11 as necessary until exit criteria are satisfied (concensus is reached that the design meets requirements)

5. **Outputs / Deliverables**

    5.1 Low-level Design Specification

5.2 Updated Test Plan

5.3 Possible revision of High-level Design Specification

5.4 Possible notification to Project Manager of required changes in the Project Plan

5.5 Invention Disclosures

5.6 Preliminary Test Plan

6. Customer

6.1 Engineering uses the outputs of this process to proceed to the code and test process

6.2 Management uses the outputs of this process to make a decision to continue funding the project

6.3 Salespeople and Project Managers use these outputs to help manage customer expectations

7. Key Measures

7.1 Estimated vs. actual elapsed time to complete

7.2 Estimated vs. actual effort to complete

7.3 Number of errors and defects

4. CODE AND TEST PROCESS DOCUMENT

Code and Test Key Process	KP008	Revision Date: 14-May-97
Accountable Function: Engineering		Revision: 1.0
		Documented by:

1. Purpose

To produce working, deliverable code for a software or firmware design that accurately implements the design specifications.

2. Scope

This applies to the development or maintenance of all software/firmware.

3. Inputs / Dependencies

3.1 Project Plan

3.2 High-level and Low-level Design Specification(s)

3.3 Industry/technical standards documents, if applicable (Institute of Electrical and Electronic Engineers (IEEE); American National Standards Institute (ANSI), etc.)

3.4 Other related Phoenix-generated or third-party specifications

3.5 Customer-supplied documents, if work is at customer request

3.6 Phoenix coding standards, both documented and undocumented

3.7 Undocumented industry standards (e.g., IBM AT compatibility)

3.8 Software Problem Reports (SPRs) and Engineering Change Requests (ECRs)

3.9 Legally-approved source code supplied by third parties, if applicable

4. **Code and Test Steps**

    4.1 Analyze all inputs

    4.2 Write (or receive) code to implement the Design Specification(s)

    4.3 Write (or receive) test programs and procedure(s) as required by the Test Plan

    4.4 Notify Project Manager if any problems were found that require changes to the Project Plan

    4.5 Identify target platform(s) for testing

    4.6 Integrate new code into the test platform

    4.7 Create test harnesses and stubs as required for testing

    4.8 Modify code as required per the code review(s)

    4.9 Perform unit testing

    4.10 Check in all new files and/or modified files

    4.11 Create Release Notes and check them in

    4.12 Issue Release Notification

    4.13 Update problem-tracking database as required

5. **Outputs / Deliverables**

   5.1 Source code that is working, tested, and reproducible

   5.2 Test programs and procedures

   5.3 Possible revision of specifications

   5.4 Release Notes and Release Notification

   5.5 Test reports

   5.6 Updates to problem-tracking database

6. **Customer**

   6.1 Release Control uses the outputs of this process to generate releases

   6.2 Source customers, engineers doing deployments

   6.3 QA uses the executable code, documentation, and test programs/procedures to validate the implementation

7. **Key Measures**

   7.1 Estimated vs. actual elapsed time to complete

   7.2 Estimated vs. actual effort to complete

   7.3 Number of errors and defects

5. TEMPLATE FOR HIGH-LEVEL DESIGN SPECIFICATIONS

Revision History

Revision	Date	Author	Description
0.1			Initial Revision

Table of Contents

1 Overview

Provide a brief summary of the project. A quality document, similar to quality software, must be designed before it is written. It is best to design a specification first in the form of an outline. For a large project, the specification outline completion date can be set as a scheduled milestone and the outline can be reviewed by other team members.

2 Related Documents

Title	Author
Initial Requirements Document for this project	

3 Terms

Define any terminology which is key to this specification.

4 Related Specifications

Discuss any other specifications that affect this design.

5 Functional Description

Provide a complete functional description of the product or feature. Be sure to cover each of the following topics:

5.1 Products Affected

Which Phoenix products or product lines are affected?

5.2 Modes

Are there multiple operating modes in this design? (e.g., normal mode vs. diagnostic mode, docked vs. undocked, etc.)

5.3 Configurations

Are there build-time options? Are there different types of hardware support?

5.4 Hardware Requirements

What type of hardware is required to support this design?

5.5 User Interface

Are there user-selectable options, or other user interface issues?

Design Parameters

Performance issues, code size limits, etc.

6. TEMPLATE FOR LOW-LEVEL DESIGN SPECIFICATIONS

Revision History

Revision	Date	Author	Description
0.1			Initial Revision

Table of Contents

1 Overview

Provide a brief summary of the project. A quality document, similar to quality software, must be designed before it is written. It is best to design a specification first in the form of an outline. For large projects, the specification outline completion date can be set as a scheduled milestone and the outline can be reviewed by other team members. For complex projects, deployment time can be minimized and debug simplified when clear, accurate descriptions and instructions are provided.

2 Related Documents

Title	Author
Initial Requirements Document for this project	
High-level Design Specification for this project	

3 Terms

Define any terminology which is key to this specification.

4 Related Specifications

Discuss any other specifications that affect this design.

5 Design Overview

Provide a detailed, top-down overview of the major design concepts. Include block diagrams or other illustrations, as appropriate.

6 Functional Interfaces

For each functional interface, specify entry and exit points, register usage, segment usage, and any other assumptions. Specify whether the interface is:

◆ An API that is available to other software programs.

◆ An inter-component interface that is available to other firmware components.

◆ A private interface that is intended to be used only within that component.

6.1 Algorithms

Describe specific algorithms that will be used to implement the functionality.

6.2 Data Structures

Define the principal data structures to be used. For complex indirect addressing, include an illustration for clarity.

6.3 Assumptions

Describe any assumptions being made that place constraints on the design, such as hardware requirements, performance limits, range of inputs, etc. Also define what the default behavior of the component or routine will be when passed input values outside of the Design Specification.

6.4 Resource Usage

6.4.1 Code Groups Used

Code groups, compressible/non-compressible, run-time/POST-time, RAM usage.

6.4.2 Data Space

Conventional RAM, SMRAM, Shadow RAM, BDA, XBDA.

6.5 Source Code Placement

Describe how the source code will be placed in the tree. Does the design contain hardware-specific pieces or platform-specific pieces?

6.6 Deployment Instructions

Include here specific directions for installing this code into an existing BIOS.

9.5 LESSONS LEARNED

With the Software Development Handbook complete, we had a complete view of what deliverables were expected from each group at each step in the software development process. The next logical question to ask was, what precisely do each of these deliverables look like? What does each contain? What criteria can be used to judge if a deliverable is complete and correct?

Some of these questions were answered in the form of document templates that provided guidance on both format and content to document authors. Templates have proven to be beneficial in several ways:

♦ Templates provide a common, professional look to all project documentation.

♦ Templates supply boiler-plate language that simplifies document creation.

♦ Templates provide guidance regarding the type of information that can be found in each type of project document.

♦ Templates promote more thorough planning and design work by prompting the author to supply all necessary information.

♦ Templates supply guidance that improves compliance with a standard set of planning and design rules.

While Phoenix has not yet reached the point where one common set of document templates are in use for all projects company-wide, the templates shown above are in use at Phoenix today.

9.6 CONTINUOUS IMPROVEMENT

With its Software Development Handbook and document templates in place, Phoenix is now in a position to work toward our goal of continuously improving our software development practices. Some of the improvements that are now on the drawing board include standardized procedures for design and code reviews, design-for-test guidelines to improve product testability, and more formal methods of identifying and collecting customer requirements.

Lord Kelvin told us that knowledge gained without measurement is unsatisfactory at best. This idea is also expressed in the management adage, "That which cannot be measured cannot be controlled." To measure our success at continuous process improvement, Phoenix has implemented an improved problem-tracking system, an engineering time-tracking system, and a project status database. These databases provide valuable data regarding defect trends, effort expended in each phase of product development, and timeliness of delivery against schedules. These tools are the yardsticks by which we measure our progress.

9.7 CONCLUSIONS

Reaching consensus and documenting the 11 key software development processes for our Software Development Handbook was a company-wide effort. This is a critical point to understand. The CST and CSE teams provided the vision and energy to continually press forward in the face of daily business emergencies and demands. The process champions worked with over 40 reviewers and senior managers to reach agreement and document the process steps and practices. All engineers attended process improvement classes, participated in internal process audits, and contributed process improvement suggestions. Executive and senior management supported the effort fully. As a result, the handbook captures the best "pooled knowledge" of all of our domestic and international sites. By using consistent processes worldwide, we have reduced the time and effort it takes to produce our product.

10

Managing Client/Vendor Relationships

International Business Systems

10.1 COMPANY PROFILE

International Business Systems (IBS) is an international, full-service software company with over 25 year's experience in wholesale distribution. IBS has a network of over 60 offices in 22 countries. More than 2,100 distribution companies use IBS software products around the globe.

IBS offers a complete range of services, including project management, implementation assistance, training, customization, and conversion, as well as software maintenance and support—available 24 hours a day, 7 days a week. We also work closely with IBM to provide complete hardware solutions that work in harmony with IBS's client/server technology.

IBS software (ASW) is written specifically for the wholesale distribution industry. IBS is the industry leader in application software and service for IBM's mid-range computers. As one of IBM's largest AS/400 Business Partners, IBS has solidified a strategic relationship with IBM, which owns 10% of IBS stock. IBS customers benefit from this close relationship because IBS will always be on the forefront of evolving technology. Currently, IBS is working with IBM on the San Francisco Project, which will provide a JAVA-based framework for ASW and other application developers to provide leading-edge software solutions.

10.2　REASON TO IMPLEMENT

10.2.1 NEW VISION

IBS wanted to reshape the traditional vision of client/vendor relationships. The goal was to rethink how a client and a vendor come together to form a team, solve problems, and create solutions. Traditionally, the client or the vendor is individually responsible for fully understanding the client's business processes as they exist, as well as the functionality of the new vendor-supplied system to determine process fit, new opportunities, and/or modification requirements. This is a time-consuming and costly approach. With the Implementation Control Process (ICP), it is the client/vendor team that is charged with this responsibility. The client brings the business knowledge. IBS brings the software package knowledge. Success is a function of how well client and vendor personnel perform—not client, not vendor, but a single solution-oriented team.

Each client brings a different amount of experience to the relationship. Some clients are very sophisticated in their understanding of the complexity of software purchases and process changes. Some have large IS staffs with well-developed methodologies, tools, and techniques. Others have very small staffs with limited experience in purchasing, converting, and implementing enterprise-wide solutions. The problem this mix of clients presents the vendor is that some amount of education must be included in the variety of services provided. It can be difficult to show how processes add value if the problems they avoid aren't understood because of inexperience. The ICP attempts to mitigate this issue with clear, consistent, and timely communication.

10.2.2 COMPETITION

The goal of IBS is to be the premier provider of distribution software and services in the world. With this in mind, we believe that client/ vendor relationships are critical to providing a clear advantage to our clients that differentiates IBS from other vendors. The ICP provides the framework for continued improvement in this vital interaction.

10.2.3 CUSTOMER SATISFACTION

We put business improvement for our customers at the top of our agenda. The ICP provides a consistent and innovative way of producing results for our clients. Real customer satisfaction comes with the realization that the new software package not only solves problems, but provides a competitive advantage.

10.2.4 TOO MANY DEFECTS

The ICP has quality initiatives built into it, not added on in the more traditional "Quality Plan" approach. Like all vendors, our goal is to provide virtually error-free software. We, however, acknowledge that the approach must be cost-effective, not simply effective.

10.2.5 TO IMPROVE OVERALL QUALITY

The ICP is a state of mind that says IBS will be better tomorrow than it was today. It will be better in products, rich in functionality, and better in processes that delivery superior customer service.

10.3 DESCRIPTION OF PROCESS

The ICP starts at the point of transition between Sales and Operations. This is where the relationship that has been established during the sales cycle is transferred to a new group of IBS employees. It's critical that all of the information gained about the client's business processes, organizational structure, team configuration, expectations, project budget, and any other constraints is communicated to the team from Operations that has been formed for this client. IBS often finds that the client feels "comfortable" with the sales staff, and in some ways, this new relationship with the operations team can be challenging.

Like any human endeavor, the initial vision and excitement of purchasing software eventually fades, as the reality of changing something as critical as business applications and processes is fully underway. As the project moves from vision to reality, it's easy to get lost in the details of the journey. The ICP attempts to keep the end result in focus for both the client and the IBS team. Our studies show that our clients are most satisfied after the return on their investment in ASW starts paying real dividends through increased revenue, cost savings, and competitive advantage. Managing communications in such a way as to continually convey the movement toward the goal of implementation is a vital aspect of the client/vendor relationship.

For the purposes of this discussion, we'll view each phase of the implementation process, not from a technical perspective, but from a client/vendor relationship perspective. We'll speak to the particular challenges that are faced in each of the phases and how the ICP guides the management of the relationship. Each phase will have purpose, relationship challenges, and germane processes. First, here is a high-level view of ICP.

The ICP has two fundamental divisions: required phases and client driven optional phases. The distinction is critical. Project Initiation is part of Phase 1, which is one of the required phases.

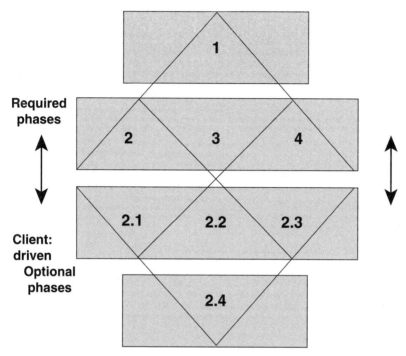

Figure 10-1: Implementation Control Process

As you can see from the Figure 10-1, the client-driven optional phases are "inserted" into the required phases as needed. The optional phases are used when the client wants IBS to modify ASW to meet specific functional and process requirements. Optional phases cover the traditional requirements, design, and development activities. This discussion will not deal with these topics from a technical development perspective, but instead focus on the client/vendor relationship management that goes on during these phases.

The required phases include Project Initiation, Solution Confirmation, Implementation, and Post-implementation. These phases provide everything needed to implement an unmodified version of our ASW software. The following is a very high-level definition of each phase, in order:

1. Project Initiation

♦ Organize the team, prepare for client site visit, and make initial contact with the customer.

♦ Conduct site visit, discuss business processes at a high level, and set project scope, objectives, and strategies.

2. Solution Confirmation

♦ Perform analysis of site visit findings, issues noted during the sales cycle, and any other client input to prepare and conduct the pilot session. During pilot sessions, key customer processes are simulated on ASW and issues to be resolved by process changes an/or modifications are noted.

3. Implementation

♦ Prepare for installation, check client responsible task completion, and verify setup and conversion preparation.

♦ Install software and conduct training.

4. Post-implementation

♦ Follow up on outstanding issues and help client to fully utilize ASW.

10.4 THE HANDOFF

The ICP provides for a Project Initiation phase, during which a turn-over meeting is held between the IBS sales staff and operations team. In advance of this meeting, the sales team prepares all of the information gathered from the client for review and presentation. The ICP provides a checklist of all items needed for review during this meeting. The checklist items are there to ensure careful attention is paid to documenting all agreements and understandings between the client and sales staff. The new team will inherit all of the information needed to begin implementation from the point where the sales team left off, including any issues that were identified during the demonstration of the product and the RFP (Request for Proposal) response.

Sales negotiates a price for the software and estimates the cost for implementation based on the required phases. It is possible that some modifications may have been defined at a high level during the sales process. If this is the case, this information and any estimates that have been produced are turned over to the implementation team as well.

An operations team introduction letter is sent to the client outlining the qualifications of the team and pointing out that every team has the full support of all IBS resources.

While the handoff between Sales and Implementation is critical, there are a number of other things that are done during this initial phase. To understand how everything fits together, let's briefly review the terminology, structure, and approach of the ICP. We'll keep the example very simple for clarity's sake.

10.4.1 TERMINOLOGY

To avoid any misunderstanding, we developed common terminology and promoted it within the staff:

◆ **Phase:** A major element in the development methodology, made up of processes.

◆ **Process:** A group of activities bound together for a common purpose.

◆ **Activity:** A series of tasks completed in the accomplishment of an end.

◆ **Task:** Unit of work with a single focus and a specific procedure.

◆ **Procedure:** Steps taken according to predetermined outline and/ or standard.

◆ **Deliverable:** The tangible result of one or more processes, activities, or tasks.

10.4.2 STRUCTURE

The ICP is designed to evolve. This evolution requires an "information architecture" so that all information related to the process can be stored and retrieved. The techniques and procedure for accomplishing various IBS-proprietary tasks are stored, retrieved, and revised as part of what IBS refers to as "Corporate Memory". The goal is to have specific information types, store them in specific places, and make them available through desktop tools that provide "in-context" access.

The ICP methodology has four levels:

1. Phase.
2. Process.
3. Activity.
4. Task.

Each level is a building block for the level above it. In this way, the structure of the methodology lends itself to statistical process control because actions can be documented as procedures. These procedures can be changed via input from quantitative and qualitative measurements of the deliverables that they create.

Below the task level, the documentation provides procedures, standards, tools, templates, and examples to support the actions at the lowest level needed to ensure a repeatable and scaleable approach, as the company grows larger. Also, procedures may change as technology changes, but the purpose is likely to be more stable. Therefore, the procedures are built and rebuilt as needed without rewriting the entire process.

Starting with Project Initiation, each section contains the Purpose, Deliverables, and Value to the Client sections, with references to standards, tools, templates, and procedures. This allows flexibility in altering our activities while the purposes and deliverables remain stable.

The methodology calls for reviews and checkpoints before and after certain critical activities. This allows the project leaders, technical leads, QA, clients, and management to reach a common understanding of the state of the work being performed. Checkpoints are mostly directed at determining if the tasks called for in the methodology outline have been completed according to the applicable standard. Reviews are used for assessing the relative merits of the work completed to gain additional experienced perspective or for reaching an agreement on a particular approach.

Not all checkpoints are monitored by QA. Different people may perform checkpoints and reviews. Team leaders perform checkpoints on items like project management, site visits, customer agreements, etc. Technical leads and project managers perform reviews on critical items like designs and PSAs (Professional Services Authorizations). QA looks at unit test completion, functional design ambiguity, and system test completion. This allocates the responsibility of monitoring projects to the people most qualified and most responsible for the outcome.

10.5 APPROACH

This section describes the ICP project management approach. Included are specific methods for dealing with project setup, client management, and project control.

Part of the development methodology contains an outline of the phases, processes, activities and tasks required to produce the deliverables demanded by the IBS agreement with our customers. Project management defines the techniques and tools used to coordinate and track the progress of both the project team and client effort over the life of the project.

Regardless of the approach used by an individual manager, there remains a core set of objectives and results that each project must obtain. The results can be summed up in a phrase, "On time, on budget with complete customer satisfaction."

The ICP methodology is based on actions. Therefore, actions need to be tracked and the results they produce quantified. To accomplish this, an "action architecture" is defined to track activities and tasks and to record the effect on requirements, designs, and agreements. This concept will be discussed in more detail later.

Here are some key principles:

♦ Every issue that needs to be resolved must be tied to a task on the project plan. If this is not true, the project has a "black hole," where time is being spent but not accounted for.

♦ When an issue is resolved, the implications of the resolution must be analyzed in terms of the impact to requirements, design, agreements, and project cost. Once the impact is understood, all related documents MUST be updated and communicated to the affected parties.

♦ Over the life of the project, tasks on the project plan will be assigned to specific people. Some tasks may be assigned to multiple people; however, the responsibility for a deliverable must be assigned to only one person. The deliverables in the methodology will be tied to specific tasks or groups of tasks. In the latter case, one of the resources must be assigned the responsibility for the deliverable. An example might be that the technical lead is responsible for a modification deliverable and the three programmers who worked on it are responsible for the coding and unit testing tasks.

♦ Requirements are never complete, but they do become "stabilized" at some point in the process. Before they are stabilized, misunderstanding and clarifications are noted as issues. The resolutions to the issues are reflected in the requirements, designs, and agreements. After the requirements are stable, resolutions are noted as change requests. The difference is critical because it has a direct effect on modification specifications, time-lines, and cost estimates. Therefore, the point at which the requirement becomes stable must be acknowledged by IBS and the client.

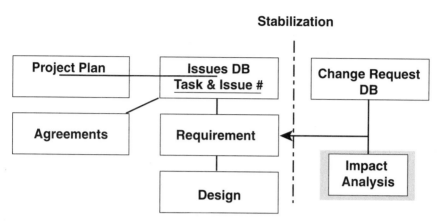

Figure 10-2: Issues and Change Request Databases

Figure 10-2 shows the Issues and Change Request databases that are kept to ensure that an impact analysis is completed for each issue or change. Also, each issue or change must be accounted for with a resolution, responsible person, and completion date.

The client's role in issue resolution is critical. Each week, the itemized list of issues that are scheduled for resolution is reviewed during a conference between IBS and client project team members. The project leader prepares the list of issues due that week and any other action items, and faxes the client a copy prior to the meeting.

Each new project starts with a project schedule for the known phases. If optional phases are selected by the client, a preliminary project plan from the project plan template is created. The purpose is to create an outline of the initial steps using a "rolling horizon" planning technique. This simply means that you can lay out the planning template and put dates on the pieces that are within the known "horizon." As more details come into view, more details are added.

The Project Initiation phase is completed to guide the startup of the project. After this, the plan is refined as specific information becomes available. If specific constraints, such as time and money are known, these can be built into the plan as soon as possible.

Continuing with the Project Initiation phase, let's review the main processes involved and the issues that arise with the client/vendor relationship.

10.5.1 PROJECT INITIATION PHASE

This phase contains the following:

◆ Start-up.

◆ Site visit.

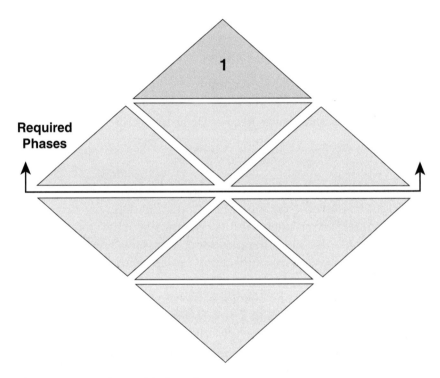

Figure 10-3: Project Initiation Phase

10.5.1.1   *Purpose of Phase*

The IBS Implementation Project Team is formed. Assistance is offered to help the client assemble their project team. Information gained during the sales process is transferred from Sales to the Implementation Project Team. A customer site visit is planned and scheduled with the client.

IBS conducts an on-site visit to the client's facilities to gain knowledge of their current business environment. During this visit, the client will have an opportunity to review with IBS any business process that they have documented or otherwise mentioned.

10.5.1.2 Relationship Challenges

The client may feel unsure or uninformed because they aren't familiar with the entire ICP process. Some time is required to set up a team, as the timing of a client signing a contract is unpredictable and resources are always in demand. This can leave a "gap" between the sales cycle and the start of the implementation process.

It is difficult and challenging to move from the contract-signing phase to a working team with ad hoc processes for communication and roles and responsibilities that are clearly defined. This is true not only for the IBS team, but also for the new client/vendor entity.

10.5.1.3 ICP Processes

IBS sends an introduction letter and conducts a phone introduction in addition to the delivery of the purchased software. A complete set of documentation is also included in this start-up process.

To effectively manage the relationship with the client, communications must be kept clear and concise. To assist with this, a number of information tracking and storage tools are set up during this phase as well. All phone conversations are logged into a database and followed up by written confirmation of decisions or conclusions that were arrived at during the call. Open issues are logged into a database designed specifically for issues that need resolution. Issues in the database can be assigned to anyone associated with the project, including members of the client team. Issues must be analyzed, solutions considered, and the impact on other facets of the project must also be understood.

In the Project Initiation phase, any issues that were discovered during the RFP process or the sales cycle become the starting point for the discovery process. It's easy to assume that all the issues were uncovered during the sales cycle because it covers a lot of functionality. However, this is where the more experienced clients realize that there is another level of detail that has yet to be fully understood. The ICP helps to show the difference in these levels of detail by tracking the issues discovered during the early cycles and comparing them to the number and complexity of the issues discovered during the Solution Confirmation phase. Learning a new application happens in stages, one leading to another. The sales cycle is a fine introduction, but it does not begin to uncover all of the hidden values that a function-rich application can provide. Another issue is that clients sometimes don't really understand their own internal processes. The site visit will help the client and IBS team in this regard because the client will be reviewing at a high level the processes that will be simulated using the new ASW software.

10.5.1.4   The Site Visit

During the site visit, the IBS team and client's team will define the goals and working processes for the project effort. The IBS team will educate the client about the ICP process, and create a communications plan to define all points and timing of contacts. They will also review any items that were turned over to the Implementation Project Team from the sales cycle for further clarification.

When the client chooses to take responsibility for certain implementation items, a clear idea of the skills required to accomplish these tasks is key to the client's success. A skill set inventory is used to help the client determine if they have the appropriate people to be successful. Reaching an agreement on which team, client or IBS, will do these necessary tasks will save an enormous amount of time and client money later. The agreements are recorded for later reference.

The Implementation Group Manager responsible for the Implementation Project Team establishes face-to-face communication with the appropriate executives within the client's firm. This ensures that a high-level exchange of information takes place on a monthly basis. A monthly executive summary is also sent to the client. In addition, a bi-weekly project status report is produced for the client's project team. This report is geared to the detailed level that the project team will find useful.

10.5.2 SOLUTION CONFIRMATION PHASE

This phase contains the following:

◆   Conference Room Pilot Session

◆   Training Plan

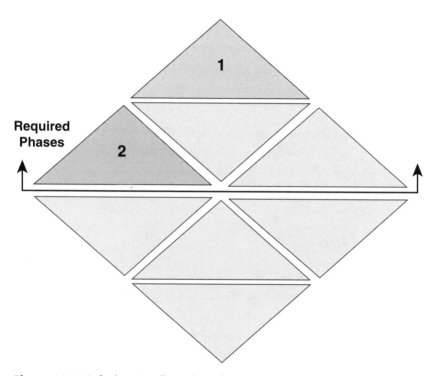

Figure 10-4: Solution Confirmation Phase

10.5.2.1   Purpose of Phase

A pilot workshop will be conducted to simulate key client processes on the new system. In addition, the client will use this phase to confirm the benefits they will be receiving from ASW and will validate their reasons for purchasing the software. IBS' responsibilities include development of a project schedule, procedures, and guidelines that will establish and set client expectations for the project. This also helps the client identify any procedural changes, software workarounds, or potential software modifications.

10.5.2.2   Relationship Challenges

It is important for everyone on the project team to be aware of the reasons why the system was purchased and to see how ASW will accomplish the goals of the client. Often, people other than the client's implementation team handle the RFP and other purchase decisions.

During the pilot process, it's critical to capture four types of information:

◆ All the things the new software does exceptionally well.

◆ The client's business processes that are to be changed to take advantage of best-in-class practices that are instantiated in the new software.

◆ Areas where the software functionality may not exactly match the existing processes but with some creativity the same purposes can be accomplished.

◆ Areas where the business specificity demands a modification to the system.

10.5.2.3   ICP Processes

To capture this information, a minimum two-person team is called for:

◆ A facilitator to run each session. This should be an industry expert.

◆ A scribe who writes down key points which are agreed upon during the meeting. Using an "Issues" database, the scribe captures all of the issues, who defined them, who they were assigned to, and when they are due to be resolved. The Issues database will be used throughout the project to ensure that every issue is resolved and that each resolution has an analysis done to determine the impact on the timeline, scope, requirements, designs, budgets, and any other constraints.

A summary of the information recorded during the Conference Room Pilot Session is gathered into a single document called a Pilot Summary. This document will guide the work that IBS does on behalf of the client. The client and IBS review and revise the summary as needed until the document represents a common understanding.

The Executive Summary and Project Status Report will also be sent during this phase providing further confirmation that the project and issues raised are on track.

10.5.3 REQUIREMENTS PHASE

This phase contains the following:

◆ Application Requirements Specification
◆ Preliminary Project Plan

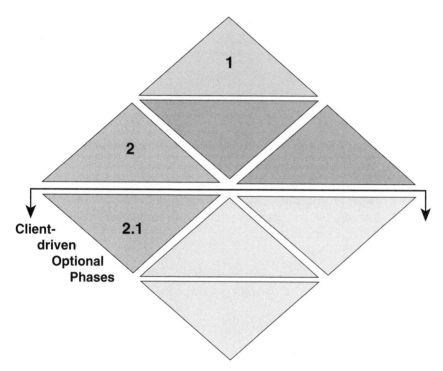

Figure 10-5: Requirements Phase

10.5.3.1   Purpose of Phase

This phase addresses those issues that arose in the Pilot Summary and determines if process changes or modifications are required. In the case of modifications, the requirements will be defined to a sufficient level of detail to allow a functional design to be created. A Preliminary Project Plan is prepared, taking into account any constraints that are known at this point.

10.5.3.2 Relationship Challenges

From a communications perspective, it's imperative that a clear point of departure from summary findings be defined. The summary may include many things, and these must be made into a list of specific items that the client is authorizing IBS to investigate, clarify, and/or define into requirements.

There's an old saying, "You can't see the forest for the trees." We find this to be the case when clients lose perspective on the impacts of their requests. When a project gets complex and there are physical distances between the client and vendor, it's easy for the client to be so involved with the details that they don't see how it's all adding up. In some ways, it's like using your credit card. You buy some gas, you stop by the store for a couple of things, a small gift is required for your son's classmate's birthday, and you pick up some new patio furniture on sale. Then the bill comes and you are astonished to see that it's a BIG number. This is human nature, and it works the same way in defining and refining requirements. One thing leads to another and if we don't continually remind our clients of the "running total," it can be a shock when a project's scope has increased dramatically.

10.5.3.3 ICP Processes

The Project Status Report and Executive Summary are designed to ensure that the client is never taken by surprise by any scope increases. If it's time, cost, or functionality, the goal of the ICP is to make sure that these decisions are done taking the full impact of the project into consideration.

A list will be created of items that need further discussion and clarification. This condensed list is called "Items to Pursue." It represents a prioritized list of significant items from the pilot summary that the client wishes IBS to resolve. This ensures a clear understanding of the client's wishes and provides approval for IBS to proceed.

A Modification Summary List in the form of a spreadsheet is prepared to track each request. ICP provides this spreadsheet as a template for each project to reuse. The template shows each modification plus its status with regard to estimated completion time, cost, degree of completion, and any associated documents. The modification summary is used as part of the biweekly status report information.

A Project Plan is prepared to show the current status of work and an early "estimate" of the time-line. The ICP calls this a "rolling horizon" plan because the plan is only specific on those items that are known or for which enough information is available to predict to a reasonable degree the expected time and effort. On other items that are unknown or little is known, there can be no estimates. This is not to be confused with constraints that are known. For example, say a client wants to go live in March. At the point where the rolling horizon of known events is approaching March, decisions will need to be made by the client on changes to the scope of the project or the constraint.

After years of experience, IBS can predict with reasonable accuracy the time it takes to do site visits, solution confirmation, and implementation for clients of various sizes and complexity. When a client wants to modify a system, the client is then in complete control of the time and cost of the effort. They are in charge of defining requirements, which are key to project scope increases. The very structure of the ICP with its client-driven optional phases defines this for the client. It is a mission-critical message that must be understood as a foundation for clear communication and accurate expectations.

10.5.4 FUNCTIONAL DESIGN PHASE

This phase contains the following:

♦ Conceptualization

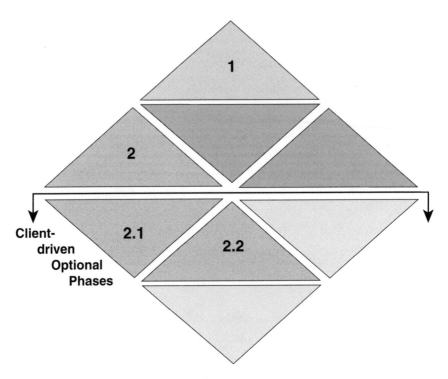

Figure 10-6: Functional Design Phase

10.5.4.1   Purpose of Phase

The Functional Design articulates required modifications to the software. The client's approval of the work is required. If the client has selected automated conversion, planning and design of these automation programs is begun.

10.5.4.2   Relationship Challenges

Communicating with the client on the purpose and specifics of functional design is the main challenge. The design must be reviewed and understood not only by the client, but also by many segments of the client's organization. The business processes that are instantiated in the design must be understood and agreed to by management. The technical aspects of the design must be agreeable to the IS team representative. The physical movement of product that may be implied by the design must be understood and agreed to by the warehouse staff. These are the three key elements in distribution software.

10.5.4.3   *ICP Processes*

Starting with the Modification Summary List, a Professional Services Authorization (PSA) will be presented to the client for approval. Upon approval, IBS will proceed with the first phase of design development for any given modification.

At each stage of the process there are four questions that need to be resolved:

◆ What does it do?

◆ How much does it cost?

◆ How long will it take?

◆ Does the client want to proceed with it?

The ICP calls for the client to authorize work, review, and sign off on a deliverable for each modification at various stages. At no time will IBS proceed on a modification without written authorization. The steps are simple:

1. After the Requirements phase, does the client authorize the vendor to proceed with a Functional Design estimate?

2. Does the client authorize the vendor to proceed with the Functional Design phase based on the estimate?

3. After review of the Functional Design, is the client satisfied with the design?

4. Considering the original estimate (and the possible revised estimate) for the total cost of the modification, does the client authorize the vendor to proceed with the Technical Design phase?

This process allows the client to be fully informed on the status of each modification. The client is in complete control of the costs associated with all work done on their behalf.

Quality is built into the designs. The ICP perspective is that the only people who can build quality are those who are actually doing the work. The QA department assures that the processes that have been defined are in fact being carried out. Therefore, designs and requirements are the most important documents the client defines or reviews. They describe the changes about to be made to ASW functionality. This communication must be as close to perfect as humanly possible. The ICP includes peer and design reviews by senior-level technical managers to ensure that each design is carefully crafted to exacting standards.

10.5.5 TECHNICAL DESIGN PHASE

This phase contains the following:

◆   Specifications
◆   Verification

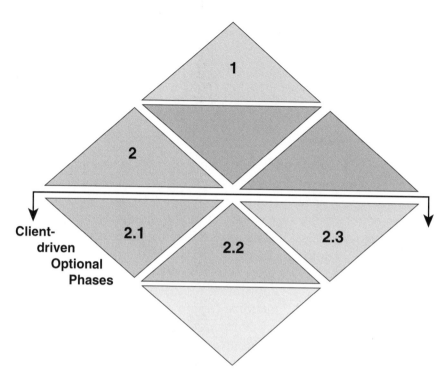

Figure 10-7: Technical Design Phase

10.5.5.1 Purpose of Phase

A Technical Design for each modification is completed in this phase. The Project Plan, Training Plan, and Testing Plan are refined.

10.5.5.2 Relationship Challenges

In this phase, the client is being asked to authorize the Technical Design. However, the Technical Design is not an easy thing to understand, especially when written over a system that the client is not yet familiar with, and written to standards that are unknown to the client, but whose level of understanding is assumed in the document.

The Project Plan needs to be understood, especially if scope changes are involved. What happened to change the time-line and/or scope of the project?

The training agenda requires some planning on the client's part because they must understand how they would like IBS to approach this vital issue.

Acceptance testing is another area where the client's plans are critical to the overall project schedule. How much assistance does the client want, if any?

10.5.5.3   ICP Processes

The Technical Design itself is designed to be largely an internal document. The document deals with very detailed descriptions of files, fields, and logic associated with the Functional Design. More sophisticated clients may want to review it, but they must take into consideration that the Technical Design assumes the person reading it is trained in ASW coding standards, tools, and techniques. It's a bit like wanting to check the Dead Sea Scrolls to ensure that the bible is accurate—probably a time-consuming task that will add little value. The Requirements and Functional Design are the key places to provide critical feedback. The ICP provides processes for tracing a requirement to its Functional Design and then to the Technical Design to insure referential integrity. This is part of the review and test planning processes.

An overall project schedule will be presented to the client based on the client-approved modifications list. The project schedule, developed by the project manager, will identify tasks in detail. Each task will also indicate the time duration of the task, the projected start and finish dates, and the resources necessary to complete each task.

The training agenda is started during the Technical Design phase to ensure timely delivery before implementation. The activities, tasks, and deliverables are noted in the Solution Confirmation phase, because a non-modified version of ASW may be implemented and this is the appropriate time begin these activities.

Project test planning involves acceptance testing by the client. To help the client do an exhaustive job of acceptance testing, ICP calls for delivery of a subset of our integration and system test scripts to the client if they wish. These scripts are traceable as described below to the various requirements and design documents. The test approach can be defined as a "V" for victory.

10.5.5.4 Testing Approach

Testing is divided into four categories:

◆ Acceptance.

◆ Systems.

◆ Integration.

◆ Unit.

Acceptance testing is traced to the requirements derived from the Pilot Summary. Systems and integration testing are traced to the specific sections in the Functional and Technical Designs, as well as the requirements they were generated to meet. Unit testing is specific for each modified object and builds the low-level testing foundation upon which all other functionality tests rely.

Figure 10-8 shows the foundation for establishing traceability from the related documents to the test suites, groups, cases, and scripts that will be generated during the test planning.

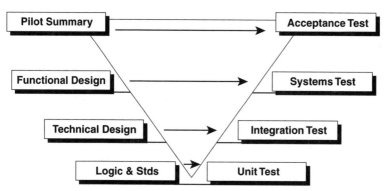

Figure 10-8: Traceability

Tracing a particular modification from the Items to Pursue, by section number through the Design Specification will insure that each modification has a corresponding test case. All modifications will be tested according to specification during integration testing. System testing will cover the overall ASW application.

Regression testing will include test suites built for non-modified modules. A subset of the systems/integration tests will be offered as a starting point for the acceptance test planning. This subset will be chosen specifically to relate to the requirements as defined in the Business Study.

This assures the client that all of the functions that are noted in the specifications are covered in the testing effort. In addition, the client is encouraged to test in any other way they think best. Some clients use this opportunity to enhance and extend their training.

10.5.6 DEVELOPMENT PHASE

This phase contains the following:

◆   Environment.

◆   Construction.

◆   Testing.

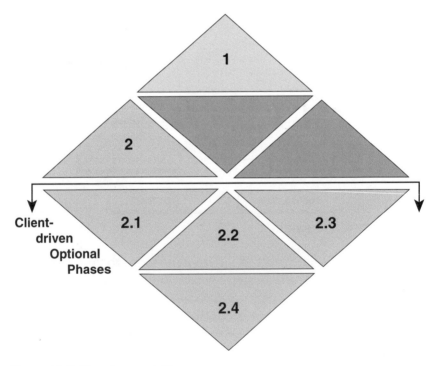

Figure 10-9: Development Phase

10.5.6.1   Purpose of Phase

A complete client project environment is generated in this phase, including development, testing, and production. Coding begins on the various programs according to the Technical Design Specification. Unit tests are required on all modified or new programs. A unit test checkpoint is scheduled with the QA department. Integration and system test results are delivered per the Project Test Plan.

10.5.6.2   Relationship Challenges

The client must stay informed on the progress of the project and must be available to resolve any issues that may arise. Also, the client is reassured that their program changes are protected and separated from any other client's project. Sometimes clients want advance versions of a modification so they can review the changes and/or design the acceptance testing.

10.5.6.3   ICP Processes

A test environment will be generated to allow the client to gain additional exposure to the software. The database used in the pilot may be copied. In addition, development and production environments are created to allow a three-tiered environmental separation.

Once the client returns program specifications and authorization to proceed, the IBS project manager begins assigning programmers to the modifications. The modifications are coded, unit tested, integration tested, system tested, and acceptance tested.

At this point, the amount of clarification required of the client is minimal to proceed, but is not non-existent. There are always fine points to be ironed out. The client may desire to see early versions of the functionality. This helps build confidence in the process and reinforce the fact that some very tangible things are being created.

Even though we've looked at this process from a "waterfall" perspective, it's likely that the project will actually be executed in several phases all at the same time. The continual updates to project status reports, executive summaries, and examination of Project Plan updates help assure the client that things are on track.

10.5.7 IMPLEMENTATION PHASE

This phase contains the following:

◆   Installation.

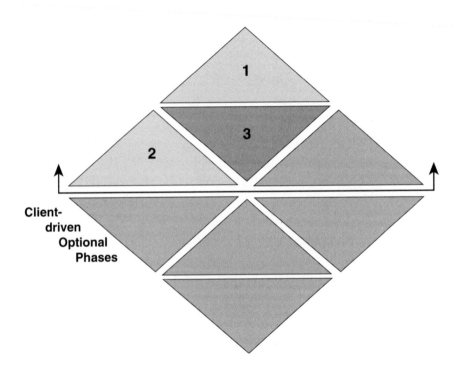

Figure 10-10: Implementation Phase

10.5.7.1   *Purpose of Phase*

In the Installation phase, all elements are completed and ready to successfully bring the client to a "live" status in their production environment. The sequence of these activities will vary from client, to client depending on preference, size, and complexity of the installation and client involvement.

IBS and the client will load and configure the new software, run and verify conversion programs or manual procedures, and "go live" with the new software.

10.5.7.2 Relationship Challenges

The issues here are in ensuring that the client is sufficiently prepared to install and go live with the new system. The ICP has a client task list that is to be reviewed far enough in advance of the live event to allow for corrections to be made. As the project progresses, communication will confirm that both sides are prepared to go live.

10.5.7.3 ICP Processes

The Implementation phase includes user training, software load and configuration, conversion, and verification activities. The client may have as much or as little help configuring the software as they want. This keeps the client in control. The acceptance testing environment should be the proving ground for setup issues, as well as testing any modifications.

The training session is conducted as planned. Always verify the schedule and available facilities in advance of the training. A reminder of this schedule is also recommended 1-2 weeks before the training. The delivery of the training in terms of timing is worked out with the client and can vary greatly. In general, it's recommended that the time between the completion of training and the go-live date not exceed 2-3 weeks.

The installation itself is coordinated with the client through the Release Control function. This is a dedicated department that uses ICP-supplied checklists to ensure consistent and accurate installation. The client is on-line with Release Control for the entire process. They may participate as little or as much as they like. This agreement is reached in advance of the event and is scheduled through the ICP Release Control database.

The IBS Implementation Project Team is on-site with the client at installation. ICP calls for an initial support that provides a safety net of on-site IBS resources to ensure immediate attention to any issues that arise. IBS personnel may perform systems administration tasks, react immediately to solve processing problems, and be available to fix any software issues.

10.5.8 POST-IMPLEMENTATION PHASE

This phase contains the following:

◆   On-going Support.

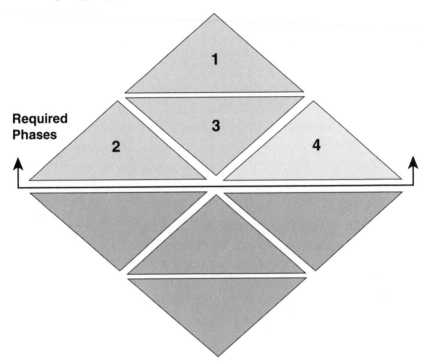

Figure 10-11: Post-implementation Phase

10.5.8.1   *Purpose of Phase*

The objective of this phase is to maintain and increase customer satisfaction through improved understanding of the client's needs and perspectives. Improved IBS products and services is another benefit of this phase.

IBS offers services to the client to help identify business process improvements that will allow them to more fully utilize ASW and gain a competitive advantage in their market.

10.5.8.2   Relationship Challenges

Every person relates what they are learning to something they already know. The greater the difference between the two, the longer the learning curve. When new software is purchased, each process is compared to what that process was like in the previous system or manual process. Oftentimes, features that appear to be cumbersome or irrelevant later are understood and turn out to be quite useful. We've all had the experience, for instance, of purchasing some software for our PCs. We create our own table of contents in Microsoft Word. Eventually, we read the manual or a co-worker will let us in on the easiest way to perform the task. We then use the built-in function to create the same table of contents. The same issues arise with commercial software installations.

After the client has become acclimated to the new ASW system, they begin to ask questions about other functions that they were not fully prepared to examine earlier. These areas can provide additional value as they are understood and included in the business processes. Providing a cost-effective way of addressing these issues is an import consideration.

10.5.8.3   ICP Processes

How can IBS proactively seek out clients and help them utilize all of the benefits of the software?

IBS has a Customer Relations department whose charter is to continue the relationship with our clients after they have successfully implemented ASW. This involves direct client contact for feedback on successes, issues, suggestions, and requests for further expert distribution assistance in changing processes and/or continued modification efforts. IBS utilizes an "Application Support Specialist," who will come to the client site if desired, to review existing business processes and uses of the new application. This person will assist the client in using the software to its fullest potential and when needed help define initial requirements for modification requests.

The Customer Relations department uses third parties to conduct unbiased surveys of a client's satisfaction on a wide range of topics. This information is collected, analyzed, and fed back to the various departments that can benefit from the information. Sometimes it's a function that's needed by the industry and the R&D department, Marketing, and Sales can review the information. Other times, it's project-related information that can be used to improve the relevant ICP processes. The client benefits in two ways: one, they will be the recipient of an improved IBS process, and two, they will enjoy the full use of the software that they purchased.

10.6 CULTURAL CHANGE

Resistance to change is a common thread in any process change. In the case of IBS, the use of acknowledged company leaders to shape the initiatives, and regular communication played a large role in the acceptance of ICP. Also major components of ICP were tested as stand-alone items in real-world situations before the official rollout. This prepared the employees to accept the new process as more of an "evolution" rather than a "revolution," because many elements were already familiar and needed only to be viewed differently.

The Quality Assurance department developed ICP with full involvement from IBS' President, Vice President, Implementation Group Managers, and key individual contributors. Some have suggested that the only way new processes can succeed is by having top down approval. We believe the only way process change can be successful is with top down AND bottom up approval. It must have both. If management is for change and employees reject it, passive resistance will prevail. If employees are for it and management rejects it, some use will be made of it but eventually it will die from lack of support and will not be integrated with other processes.

10.7 PROJECT PLAN/TIME-LINE

Description of how the best practice was implemented:

◆ Who was in charge of implementation?

    ❏ The QA Department Manager.

◆ How was the training given?

❏ Large group overviews followed by project focus groups as the new process was rolled out on new projects. Older projects were "grandfathered" in, based on potential benefits.

◆ Who ensured the implementation guideline was followed by all participants?

❏ IBS has an organizational structure that includes an Implementation Group Manager (IGM). This position oversees a balanced team of project managers, technical leads, and programmers. The IGMs are responsible for insuring compliance. The QA organization monitors each project for compliance, passing non-compliance issues back to the IGMs for resolution.

◆ How long did it take to implement the new process?

❏ Approximately six months.

10.8 RESULTS

IBS and our clients are benefiting from a cost-effective and consistent implementation process that guides the vendor/client relationship in a positive and productive way. We are very proud to present the following tangible results:

◆ Over the two years of the ICP's existence, the ratio of Application License fees versus Professional Services has positively changed from 1 to 4.6 in 1996; 1 to 2.3 in 1997; and is currently at 1 to 1.1 in 1998.

◆ The time from the start of a project to the point where a specific list of issues is compiled (delta between current process and ASW functionality is created) has been reduced by 50%.

◆ The ratio of clients that had cost overage conversations with IBS has been tremendously reduced from 1 in 3 during 1996 to 1 in 10 during 1998.

10.9   LESSONS LEARNED

Children often play with little toy steering wheels while riding in a child's car seat. Everyone in the car sees the toy wheel and understands that it's a toy, and doesn't actually do anything except possibly make noise when the horn is honked. The child pretends that turning the plastic wheel actually turns the car.

This is somewhat like upper-level management when they decide to change a documented process and they assume that the results will actually change because they "turned the plastic wheel." In some cases this may be true, but often the employees are turning the real "informal" process wheel and that is the one that is steering the car. This problems arises when processes are overly complex, hard to interpret for a given situation, and stored on a media that does not provide easy "in-context" access. The trick is to be sure that the processes are actually being used to do work, not to placate management by providing the correct-looking deliverable while the work that created it is not done according to the prescribed process. The saying, "Whatever you monitor will continue, whatever you measure will improve" just about covers it.

10.10 CONCLUSIONS

At IBS, the "circle" has become an inside joke to some degree because we constantly refer to it when assessing the effect of a process change. This adds a little fun, which is good, but it also helps to keep the image of the circle in our minds. If we want to change the type of candy in our vending machine, where does it go in the circle?....yes some things can be taken too far!

Every process needs to be viewed holistically. Every organization has a connection to every other. When designing the ICP with client relationships in mind, what interactions come before, during, and after with the other departments at IBS was a topic that needed a lot of debate, review, and investigation. Sometimes you are truly amazed at what really goes on in other departments.

The following questions should be answered for each process change:

- How does it fit with the organization structure?
- Will it require a new skill set?
- Will it require new and/or revised job descriptions?
- How does it fit with other processes, especially those that cross organizational boundaries?
- How does it fit with your current tools set?
- How does it fit with your current information architecture?
- Does the new terminology conflict with existing terminology?
- How will it fit with your future plans, both technically and conceptually?

Acronyms/Abbreviations

- AC: Authentication Center
- AM: Account Manager
- ASW:International Business Systems' Software
- ATM: Asynchronous Transfer Mode
- AV: Anti-virus
- CA: Customer Advocacy
- CCB: Change Control Board
- CMM: Capability Maturity Model
- CPU: Central Processing Unit
- CR: Change Request
- CRD: Cyclic Redundancy Check
- CSE: Corporate Systems Engineering
- CSO: Customer Service Order
- Dir: Director
- Doc: Documentation
- DOS: Disk Operating System
- FCS TTM: First Customer Ship Time To Market
- FCS TTV: First Customer Ship Time To Volume
- EFT: Early Field Trial
- Eng: Engineering
- FI/CO: Finance and Control

- FP: Function Point
- FT: Field Trial
- 4GL: 4th Generation Language
- GUI: Graphic User Interface
- HF: Human Factors
- HLR: Home Location Register
- ICP: Implementation Control Process
- IE: Information Engineering
- ISO: International Organization for Standardization
- IT: Integrated Technology
- JCL: Job Control Language
- JAD: Joint Application Development
- LAN: Local Area Network
- LDVP: LANDesk Virus Protect
- MAC: Macintosh
- MBR: Master Boot Record
- Mfg: Manufacturing
- Mgr: Manager
- Mktg: Marketing
- MM/PP: Material Management/Production Planning
- MMTF: Mean Time To Failure
- MTTR: Mean Time To Repair
- MRD: Marketing Requirements Document
- NDA: Non-Disclosure Agreement
- NPD: Network Products Division
- OEM: Original Equipment Manufacturer
- Ops: Operations
- PC: Personal Computer
- PDT: Product Development Team
- PLC: Product Life Cycle
- PMI: Project Management Institute
- PRD: Product Requirements Document
- Prod: Product
- PSE: Product Support Engineering
- PSL: Problem Severity Level
- Pubs: Publications
- QA: Quality Assurance

- R&D: Research and Development
- S&T: Systems and Technology
- SAP: Systems, Applications, and Products in Data Processing
- SDLC: System Development Life Cycle
- SE: Serviceability Engineer
- SEI: Software Engineering Institute
- SLT: System Level Test
- SMD: Systems Management Division
- Spec: Specification
- SRE: Software Reliability Engineering
- Sys: System
- SW: Software
- TAC: Technical Assistance Center
- Tech: Technical
- TPMP: Technology Project Management Process
- VP: Vice President
- WAN: Wide Area Network

References

CHAPTER 2

[Box98] BOX, Don, *Essential COM*, Addison-Wesley Longman, Inc., Reading, MA. 1998.

[Chess96] Chess, David M., *Things that Go Bump in the Net,* Virus Bulletin Conference ©1996 Virus Bulletin Ltd, The Pentagon, Abingdon, Oxfordshire, OX14 3YP, England.

[Crandall87] CRANDALL, Vern J., Computer Science 427: Software Design and Implementation, Lecture Notes, Alexander's Print Shop, Provo, Utah. 1987.

[DeMarco96] DEMARCO, Tom, *Software Risk Management*, NetFocus: Software Technology Highlights, No 212, December 1996.

[Grebert97] GREBERT, Igor, *The Changing Face of Virus Protection in the 21st Century*, Virus Bulletin Conference ©1997 Virus Bulletin Ltd, The Pentagon, Abingdon, Oxfordshire, OX14 3YP, England.

[Grove96] GROVE, Andrew S., *Only the Paranoid Survive*, Doubleday, New York, NY. 1996.

[Hayes97] HAYES, Linda, "Don't let your business processes regress," *Datamation*, July 1997, p. 34.

[Humphrey89] HUMPHREY, Watts S., *Managing the Software Process*, Addison-Wesley, Reading, MA. 1989.

[Isaacson97] ISAACSON, Walter, *TIME Magazine*, Dec. 29, 1997 / Jan. 5, 1998.

[Jarvis97] JARVIS, Alka, and Vern J. Crandall, *Inroads to Software Quality: A "How To" Guide with Toolkit*, Prentice Hall, Upper Saddle River, NJ. 1997.

[Kephart97] KEPHART, Jeffrey O., Gregory B. Sorkin, Morton Swimmer, and Steve R. White, *Blueprint for a Computer Immune System*, Virus Bulletin Conference ©1997 Virus Bulletin Ltd, The Pentagon, Abingdon, Oxfordshire, OX14 3YP, England.

[Lundburg95] LUNDBURG, Gary B., and Joy Saunders Lundberg, *I Don't Have to Make Everything All Better*, Riverpark Publishing, North Las Vegas, NV. 1995.

[Myers79] MYERS, Glenford, *Reliable Software Through Composite Design*, Van Nostrand-Reinhold, New York. 1979.

[Norman88] NORMAN, Donald A., *The Design of Everyday Things*, Doubleday, New York. 1988.

[Parnas72] PARNAS, D. L., "On the Criteria to be Used in Decomposing Systems into Modules," *Communications of the ACM*, December 1972, pp. 1053 - 1058.

[Peters87] PETERS, Lawrence, *Advanced Structured Analysis and Design*, Prentice Hall, Englewood Cliffs, NJ. 1987.

[Roberts85] ROBERTS, Wess, *Leasership Secrets of Attila the Hun*, Warner Books, Inc., New York. 1985.

[Slade97] SLADE, Robert M., *Intel Corporation, LANDesk Virus Protect Family of Products, Phase 1 Report*.

[Snow97] SNOW, Cindy, Alka Jarvis, and Vern J. Crandall, *A New Paradigm for a Product Delivery Process*, The Journal of the Quality Assurance Institute, October 1997, p. 30.

[Stevens74] STEVENS, Wayne, Larry Constantine, and Glenford Myers, "Structured Design," *IBM Systems Journal*, Vol. 13, No. 2, p. 115-139.

[U. of Hamburg97] UNIVERSITY OF HAMBURG'S Virus Test Center, http://agn-www.informatik.uni-hamburg.de/pub/texts/macro/.

[Wells97] WELLS, Joe, *Monthly In-the-Wild List*, http://www.virusbtn.com/WildLists/199712.html.

[White96] WHITE, Steve R., Jeffrey O. Kephart, and David M. Chess, *The Changing Ecology of Computer Viruses*, Virus Bulletin Conference ©1996 Virus Bulletin Ltd, The Pentagon, Abingdon, Oxfordshire, OX14 3YP, England.

CHAPTER 5

[Deming86] DEMING, W. Edwards, *Out of the Crisis*, Cambridge University Press, Cambridge, England. 1986.

[Fagan76] FAGAN, Michael E., *Design and Code Inspections to Reduce Errors in Program Development, IBM Systems Journal*, Vol. 15, No. 3, 1976.

[Gilb88] GILB, Tom, *Principles of Software Engineering Management*, Addison-Wesley, Wokingham, England. 1988.

[Gilb93] GILB, Tom and Dorothy Graham, *Software Inspection*, Addison-Wesley, Wokingham, England. 1993.

[Hammer93] HAMMER, Michael, and James Champy, *Reengineering the Corporation*, Nicholas Brealey Publishing, London. 1993.

[Juran88] JURAN, J.M., *Juran on Planning for Quality*, Macmillan, New York. 1988.

[Paulk93] PAULK, Mark C., Bill Curtis, Mary Beth Chrissis, and Charles V. Weber, *Capability Maturity Model for Software, Version 1.1*, CMU/SEI-93-TR-24, Software Engineering Institute, Carnegie Mellon University, Pittsburgh, PA. February 1993.

[Peters92] PETERS, Tom, *Liberation Management*, Macmillan, London. 1992.

[Petrozzo94] PETROZZO, Daniel P., and John C. Stepper, *Successful Rengineering*, Van Nostrand Reinhold, New York. 1994.

CHAPTER 6

[Abrahamson92] ABRAHAMSON, S. R., et al., "Customer Satisfaction-Based Product Development," Proceedings International Switching Symposium, Vol. 2, Institute Electronics, Information, Communications Engineers, Yokohama, Japan, 1992, pp. 65-69.

[Brooks95] BROOKS, Frederick P., *The Mythical Man-Month, Anniversary Edition*. Addison-Wesley: Reading, PA. 1995.

[Crandall93] CRANDALL, Vern J., "The Cost-Effectiveness of Software Testing: Making a Case to Management," The Journal of the Quality Assurance Institute, October, 1993, pp. 8-20.

[Crandall94] CRANDALL, Vern J., "Handling Risk in Software Development Part I: Identifying and Managing Risk," The Journal of the Quality Assurance Institute, January 1994.

[Humphrey95] HUMPHREY, Watts S., *A Discipline for Software Engineering*, Addison-Wesley, Reading, PA. 1995.

[IEEE95] IEEE, Charter and Organization of the Software Reliability Engineering Committee, 1995.

[Jarvis97] JARVIS, Alka, and Vern J. Crandall, *Inroads to Software Quality: A "How to" Guide with Toolkit,* Prentice Hall, Upper Saddle River, NJ. 1997.

[Lyu95] LYU, Michael R., Ed. *Handbook of Software Reliability Engineering*, IEEE Computer Society Press, Los Alimitos, CA [McGraw-Hill, New York]. 1995.

[Musa87] MUSA, John D., Anthony Iannino, and Kazuhira Okumoto, *Software Reliability: Measurement, Prediction, Application*, McGraw-Hill, New York. 1987.

[Musa97] MUSA, John D., and James Widmaier, "Software Reliability Engineered Testing," Journal of the Quality Assurance Institute, October, 1997, pp. 26-29.

[Snow97] SNOW, Cindy, Alka Jarvis, and Vern J.Crandall, "A New Paradigm for a Product Development Process Part I," Journal of the Quality Assurance Institute, October, 1997, pp. 30-39.

Index

A

accountability 44-45, 213
acronyms/abbreviations 335-37
administration 111
agenda 116
auditing 213
automatic feedback loop 161
automation 141-42
availability of information 69-73, 129

B

benchmarking 108, 118, 132
beta test plan 59
brainstorming 161, 164
business partner alignment 135
business process engineering 149
business process model 10-12

C

Capability Maturity Model 150-51
change activity 113
change management 61, 122-23
client/vendor relationship
    checkpoints 306-07
    cultural change 330
    development phase 324-25

functional design phase 317-24
handoff 304-07
implementation control 303
implementation phase 326-27
initiation phase 310-12
issue resolution 309
key principles 308
post-implementation phase 328-30
process 302-04
project management approach 307-330
project plan 317, 330-31
project schedule 309
questions for process change 333
reasons to implement 300-01
regression testing 323-24
relationship challenges 311, 314, 316, 318, 321, 325, 327, 328
requirements phase 315-17
site visit 312
solution confirmation phase 313-15
technical design phase 320-24
testing 323-24

traceability 323
communication 75-76
communications plan 138-39
competence 129
competition 301
competition wall 49-50, 53
completion review 143-44
compounded cumulative risks 21
confidence rating 263-66
configuration management plan
   140
conflict resolution 14-15
conformance with standards 129
consensus 145
continuous process improvement
   48, 76-77, 140, 154, 166, 215, 296-97
contract management plan 139
cooperation 145
correctness 129
cultural change 86-87, 133-36, 169,
   187-89, 207-12, 251, 276-78, 330
customer
      involvement 78-79, 102, 115-16
      preserving relationship 277
      satisfaction 142-44, 301
      service 74, 188
      support training plan 60

D

defect
      defined 199
      detection 158-59
      prevention 165
Deming plan 48, 61, 76-77, 165-66,
   201-02
dependability 129
dependencies 109
dictated vs. adopted change 21
document control plan 140-41
document inspection
      administration 159
      artifacts 161-62
      automatic feedback loop 161
      brainstorming 161, 164
      continuous process

improvement, 166
   defect detection 158-59
   defect prevention 165
   documentation 163
   objective 158-59
   procedure 160
   roles 159-60
   Shewhart/Deming Cycle 165-66
   sub-processes 164
   synthesis 166-67
   system attributes 166-67
   written rules 159
documentation 71-73, 81-82, 120-21
documentation development plan
   59

E

efficiency 129
error 199
ethical standards 85

F

failure 198
fault 199
feedback 145
filter 201
financial management plan 139
flexibility
      benefits 85-86
      cultural change 86-87
      quality 129

H

hardware
      resource requirements 107
      upgrades 106

I

identity 145
impact evaluation 80, 102-05
impact table 105
implementation 88-89, 100, 135
incremental change 21
information gathering 77-78

information hierarchy 9-10
inspections
    cultural change 187-89
    need 148-49
    process 156-67
    software quality 150-56
    start-up 167-76
    strategic planning 189-94
integrated requirements 22
inventory 121

J

Juran Trilogy Diagram 151, 166

K

key dates 109

M

maintainability 129
management
    approval 46, 78, 87, 110, 132,
        210-12
    culture 23-24
    defined 96
    involvement 100-01
manual updating 120
marketing requirements document
    50-53
mass inspection 76
mean time to failure 198
mean time to repair 198
metrics 9-10, 140, 144
milestones 109, 114
mission statement 49-50
multi-disciplinary team
    defined 29
    planning 64
    responsibilities 53
    types 30-32
    vertical management
        accountability 30

N

name recognition 9
no blame 7
non-disclosure 55

O

ongoing requirements
    management 19-20
outside consultant 7
outsourcing 68-69

P

participation 145
peer review 113-14
people resources 107
plan approval 110
planning 77-78, 96
points of contact 138-39
probability distribution 204
procedural changes 105-06
process
    documentation 158
    generic 156-58
    management 135, 139
    meta 156
    production 156
product life cycle
    beta test plan 59
    change management 61
    customer support training
        plan 60
    development 61
    documentation development
        plan 59
    engineering design 52-53
    marketing business plans 49
    marketing product
        requirements 49
    marketing requirements
        document 50-53
    product requirements
        document 52-53, 59
    project plan 60
    prototyping 54-60
    support/maintenance plan 60
    supporting others' needs 9
product requirements document
    52-53, 59
production 17-19
progress monitoring 112-13
project administration
    change activity 113

defined 111
milestones 114
peer review 113-14
planning 71-73
progress monitoring 112-13
project plan 112
status reporting 114-15
support 113-14
testing plan 113
update activities 112
project completion
    benchmarking 118
    cleanup 118-19
    defined 117-18
    documentation 120-21
    finishing 118
    inventory 121
    planning 71-73
    product manual updating 120
    workbook 121-22
project initiation 71-73, 98-99
project office
    mandate 136
    practices and procedures 137-41
    staff 137
project planning
    accountability 44-45
    administration 112
    communication 65
    components 109
    continuous process
        improvement 48
    goal 108-09
    information sharing 45
    integration 64-65
    management approval 46
    product life cycle 48-61
    team goals 47-48, 50
    technology project managing
        69-73
    think-tank meeting 44, 66
prototyping
    communication 54
    creation 55
    engineering design stage 58-59
    final project plan 58

finalized architecture 57
importance 65-66
non-disclosure 55
parallel efforts 56, 64
scheduling 58

Q

quality
    factors 129
    improvement 154
    measurement 154
    need 128

R

regression testing 323-24
relationship challenges 311, 314,
    316, 318, 321, 325, 327, 328
release metrics
    assessment 258-59
    confidence rating 263-66
    buy-in 257-58
    implementation 267-69
    management 269-71
    rating components 260-63
    reasons for implementation
        255-57
    special handling 267
    test effort 266
release planning
    checkpoints 232-50
    cultural change 251
    defining 227-28
    documentation 226-27
    field trial 240, 245-46
    meetings 226, 230-31
    priorities 228-30
    process 225-50
    reasons to implement 222-24
    schedule 17-19
    team leaders 225-26
repetition
    among projects 69-73, 99
    benefits 82-83
    determining repetitiveness
        123
    formalized procedure 124
    procedure 83-85

project completion 123-24
project or task 83-84, 99-100
service request 83
requirements
  "bare bones" approach 6
  business driven process 9
  business process model 10-12
  characteristics of good
    requirements 24
  compounded cumulative risks
    21
  conflict resolution 14-15
  defined 2-3
  dictated vs. adopted change 21
  elicitation 8
  functionality 13
  gathering 100-01
  information hierarchy 9-10
  integrated requirements 22
  management 137-38, 141
  management culture 23-24
  metrics 9-10
  name recognition 9
  no blame 7
  ongoing requirements
    management 19-20
  outside consultant 7
  production 17-19
  requirements representation
    12-15
  resources 77-78
  responsiveness 22
  rewards 22
  roll off from consultant 7
  rolling release 5, 7, 17, 23
  script 13
  steps in process 24
  testing template 13
  time box 5, 7, 23
  validation 16-17
resource integration 77-78, 105-08
resource management plan 139
responsibility 145
responsiveness 22, 129
risk evaluation
  complexity 103
  defined 77-78
  impact evaluation 80, 102-03

  management plan 139
  overall risk level 80
  plan approval 110
  risk table 80, 103-04
  standardization 85
  time 103
rolling release 5, 7, 17-19, 23

S

scope of project 101-02
security 129
service
  defined 198
  quality 76-77, 129
  request 81-82, 83
Shewhart/Deming Cycle 165-66
site visit 312
software
  attributes 152-53
  Capability Maturity Model
    150-51
  communicating attributes
    155-56
  externally-focused attributes
    155
  inspection against
    documented criteria 151-52
  internally-focused attributes
    155
  Juran Trilogy Diagram 151,
    166
  metrics 152
  productivity 153-54
  quality 150-56
  quantified system attributes
    154-56
  reliability 153-54
  resource requirements 107-08
  upgrades 106
software development process
  handbook
    continuous improvement 296-
    97
    cultural change 276-78
    drafting 278-95
    high-level design
      specifications 292-93
    low-level design specifications

294-95
reasons to implement 276
template 296
software reliability engineering
    auditing 213
    basic steps 199-200
    cultural change 207-12
    defined 198
    deliverable 203-04
    filter 201
    goals 198-200
    implementation 214-16
    management approval 210-12
    probability distribution 204
    project timeline 212-13
    reasons to implement 200-04
    solutions 205-07
    testing 203
    training 215
standardization
    benefits 85, 97
    flexibility 86
    documentation 84-85
start-up
    activities 167-68
    quantified system attributes
      168-74
status reporting 69-73, 114-16, 138-
    39
support/maintenance plan 60
support office
    business partner alignment
      135
    challenges 141-42
    manager 135
    mandate 136
    ongoing implementation
      support 135
    process management 135
    strategic approach 134-35
system attributes
    criteria 172
    external 168-72
    internal 168-72
    measurement 173-74
    processes 174-75
    support system 176
    training 175

T

task 96
team building 145
team goals 47-48, 50
technology project management
    cultural change 86-87
    implementation 88
    outsourcing 68-69
    process 74-86
    reasons to implement 69-73
    sample process 91-126
    scope 101-02
template 296
testing plan 113
time box 5, 7, 23
traceability 323
training 60, 140, 175, 215

U

usability 129

V

validation
    business risk areas 16
    irresolvable issues 17
    testing 16
vendor information 107

W

workbook
    benefits 97
    documentation 121-22
    standardization 84-85
workload appropriation 110